THRESHOLD PHENOMENA

Threshold Phenomena

DERRIDA AND THE QUESTION OF HOSPITALITY

Michael Naas

FORDHAM UNIVERSITY PRESS   NEW YORK 2024

Copyright © 2024 Fordham University Press

Fordham University Press has no responsibility for the persistence or accuracy
of URLs for external or third-party Internet websites referred to in this
publication and does not guarantee that any content on such websites is, or
will remain, accurate or appropriate.

Fordham University Press also publishes its books in a variety of electronic
formats. Some content that appears in print may not be available in electronic
books.

Visit us online at www.fordhampress.com.

Library of Congress Cataloging-in-Publication Data available online at https://
catalog.loc.gov.

Printed in the United States of America
26 25 24 5 4 3 2 1
First edition

Dedicated to the Memory of
Darrell Gibbs
(1959–2022)

A friend like no other,
Who lived life always on the threshold,
With the spirit of Kerouac and the serenity of the Dalai Lama,
Teaching us all to heed what lies beyond the phenomena.

Contents

III. The Wall, the Door, the Threshold, the Hotspot

Abbreviations of Works by Jacques Derrida

"AANJ" "Above All, No Journalists!" Trans. Samuel Weber. In *Religion and Media*, ed. Hent de Vries and Samuel Weber, 56–93. Stanford, CA: Stanford University Press, 2001. (*Cahier de l'Herne: Derrida*. Ed. Marie-Louise Mallet and Ginette Michaud, 35–49. Paris: Éditions de l'Herne, 2004.)

"AED" "Accueil, éthique, droit et politique." Interview with Michel Wieviorka. In *Manifeste pour l'hospitalité—aux Minguettes, Autour de Jacques Derrida*, ed. Mohammed Seffahi, 143–54. Grigny: Éditions Paroles d'Aube, 1999. Reprinted in *Derrida-Levinas: An Alliance Awaiting the Political / Une alliance en attente de politique*, ed. Orietta Ombrosi and Raphael Zagury-Orly, 309–16. Mimesis International, 2018.

AEL *Adieu: To Emmanuel Levinas*. Trans. Pascale-Anne Brault and Michael Naas. Stanford, CA: Stanford University Press, 1999. (*Adieu à Emmanuel Lévinas*. Paris: Éditions Galilée, 1997.)

"AIP" "As If It Were Possible, 'Within Such Limits' . . ." Trans. Rachel Bowlby. In *PM* 73–99.

AP *Aporias*. Trans. Thomas Dutoit. Stanford, CA: Stanford University Press, 1993. (*Apories*. Paris: Éditions Galilée, 1996; first version published in *Le passage des frontières, autour du travail de Jacques Derrida*, 309–38. Paris: Éditions Galilée, 1993.)

ATT *The Animal That Therefore I Am*. Trans. David Wills. New York: Fordham University Press, 2008. (*L'animal que donc je suis*. Édition établie par Marie Louise Mallet. Paris: Éditions Galilée, 2006.)

"CHM"   "Cogito and the History of Madness." In *Writing and Difference*,
        trans. Alan Bass, 31–63. Chicago: University of Chicago Press, 1978.
        (*L'écriture et la différence*, 51–97. Paris: Éditions du Seuil, 1967.)

"D"   "Discours du Professeur Jacques Derrida." Discourse given upon the
        conferral of an honorary degree at the University of Silesia, Kato-
        wice, Poland. In *Jacques Derrida: Doctor honoris causa, Universitatis
        Silesiensis*, 108–24. Katowice, 1997.

DE   *Deconstruction Engaged: The Sydney Seminars*. Ed. Paul Patton and
        Terry Smith. Sydney: Power Publications, 2001.

"F"   "*Fichus*: Frankfurt Address." In *PM* 164–81. (*Fichus : Discours de
        Francfort*. Paris: Éditions Galilée, 2002.)

FS   *For Strasbourg: Conversations of Friendship and Philosophy*. Trans.
        Pascale-Anne Brault and Michael Naas. New York: Fordham Univer-
        sity Press, 2014. Includes "The Place Name(s)—Strasbourg" (2004).

FWT   *For What Tomorrow. . . .* With Elisabeth Roudinesco. Trans. Jeff
        Fort. Stanford, CA: Stanford University Press, 2004. (*De quoi de-
        main . . . : Dialogue*. With Elisabeth Roudinesco. Paris: Libraire
        Arthème Fayard et Éditions Galilée, 2001.)

GL   *Glas*. Trans. John P. Leavey Jr. and Richard Rand. Lincoln: Univer-
        sity of Nebraska Press, 1986. Also translated into English by Geoffrey
        Bennington and David Wills as *Clang*. Minneapolis: University of
        Minnesota Press, 2021. (*Glas*. Paris: Éditions Galilée, 1974.)

H 1   *Hospitality 1, Seminar of 1995–1996*. Trans. Ellen Burt. Chicago:
        University of Chicago Press, 2023. (*Hospitalité 1, Séminaire (1995–
        1996)*. Ed. Pascale-Anne Brault and Peggy Kamuf. Paris: Éditions du
        Seuil, 2021.)

H 2   *Hospitality 2, Seminar of 1996–1997*. Trans. Peggy Kamuf. Chicago:
        University of Chicago Press, 2024. (*Hospitalité 2, Séminaire (1996–
        1997)*. Ed. Pascale-Anne Brault and Peggy Kamuf. Paris: Éditions du
        Seuil, 2022.)

"HI"   "Une hospitalité à l'infini." In *Manifeste pour l'hospitalité—aux
        Minguettes, Autour de Jacques Derrida*, ed. Mohammed Seffahi,
        97–106. Grigny: Éditions Paroles d'Aube, 1999.

"HJR"   "Hospitality, Justice, and Responsibility: A Dialogue with Jacques
        Derrida." In *Questioning Ethics: Contemporary Debates in Philoso-
        phy*, ed. Richard Kearney and Mark Dooley, 65–83. London: Rout-
        ledge, 1999.

"HSC"   "Une hospitalité sans condition." In *Manifeste pour l'hospitalité—
        aux Minguettes, Autour de Jacques Derrida*, ed. Mohammed Seffahi,
        133–42. Grigny: Éditions Paroles d'Aube, 1999; reprinted in *Derrida-*

Levinas: An Alliance Awaiting the Political / Une alliance en attente de politique, ed. Orietta Ombrosi and Raphael Zagury-Orly, 317–22. Mimesis International, 2018.

"K"   *"Khōra."* In *On the Name,* ed. Thomas Dutoit, 87–127. Stanford, CA: Stanford University Press, 1993. (*Khōra.* Paris: Éditions Galilée, 1993.)

MO   *Monolingualism of the Other; or, The Prosthesis of Origin,* trans. Patrick Mensah. Stanford, CA: Stanford University Press, 1998. (*Le monolinguisme de l'autre: ou la prothèse d'origine.* Paris: Éditions Galilée, 1996.)

N   *Negotiations: Interventions and Interviews, 1971–2001.* Ed. Elizabeth Rottenberg. Stanford, CA: Stanford University Press, 2002.

"NU"   "Not Utopia, the Im-possible." Interview with Thomas Assheuer. In *PM* 121–35. ("Non pas l'utopie, l'im-possible." In *Papier Machine* 349–66.) First published in a slightly abbreviated version in German translation in *Die Zeit,* March 5, 1998.

OCF   *On Cosmopolitanism and Forgiveness.* Trans. Mark Dooley and Michael Hughes. London: Routledge, 2001. Includes "On Cosmopolitanism," 1–24. (*Cosmopolites de tous les pays, encore en effort!* Paris: Éditions Galilée, 1997); "On Forgiveness," 25–60. (*Le Monde des débats,* December 1999.) Much of "On Cosmopolitanism" was first presented during the seminar session in *H 1* of March 20, 1996.

OG   *Of Grammatology.* Trans. Gayatri Chakravorty Spivak. Baltimore, MD: Johns Hopkins University Press, 1976. (*De la grammatologie.* Paris: Éditions de Minuit, 1967.)

OH   *Of Hospitality.* With Anne Dufourmantelle. Trans. Rachel Bowlby. Stanford, CA: Stanford University Press, 2000). (*De l'hospitalité.* With Anne Dufourmantelle. Paris: Calmann-Lévy, 1997.) Includes revised versions of the *H 1* sessions of January 10 and 17, 1996.

P   *Positions.* Trans. Alan Bass. Chicago: University of Chicago Press, 1981. (*Positions.* Paris: Éditions de Minuit, 1972.)

PF   *Politics of Friendship.* Trans. George Collins. New York: Verso, 1997. (*Politiques de l'amitié.* Paris: Éditions Galilée, 1994.)

"PH"   "The Principle of Hospitality." In *PM* 66–69. ("Le principe d'hospitalité." In *Papier Machine* 273–77.) First published as "Il n'y a pas de culture ni de lien social sans un principe d'hospitalité," *Le Monde,* December 2, 1997.

PM   *Paper Machine.* Trans. Rachel Bowlby. Stanford, CA: Stanford University Press, 2005. (*Papier Machine: Le ruban de machine à écrire et autres réponses.* Paris: Éditions Galilée, 2001.)

"Q"   "Quand j'ai entendu l'expression *'délit d'hospitalité'. . .*" In *Plein
          Droit* 34 (April 1997): 3–8; reprinted in *Marx en jeu*, with Marc
          Guillaume and Jean-Pierre Vincent, 73–91. Paris: Descartes & Cie,
          1997.

S   *Sur Parole.* Paris: Éditions de l'Aube, 1999; includes the transcrip-
          tion of a series of radio interviews with Catherine Paoletti on France
          Culture conducted on December 14–18, 1998, along with four radio
          programs produced by Antoine Spire on various themes in Derrida's
          work, including a program from December 19, 1997, on hospitality
          (63–74).

SQ   *Sovereignties in Question: The Poetics of Paul Celan.* Ed. Thomas
          Dutoit and Outi Pasanen. New York: Fordham University Press,
          2005. Includes "Language Is Never Owned: An Interview," trans.
          Thomas Dutoit and Philippe Romanski, 97–107. ("La langue n'ap-
          partient pas." *Europe* 861–62, special issue, "Paul Celan" (January–
          February 2001): 81–91.)

"SST"   "Some Statements and Truisms about Neologisms, Newisms,
          Postisms, Parasitisms, and Other Small Seismisms." Trans. Anne
          Tomiche. In *The States of "Theory": History, Art, and Critical Dis-
          course,* ed. David Carroll, 63–94. New York: Columbia University
          Press, 1990. (*Derrida d'ici, Derrida de là.* Ed. Thomas Dutoit and
          Philippe Romanski, 223–252. Paris: Éditions Galilée, 2009.)

TS   A *Taste for the Secret.* With Maurizio Ferraris. Trans. Giacomo
          Donis. Ed. Giacomo Donis and David Webb. Cambridge: Polity,
          2001.

"UG"   "Ulysses Gramophone: Hear Say Yes in Joyce." Trans. Tina Kend-
          all and revised by Shari Benstock. In *Acts of Literature.* Ed. Derek
          Attridge. London: Routledge, 1992, 253–309.

"US"   "Unconditionality or Sovereignty: The University at the Frontiers of
          Europe." Trans. Peggy Kamuf. *Oxford Literary Review* 31 (Decem-
          ber 2009): 115–31. (*Inconditonnalité ou souveraineté : L'université aux
          frontières de l'Europe.* Athens: Editions Patakis, 2002.)

"UWC"   "The University without Condition." In *Without Alibi,* ed. and trans.
          Peggy Kamuf, 202–37. Stanford, CA: Stanford University Press, 2002.
          (*L'Université sans condition.* Paris: Éditions Galilée, 2001.)

VP   *Voice and Phenomenon: Introduction to the Problem of the Sign in
          Husserl's Phenomenology.* Trans. Leonard Lawlor. Evanston, IL:
          Northwestern University Press, 2011. (*La voix et le phénomène.* Paris:
          Presses Universitaires de France, 1967.)

THRESHOLD PHENOMENA

Introduction

Fist Bumps and Pandemic Bubbles

> Now we begin, or we pretend to open the door of the seminar. We are
> on the threshold [*le seuil*]. (H 1 7/26)

The pandemic of the past few years changed just about everything about our
daily lives, in some cases just for a short period of time and in others more
permanently. It changed how we work and travel, how we eat and drink, how
we greet and communicate with one another, how we live with and even
how we mourn one another. And, of course, it changed just about everything
having to do with hospitality. For a time, we no longer invited others into
our homes; we restricted our circle of friends and acquaintances to what we
quaintly called our "bubble"; we socially distanced ourselves from one another, and, for a time, we washed and sanitized our hands after every contact
with anyone or anything that we suspected may have come into contact with
anyone or anything suspected of having COVID-19. We even quarantined
ourselves, sometimes even within our own homes, for days and sometimes
even weeks. And then there were, of course, all the regulations and restrictions
placed on how and when we might go into public spaces, regulations having
to do with the wearing of masks, getting tested or vaccinated, and even when
or how we might visit our loved ones in hospitals or accompany them, or not,
to their final resting place.

In the United States, and no doubt elsewhere throughout the world to vary-
ing degrees, all these changes and regulations brought about by the pandemic
in late 2019 and early 2020 converged with questions and issues that were
already at the center of public discourse well before COVID-19, questions of
"reception" or "contagion" of another type, that is, questions of immigration,

of whether or how to restrict access to the body politic: in the United States, for example, the whole question or polemic surrounding the building of a wall along our southern border to keep out aliens and foreigners, migrants and asylum seekers, from Mexico, Latin and South America, Haiti, and elsewhere. COVID thus became in the United States a Petri dish for all these questions, as those in favor of building that famous wall often became virulently against the wearing of masks, and those who looked for stricter government guidelines to combat the virus were often the first to ask for a more liberal policy regarding the acceptance or even the welcoming of strangers upon our shores. In addition, the pandemic caused all of us to assess or reassess just what home is, what it is for and where it should be, whether it makes sense to make our home in the city or the suburbs or the country, close to other people or as far away as possible.

The pandemic thus caused us all, in short, to rethink the limits, boundaries, and restrictions we place on our nation-states, our communities, our homes, our bubbles, and our bodies, everything from what mandates should be imposed on all these places to what shibboleths should be uttered when crossing over the threshold of any of them, shibboleths like: "Don't worry, I'm double-vaccinated, Pfizer, if you want to know, I've even been boosted"—those kinds of reassurances. The pandemic thus changed, in the short or the long run, nearly everything having to do with hospitality, everything from our daily gestures to our everyday language. And the irony, of course, is that the whole pandemic was in many ways the result of nothing other than our very gregarious—indeed, one is tempted to say our very *hospitable*—nature with regard to other human beings, though also, it has to be said, with regard to the virus itself.[1]

Now, it so happens that Jacques Derrida spent a good deal of time in the mid-to-late 1990s thinking, writing, and teaching about all these questions of hospitality—including and perhaps especially these questions of a more sociopolitical nature, questions of immigration, of border control, of asylum cities, of cosmopolitanism, and so on. He did this in a series of short texts that have been known, studied, and written about for more than twenty years now, *Of Hospitality*, for example, a text written together with Anne Dufourmantelle; *Cosmopolitanism and Forgiveness*; "Une hospitalité à l'infini"; "The Principle of Hospitality"; and several others.[2] But he also did this over the course of two full years of a seminar at the École des Hautes Études en Sciences Sociales (EHESS) in Paris on the topic of hospitality, a seminar that ran roughly from November 1995 to May 1997. While a small number of sessions from that seminar have been previously published (two of them, for example, in *Of Hospitality*), it was only in 2021 and 2022 that the two years of the seminar were published in their entirety in French, with their English translations following in 2023 and 2024. These recent publications are thus already causing us to re-assess or rethink what Derrida thought about hospitality, and, as a result, they are already causing us to rethink or reframe the kinds of questions that were circulating in the 1990s and that have lost none of their urgency or actuality in the intervening three decades.

This work focuses primarily, though not exclusively, on the first year of Derrida's seminar, which was given in Paris from mid-November 1995 to mid-May 1996, along with several related works from around the same period, including *Of Hospitality* and *On Cosmopolitanism and Forgiveness*. As I will argue, the seminar *Hospitality* as a whole, and the first year in particular, war-rants such attention for the way it both raises the philosophical, political, and ethical dimensions of the question of hospitality and illuminates in exemplary fashion Derrida's work more generally. Moreover, this particular seminar, like the texts associated with it, was largely motivated—indeed perhaps like no other—by world events, and particularly events in Europe and France, by the arrival of more and more immigrants to France and other European nations, and so by questions related to asylum and to offering hospitality to migrants or foreigners, questions that were becoming more and more central to French and European public discourse in the mid-1990s, as some on the left argued for more liberal and open policies to address these problems and others on the right began to argue for much stricter immigration policies, a strengthening of borders, and a radical reassessment of just what European or French identity meant. All this called not just for a political response but also for a philosoph-ical response, in the form of an analysis of the terms and questions that were becoming more and more central to those public discourses. Derrida's two-year seminar on hospitality can be read as just such a philosophical response.

Derrida's work on hospitality thus has a unique genesis, and it is marked by its time in an indelible way. And yet its themes could not be more current or timely. When reading Derrida's seminar one cannot but be driven to con-sider some of our own attitudes and policies with regard to "hospitality" in all its guises, at once private and public, everything from how we treat those around us, our neighbors and those and in communities, to immigration and refugee policies to controversies surrounding the building of walls and the es-tablishing of sanctuary cities. With refugee crises growing in size and number throughout the world, with literally millions of homeless, stateless, displaced, or migrant peoples on the move as I type these words, in Mexico, South Amer-ica, and Latin America, in northern Africa, Syria, Afghanistan, Ukraine, and Gaza, to name just the most visible at the present moment, there will con-tinue to be, unfortunately, no shortage of contemporary examples for us to try to think through in conjunction with Derrida's rethinking of hospitality. While Derrida reminds us in *Sur Parole* that we must "constantly distinguish the problem of hospitality in the strict sense from problems of immigration, control over the flow of migrants," and so on, he also goes on to say that "the two are inseparable" (S 71).

This work aims to treat these questions of hospitality "in our times" in a philosophical way, one that will not be devoid of pathos but that will not, or at least this is the hope, give in entirely to that pathos. For as Derrida well knew, no one can claim the moral high ground by arguing that they are *for* hospitality while others are *against* it. In the end, everyone is *for* it, and people differ only in their social and political positions with regard to it and, especially relevant here, their philosophical understanding of it and the philosophical assumptions that determine that understanding (see *H* 1 131/181).

This work bears the title "Threshold Phenomena: Jacques Derrida and the Question of Hospitality" because the threshold is always the place from which the question is posed, and not just the question of hospitality but the question in general, including the question of whether and how to address others from the threshold and the question of philosophy's commitment to the question as its primary mode of engagement. All this suggests that hospitality is not just one question among others for Derrida or for deconstruction but, perhaps, the very work and promise of deconstruction. For if "ethics" is always, as Derrida argues, a question of the "ethos," that is, a question of inhabiting, of sojourning, then "every ethics is no doubt an ethics of hospitality" (*H* 1 16/60), and deconstruction, which is always a question of ethics, is always a deconstruction of hospitality, or indeed, as we shall see, a deconstruction *as* hospitality.

What Derrida gives us in the texts he devoted to hospitality, and especially in the two-year seminar of 1995–1997 on this question, is a *philosophical* account of the notion or the concept of hospitality. I underscore "philosophical" because Derrida's seminar can today be read, to the delight of some and no doubt the consternation of others, as a sort of primer or handbook on how to do a certain "Continental Philosophy." What we see in the seminar is not quite Derrida's *method* but rather his way of approaching the question from multiple directions, on multiple paths, with multiple resources, and oftentimes within the course of a single seminar session, approaching it and then backing off, trying one approach and then another, always advancing but somehow always returning to the point of departure. This perpetual back and forth between different texts and approaches often looks pretty seamless, but when one steps back a bit one can see the sort of high-wire act Derrida is engaged in and the peril he constantly faces of mixing genres, texts, and sources in a way that would be more confusing or distracting than enlightening. If Derrida always manages to avoid falling off that high wire, if he manages always to illuminate rather than confuse, it is not because he ever stops juggling all these sources, texts, and approaches in order to concentrate on just one. Indeed, all the balls that are thrown into the air in the course of the very first session of the first year remain in the air until the very end of the seminar. Here are just some of these, which I take some time to enumerate and explain because I believe that the *Hospitality* seminar, while not unique, is *exemplary* of a certain way of doing philosophy and because I think explaining Derrida's approach, his *démarche*, is the best way of immunizing oneself against the very silly but also very dangerous thinking of deconstruction as merely playful, or as destructive or nihilist, or, indeed, as the French minister of education referred to it in early 2022, as a *virus* from which one needs to be inoculated.[3]

In just the first year of the seminar, there is, first of all, and those who have read the little book *Of Hospitality* will recall this, an attempt to develop a sort of *formal logic* that relates what Derrida will characterize as two different regimes or regimens of hospitality, an unconditional hospitality and a conditional one, that is, an unconditional, absolute, hyperbolic, infinite hospitality and a conditional, conditioned, limited, historically embedded, and effective hospitality, these two poles or regimes of hospitality being related in what Derrida will call an aporetic way, in much the same way that, for example, justice is related to law in other texts.

In addition to this attempt to develop a logic, as it were, of hospitality, there are multiple returns, as one might expect, to the *history of philosophy*, both texts that speak of hospitality explicitly, Kant's *Perpetual Peace*, for example, with which Derrida opens the seminar and to which he returns repeatedly, or Levinas's *Totality and Infinity*, or Nietzsche's *Of Zarathustra*, and texts that use the *lexicon* of hospitality, for example, the dialogues in which Plato uses the term "foreigner" or "stranger," *xenos*, including those that have a central character who bears that name. In addition to these insights from and references to the history of philosophy with regard to hospitality, Derrida will frequently recall, through a sort of shorthand, things he will have argued elsewhere regarding Husserl and phenomenology, the phenomenon of hearing-oneself-speak, for example, and the phantasm that is commonly produced by it, the phantasm, for example, of a voice or even a language that would be naturally ours, like a mother tongue.

Then there are texts of literature, at once ancient works, such as Sophocles's *Oedipus at Colonus*, more modern, Molière's "Don Juan or the Feast of the Stone" and La Bruyère's "Le Distrait," and relatively contemporary, Pierre Klossowski's *Roberte ce soir*.[4] These works of literature will be used by Derrida to help illustrate certain key points in his philosophical analysis, and they will be used to develop and mobilize that analysis—the relationship between hospitality and both sovereignty and mourning in *Oedipus at Colonus*, for example; the notion that we are always at home in the home of the other in La Bruyère's "Le Distrait"; and the fact that hospitality must always be open to a certain pervertibility, to the possibility that a host, for example, can always become the hostage to his guest, in *Roberte ce soir*.

Philosophy, literature, but then also biblical sources, the story of Lot and his daughters, which is then contrasted with Kant, not *Perpetual Peace* this time but his text on lying. And then there are etymologies, which could easily appear to be distractions or detours from that more formal approach but which demonstrate that there can be no thinking of hospitality without considering the *language* of hospitality, its history, its tropes, and its lexicon. As is often the case for Derrida in the 1990s, Benveniste's *Dictionary of Indo-European Concepts and Society* will be the text of reference.[5] Etymologies for the word *hospitality*, for example, with all of its Indo-European roots, *hospitality* being related both to the word *hostes*, which can mean either *host* or *guest*, both *host* and *guest*, and to the power, the despotic power, of the one who—as master of the house—is *able* or has the *capacity* to offer hospitality.

In addition, Derrida will make constant reference to other kinds of linguistic analysis, from speech act theory to the question of the question, and then, of course, the question of the relationship between language and hospitality more generally, which will lead to questions regarding the mother tongue, the idiom, and, finally, translation. This will raise, for example, the whole question of whether hospitality must always pass by way of one's own language, by way of the language of the host, or whether it can or even must exceed that language, since a hospitality that assumes that the other can understand my invitation already draws hospitality into a circuit of exchange and identification.

Philosophy, literature, biblical texts, etymologies, a more formal conceptual analysis, linguistic analyses of all kinds, but then also multiple examples from everyday culture, current events, as we might call them, mostly from France but not exclusively, contemporary projects or proposals of law having to do with immigration in France, stories of migrants seeking asylum in Parisian churches, the contemporaneous deaths of friends, such as Gilles Deleuze, and public figures, such as François Mitterrand, as well as the then very contemporary question of cloning. These references to current events, to stories in the press, are clearly an attempt to bring the question of hospitality up to date, to make it more relevant, which is always a good thing in teaching, but they also help illuminate, as we will see, the essential perfectibility/pervertibility of the laws of hospitality that Derrida tries throughout to articulate in a more formal way.

And then, finally, there are brief *autobiographical* moments, particularly but not exclusively in oral asides, some quite poignant and powerful and others rather colorful and humorous. The seminar format lends itself to these more personal or autobiographical comments, which are relatively infrequent but which nonetheless punctuate the entire two years of the seminar. We hear, for example, of Derrida's recent trip to Heidegger's hut in the fall of 1995. We later get a rather detailed account of questions surrounding citizenship and cultural and religious integration in Derrida's native Algeria from 1830 up to the mid-1990s, including Derrida's own experience of these (*OH* 141–47/125–29; see *H* 1 122–24/168–71), as well as an account of Derrida's experience of language, his difficulty learning German and Hebrew, for example, in the course of a brief survey of thinkers (Levinas, Arendt, Rosenzweig) who either adopted the tongue of another as their own or who clung more tightly to their so-called mother tongue (see *H* 1 165/225).

So, philosophical analysis, literature, etymologies, biblical stories, current events, personal anecdotes . . . It is an impressive array of sources and materials, and they are not simply lined up sequentially, one after the other, but juxtaposed or combined in almost every session, the one often interrupting or helping to introduce the other. Only a few pages into the seminar, for example, we will have had Kant, Benveniste and his etymologies, Klossowski, and Levinas, so many balls that Derrida puts into the air in those opening pages and will continue to juggle right up to the end of the seminar. And, as is also always the case with Derrida, all these sources and texts, all these approaches to the singular question of hospitality, will become the occasion for Derrida to rethink and reinscribe within the context of hospitality so many well-known Derridean themes and terms: not just the conditional and the unconditional but law and justice, immunity and autoimmunity, purity and impurity—as well as the trace, auto-affection, spectrality, the phantasm of presence in the spoken voice, messianicity without messianism, and the democracy to come, to name just a few.

The *Hospitality* seminar is, therefore, a stunning example of a certain Continental Philosophy, exhilarating for those inclined to doing philosophy in this way yet liable to being greeted with frustration by anyone hoping to find in the seminar a single, simple definition of hospitality or a series of concrete proposals for how hospitality should or should not be offered in our homes, our cities, and our states. (To whom exactly? In what way? In what numbers? With what expectations? And so on.) Some will thus say that while there is the appearance of progress in Derrida's pursuit of the nature of hospitality, with each of these sources—philosophical, literary, biblical, linguistic—providing the opening to move forward, to advance toward a definition or a more comprehensive and complete understanding, we always end up returning to where we began. No matter how many steps we take toward hospitality, we are perpetually sent back to the *threshold* from which we set out. As Derrida writes at the beginning of the fifth session of the seminar, *pas d'hospitalité*, that is, there are steps (*pas*) forward yet also no (*pas*) steps at all, advances and no advances at all, forays out beyond an initial threshold and perpetual returns to that threshold.

But I would like to suggest here at the outset, here on the threshold, that rather than take this as a shortcoming or source of frustration, we may want to ask what this approach teaches us about hospitality, if not about philosophy or teaching, itself, that is, what this notion of the *pas d'hospitalité* teaches us both about that formal logic to which we will return later and about the centrality—indeed the necessity—of this notion of the threshold for any philosophical thinking of hospitality. As we will see, the threshold—a thinking of the threshold—will be absolutely crucial to Derrida's approach to hospitality, though also, as I will wish to argue, to Derrida's thinking in general, as if the threshold—as a place or nonplace of difference—were what Derrida's thinking has been about, that around which his thinking had turned, from the very beginning.

This work makes no claim to treating Derrida's entire thinking on hospitality, or even the two years of the *Hospitality* seminar, in an exhaustive way. It attempts instead to work through the major themes of the seminar, and especially the first year, often with the help of texts written on the topic from around the same time, though sometimes from texts much earlier or later than the seminar. My aim is to work not chronologically but *thematically* through the seminar, beginning with some of the language and premises necessary to understanding the seminar, working in detail through its central claims or arguments, and then following some of the major consequences of the seminar for Derrida's work but also for thinking about contemporary questions in relation to hospitality.

Since the central claim of this work is that essential to Derrida's rethinking of hospitality is a reinscription or redeployment of the notion of the *threshold*, the place where hospitality is typically granted or refused, we begin with a series of "Pre-liminaries." Chapter 1 thus looks briefly at something Derrida does not, the role of hospitality—and especially the place of the threshold—in the very first works of the Western tradition, namely, in Homer. We then turn in Chapter 2 to the question of translation in relation to hospitality, both to the way translation—speaking or not speaking the language of the host—is always central to the question of hospitality and to the problems of translating certain key words in the lexicon of hospitality, problems that Derrida's seminar broaches and problems that any translation of Derrida's seminar must also try to confront. We will thus need to take up here the question not just of language or the idiom in general but of Derrida's own *practice*, as it were, of the idiom, and particularly the French idiom, in phrases such as *la question de l'étranger* or *pas d'hospitalité*. We will see that while placing such emphasis on the original language of a text is never enough for truly thinking through a text, such emphasis is often indispensable—and for philosophical reasons—to such thinking, and this is particularly true of texts by Derrida. Chapter 3 develops the relationship between hospitality and a certain conception of mastery or sovereignty, what Derrida calls here and in other later texts *ipseity*. The following chapter then takes up the relationship between the stranger or the guest, the *xenos*, and guest-friendship, *xenia*, at once by following Derrida's analyses of Benveniste on the topic and by taking up an example, once again from Homer's *Iliad*, that Derrida does not mention but that illustrates the stakes of guest-friendship that Derrida underscores. We will also see at the end of this chapter the way Plato in the *Symposium* not only refers to this very same example from the *Iliad* but radically reworks it, reinscribing it into philosophy and thereby transforming the very meaning of hospitality.

Chapters 5 and 6 turn back one last time to the Greek world. The first looks at Sophocles's *Oedipus at Colonus*, which is for Derrida a central work for asking questions about public hospitality and its relation to private mourning, which itself then leads to the differences between thinking hospitality on the basis of birth and citizenship and thinking it on the basis of death and dying, the place where one—or one's ancestors—will die and be buried rather than the place where one was born. Chapter 5 then considers the role of the foreigner or stranger in Plato more generally and the Platonic appropriation and transformation of the Greek—and especially Homeric—notion of hospitality by means of the "what is," or *ti esti*, question.

In Part II, we consider in some detail the "concept"—the self-deconstructive, autoimmune "concept"—of hospitality. Having seen in the preceding chapters the premises for rethinking the question of hospitality in relation to the threshold, we begin in Chapter 7 by taking up the question of the question in relation to hospitality, that is, the question of both how to approach the topic of hospitality and how to approach the foreigner or stranger him- or herself. Having seen the importance of the question—the ontological question—for Plato, we will be better able to distinguish the various valences of the phrase with which Derrida begins one of the sessions of the seminar, that is, *la question de l'étranger*, "the question of the foreigner," which will lead us to ask about the role that questioning should play in a philosophical interrogation of hospitality, in any politics of hospitality, or in any private hospitality.

In Chapters 8 and 9, we analyze in some detail the central relationship or logic between what Derrida calls throughout the first year of the seminar *conditional* and *unconditional* hospitality, that is, a limited, conditioned hospitality and a pure, open, absolute, and unconditioned hospitality. We will spend a good deal of time tracking Derrida's language with regard to these two hospitalities in order to show that while the two types or regimes of hospitality must remain distinct, they are both necessary and so must be thought in some way together. Hence the need for what Derrida calls mediating "schemata" between the two kinds of hospitality, as well as, as we see in Chapter 10, the need to think these schemata as part of what Derrida calls an "art" or a "poetics" of hospitality. We then ask in the following chapter about the centrality of Kant to the first year of the seminar, the reasons why Derrida, despite his critique of Kant, considered the project of *Perpetual Peace* to be so necessary. This will then lead us to ask, some quarter of a century after the seminar was first given, about the relevance of projects such as Kant's *Perpetual Peace* at a time when such international, cosmopolitical projects are being questioned or outright rejected by so many nation-state nationalisms.

Chapter 12 tries to pull together the various threads of the preceding analysis in order to ask about the relationship between hospitality and deconstruction, that is, about hospitality as a special theme for deconstruction and deconstruction as a kind of hospitality. We thus bring together here many of the terms commonly associated with deconstruction—aporia, antinomy, undecidability, double bind, pervertibility and perfectibility, historicity, event, messianicity without messianism, democracy to come, desire, justice, immunity and autoimmunity—all reframed or rethought in the context of hospitality. One very telling sign, for example, of the ineradicable pervertibility or autoimmunity in the very concept of hospitality, one indication of the essential relation between hospitality and its contrary, namely, a sort of hostility, can be seen in Derrida's initial inclination to give as a general title to his seminar not the everyday name "hospitality" but the neologism "hostipitality."[6]

In the final part of the work, "The Wall, the Door, the Threshold, the Hotspot," we turn to some of the most urgent sociopolitical problems and questions raised by the *Hospitality* seminar. In Chapter 13, we return to the question of the relationship between hospitality and sovereignty, but thought here in relation to property, properness, purity, and propriety. Derrida asks why the foreign or the foreigner is often considered not only improper but "dirty," repugnant, and so in need of being purified or purged from the body politic. In the following chapter, we turn to the theme of teletechnology in relationship to hospitality, a theme that runs throughout the entire seminar, and then, in Chapters 15 and 16, to the relationship between various contemporary teletechnologies—including, and especially, the cell phone or, rather, the *mobile* phone—and hospitality. We also return in these chapters to some of Derrida's earliest works on the auto-affection of the human voice and the phantasms to which it gives rise, including those related to the so-called mother tongue—all this with the aim of illuminating the related phantasms brought about by contemporary teletechnology.

In Chapter 17 we turn to Derrida's interest in and contribution to a new "cosmopolitan" project for establishing "cities of refuge" throughout the world to help address the problem of political asylum for intellectuals and writers persecuted in their home countries but also in order to pave the way for a new thinking of immigration policy more generally. In Chapter 18, we turn to Derrida's questioning of the limitation of hospitality, in Kant and others, to the human. We thus take up in the question of whether it makes sense to offer hospitality to animals, plants, and gods, and at the end of the chapter we turn to the curious question of clones, which arises somewhat unexpectedly at the end of the seminar's second year.[7] Finally, in the conclusion, we return to the place from which we set out, the figure of the threshold, and to its implications not simply for the seminar on hospitality but for the question of teaching more generally.

This is, to be sure, a large and wide-ranging set of themes and questions, but we will end up returning each time to this question of the threshold in relation to each of them, the question of what delimits or demarcates—or is assumed to do so—an inside from an outside. As we will see, there can be no thinking of hospitality, or indeed of deconstruction, without a thinking of the relationship between an inside and an outside, that is, without a thinking of the frontier, border, barrier, wall, gate, or door that separates—or is thought to separate—an inside from an outside, that is, without the threshold that marks the place of transition or transit, the place of invitation or acceptance, of arrival or departure, the place from which hospitality is typically offered or accepted. The question of hospitality, then, like the question of deconstruction, is always the question of the threshold, the question of the phenomenon of the threshold and the question of what lies beyond the threshold as a phenomenon.[8]

Though we will be unable to do justice to the seminar as a whole, the aim of this work is to give the reader some idea of what is in the seminar and make some suggestions about how it might be read, both for itself and for what it might tell us or help us think concerning, for example, the United States' or

Europe's situation with regard to immigration. It will also teach us a great deal about how to treat in a *philosophical* way such limits related to hospitality as, to name just three figures, the *wall*, the *door*, and, especially, the *threshold*, everything from that famous wall that never got built on the United States' southern border with Mexico, to the door that opens or closes in every immigration office, to, finally, the threshold that marks the limit of every house, city, or nation-state, the threshold as the place from which, as we will see, everything gets decided, a threshold that is at once singular and multiple, separating inside from out, the public from the private, in short, the threshold as the place from which everything must be thought.

One last word about Derrida's *Hospitality*: Though this is, of course, purely a coincidence, Derrida's seminar has been published in French not with Édi-tions Galilée, where Derrida published most of his books during his lifetime and where his seminars were being published up until 2019, but with Éditions du *Seuil*, that is, if one may be allowed to translate this proper name into English, with "Threshold Editions."[9] To put it in an even more French idiom, the seminar has been published or has come out "chez Seuil"—those two words, *chez*, "at home," and *Seuil*, "threshold," being two of the central words of the seminar itself. Again, it is purely a coincidence that Derrida's seminar on hospitality has been published with Les Éditions du Seuil, but it is a very fortu-itous one, for Derrida marks and remarks this term *seuil*, "threshold," from one end of the seminar to the other—at once using it and mentioning it—turning it into something like a nonsynonymous substitute for what he elsewhere calls "margin" or "trace" or even "*différance*." This term is thus at once thematic and operative throughout the seminar, marking out a difference, it seems, between an analysis of hospitality that moves forward methodologically with-out looking back or at least without return and one that necessarily interrupts itself, returns to, or doubles back on itself. Though Derrida himself does not put it this way, we might understand this to be a difference between a *method-ological* treatment of the topic and a different kind of *approach*, a difference that might be heard in or between two nearly identical Greek words, *hodos* (ἡ ὁδός)—the word at the basis of our word "method" (from *meta-hodos*), *hodos* meaning a path or a road, a *chemin*, a path that should be followed straight to the end whenever possible, as Descartes advises in his *Discourse on Method*, and the nearly identical word *odos* (ὁ ὁδός or ὁ οὐδός), meaning "threshold," which is spelled exactly the same way and so differs only in its breathing or aspiration and in its gender, with *hodos* being feminine and *odos* masculine.

Odos, then, or *seuil*, in German *Schwelle*, in Spanish *umbral*, and, of course, in English *threshold*. The *OED* (*Oxford English Dictionary*) defines this latter as "the piece of timber or stone which lies beneath the bottom of the door, and has to be crossed in entering a house; the sill of a doorway; hence the entrance to a house or doorway." And from this we get, of course, the more figurative sense of "border, limit (of a region); the line which one crosses in entering (Old English)," and in reference "to entrance, the beginning of a state or action, outset, opening." As for the "thresh" of "threshold," it would apparently come from "thrash," in which case it would be related not simply to thrashing as beating, flogging, or belaboring but, again according to the *OED*, to various mechanical means of separating elements by rubbing, shaking, trampling, stamping, beating, or applying intermittent pressure. The threshold would thus be a sort of threshing floor where things are agitated and separated out, the good elements from the bad, we might think, the wheat from the chaff, or in the case of a certain hospitality, those who look like us or who are to our liking and those who do not and are not, a threshing that takes place always on the threshold between inside and out, in the place where we distinguish, filter, and select those who will enter our houses, cities, and states and those who will not.[10]

Between *hodos* and *odos*, *chemin* and *seuil*, path and threshold, method and approach, methodological progress and, let us say, a certain approach or, better, a certain *démarche*, the difference in inflection or aspiration can perhaps be heard to mark two different ways of thinking hospitality and, perhaps, two different ways of doing philosophy, the first, again, a philosophy with a certain method, a *hodos*, an attempt to follow a single path from beginning to end, and the second an approach or a *démarche* that returns us perpetually to the threshold, that is, to the *odos*. Between *hodos*, with a rough breathing on the omicron, and *odos*, with a smooth breathing, one could say that it is a difference between two omicron variants, to recall once again the language of the pandemic, the first giving us a word that suggests a movement toward somewhere determinate and the second not, though it may be this latter that best teaches us how to negotiate the threshold of a hospitality that perhaps "is," in the end, nothing other than the movement of the threshold itself.

PART I

Preliminaries: Questions on the Threshold

1

Hodos and Odos (Homeric Hospitality 1)

> What do these strange steps of hospitality mean, these interminable
> thresholds and these aporias of hospitality? (*H* 1 102/145)

Since we are still on the threshold, on the *odos*, I propose taking a very brief
detour through a very old interest of mine that has been rekindled by Derrida's
hospitality seminar, namely, Homer, our first great poet in the Western tradition and, indisputability, our first great thinker of hospitality. I thus propose
returning, very briefly, to the threshold of Western literature and thought in
order to consider the role or the place of the *odos*, the threshold, in the *Iliad*
and the *Odyssey*, the threshold of a door or a gate or, as we will see, the threshold of old age, just one threshold before, it seems, the threshold that separates
life from death.[1]

But before focusing on the *odos* itself, let me simply recall how hospitality
figures as a central theme of both Homeric poems. Indeed, it is no exaggera-
tion to say that the entire premise of the *Iliad*, this first great work of literature
in the West, is a transgression of the laws or customs of hospitality. Indeed,
the entire Trojan War is triggered by the foreigner or the guest-stranger who
is Paris abusing the friendship and hospitality that had been accorded him by
his Greek host, Menelaus, in Sparta, by abducting or seducing (there are various versions of the tale, but it's bad either way) his host's wife, Helen. In the
third book of the poem, Menelaus, preparing to confront the very same Paris
in a man-to-man duel some nine to ten years into the war, asks Zeus to help
him avenge himself on Paris so that "many a one even of men yet to be may
shudder to work evil to his host [*xeinodokon*], that hath shown him friendship
[*philotēta*]" (*Iliad* 3.353–54). Later in the poem, Menelaus recalls that Zeus,

as the "god of hospitality [*xeiniou*]," will destroy Troy because of Paris's deeds (*Iliad* 13.625–27). Hence the *Iliad* is motivated by a scene of hospitality in Sparta that gets perverted by Paris, this friend or guest-friend who is granted hospitality and friendship in Menelaus's home and who, having spurned or betrayed that hospitality, becomes a hated enemy.

As for the *Odyssey*, it too revolves in large part around questions of hospitality, with two scenes of hospitality—the one more or less proper and traditional, the other perverse—being juxtaposed by Homer. The traditional scene occurs when Odysseus washes up on the shores of the Phaeacians and is brought by the princess Nausicaa to the palace of the Phaeacian king, where he is given food and wine and is entertained with athletic contests and the singing of a bard for several days without anyone ever asking his name. Indeed, it is not until Alcinous, the Phaeacian king and Nausicaa's father, sees Odysseus weeping while listening to a story about Troy told by the Phaeacian bard Demodocus that he is inclined to ask him about his lineage. Odysseus on the island of the Phaeacians is thus, we could say, received without any conditions, without even having to say who he is. It is only after having been given food and drink and shelter that Odysseus is even asked who he is.

Homer seems to contrast this remarkable scene of hospitality in books 6–8 with what Odysseus himself in book 10 recounts happened to him and his men when they encountered Polyphemus, the Cyclops, whose circle of kinship seems to extend no further than his cave. Though Odysseus will remind the Cyclops that "Zeus is the avenger of suppliants and strangers—Zeus, the strangers' god—who ever attends upon revered strangers" (*Odyssey* 9.270–71), the Cyclops will not heed the reminder and will be punished as a result.[2]

When Odysseus and his men enter the cave of Polyphemus, who lives alone and is out tending his goats, they resist the urge to steal some of the many cheeses and other provisions stored there. They instead wait for Polyphemus to return in order to ask him to provide them with some gift, some show of hospitality. But Polyphemus spurns the request and ends up inverting all the codes of hospitality. Instead of offering them hospitality without asking who they are, the Cyclops asks them to identify themselves, which Odysseus does, calling himself and his men "Achaeans." Instead of then offering food and drink to his guests, Polyphemus then commits the outrage of killing and gobbling up some of Odysseus's men for his evening and morning meals. Instead of offering shelter to his guests, he imprisons Odysseus and his comrades, who are to be his future victuals, in his cave, blocking the entrance with an enormous stone. It is in the wake of these breaches of the codes of hospitality that Odysseus, inverting things on his own, gets the Cyclops drunk on wine that he had brought from his own ship and, when pressed by the Cyclops to tell him his name, gives him the fake name Nobody, *Ou tis*, a name that will later be repeated with a slight difference, another negative, *Mē tis*, meaning both Nobody and Ruse, when the Cyclops, having been blinded by Odysseus, who puts a fire-hardened, smoldering stick into his single eye, calls out for help to the other Cyclopes on the island to complain that Nobody has harmed him.

Scenes of hospitality are thus central to these poems situated at the beginning or on the threshold of Western literature and culture, as is the figure of the *odos*, of the threshold, which marks both poems from beginning to end and punctuates, as it were, both narratives. For whenever someone crosses a threshold in Homer, however insignificant or unremarkable it may first appear, some ritual is being enacted, some rite of passage performed. Whenever someone crosses a threshold, some relationship is being established, renewed, or severed, be this a relationship with another human being, with the gods, or with life itself. And so whenever a threshold, an *odos*, is mentioned in the *Iliad* and *Odyssey* it almost always functions to mark a critical transition between, for example, exile and return, mortals and the gods, or life and death. A threshold is thus almost never simply part of a mere description, part of a catalogue of the elements of a house, for example, but rather a marker that actually gives force and rhythm to the narrative and all the distinctions within it.

The tale of the *Odyssey* essentially opens, in fact, on a threshold. Odysseus has been away from his native Ithaca for some nineteen years, and the gods have decided that it is finally time for him to return home. Descending from Olympus to Ithaca in order to incite Telemachus to look for his father, Athena takes her stand "at the outer gate of Odysseus, on the threshold [*oudos*] of the court," a female goddess in the guise or the likeness of a foreigner or stranger, a *xenos*, precisely, the leader of the Taphians who goes by the name of Mentes (*Odyssey* 1.103–5). From this threshold, Athena, disguised as a *xenos*, that is, as a foreigner but also a guest—*xenos* being a key term for hospitality—speaks to Telemachus and sets in motion the entire sequence of events that will eventually conclude with Odysseus's return.

This is just the first inscription in the narrative of a threshold that, in both the *Odyssey* and the *Iliad*, marks a place of transition, difference, or distinction between exile and return, life and death, male and female, mortals and the gods.[3] This threshold on which Athena appears at the beginning of the *Odyssey* is later recalled when Odysseus returns to Ithaca. Disguised as a beggar, he sits down "upon the ashen threshold within the doorway" (*Odyssey* 17.339), the place traditionally reserved for beggars, suppliants, foreigners, and travelers (see *Odyssey* 10.62, 18.17)—in short, the place where hospitality is asked for and offered or else asked for and denied. Later, it is the threshold to Odysseus's treasure chamber—the place where the great bow is stored—that is remarked upon by the narrator-poet, as if to signal to the reader that something important is in storage there and, as a result, something important is in store for the narrative (*Odyssey* 21.43). It is then once again from a threshold, right on a threshold, that Odysseus, having returned home but still in disguise, strips off his beggar's rags and begins his assault on the suitors with the great bow that he has retrieved from the treasure chamber at Penelope's suggestion (*Odyssey* 22.2).

The threshold, rather than the home or palace itself, is thus the place of return, or at least of transition, the place between inside and outside, past and present, the rightful owner of the palace and the pretenders to it. It is almost as if the threshold came *before* the two spaces or times on either side of it, as if the threshold came *first* and the palace or the narrative was built around it, not unlike the olive tree around which Odysseus's chamber and palace were built. Indeed, it is almost as if human life itself must be thought first and foremost on the basis of the threshold that marks our *entrance* into or our *exit* of it.

When Odysseus returns to his native Ithaca, he asks about his mother and father, whom he had left behind, as he says, "on the threshold of old age." "Are they haply still living beneath the rays of the sun? or are they now dead and in the house of Hades?" (*Odyssey* 15.348–50). The difference between life and death is here conceived neither biologically nor metaphysically but as a relation between light and darkness, between walking beneath the rays of the sun and being stretched out beneath the earth in Hades, in short, between being on one side or the other of that ultimate threshold.

But what does it mean to be "on the threshold of old age"—a phrase that appears several times in Homer?[4] It seems to suggest not a threshold *to* old age but the threshold that old age *is*, a state that *borders* on or is on the *verge* of death, on the threshold of the house of Hades. It is a threshold, then, where one might live or linger for a time, near the end of life, though there are some who die too early and so never have the chance to reach and linger there (see *Odyssey* 15.246–47). Penelope herself laments over the nearly two decades lost with her husband Odysseus: "It is the gods that gave us sorrow," she says, "the gods who begrudged that we two should remain with each other and enjoy our youth, and come to the threshold of old age" (*Odyssey* 23.210–12).

The threshold is thus a place both of joy and pain, return and loss. A glance back over one's life from "the threshold of old age" can thus be an occasion for joyful recollection or sorrowful remembrance. Priam, king of Troy, prays to his most beloved son Hector as he is about to be slain by Achilles: "Have compassion on me that yet can feel—on wretched me whom [Zeus] will slay by a grievous fate on the threshold of old age, when I have beheld ills full many"

(*Iliad* 22.59–61). And at the very end of the *Iliad* this same Priam asks Achilles to take pity on him and return the body of his son Hector by remembering his own father "on the grievous threshold of old age" (*Iliad* 24.487). A father on the threshold of old age who has lost his dearest son thus asks pity from the man who has slain that son by recalling that that man's own father is himself on the grievous threshold of old age.

The threshold thus always marks in Homer a point of transition or transformation between different times of life or different phases of narrative. We hear that Agamemnon learned something of the future "in sacred Pytho, when he passed over the threshold [*oudon*] of stone to enquire of the oracle" (*Odyssey* 8.79–80), the threshold here marking a limit between human knowledge and the knowledge of the gods. In the *Odyssey*, the threshold even seems to mark the transition from everyday life to poetry itself, from the ordinary to the fantastic, as Odysseus stands in awe before the threshold of Alcinous's mythical palace (*Odyssey* 7.82–83, 88–89, 130, 135), the place where Odysseus will recount much of his long journey back to Ithaca (see also *Iliad* 6.375; *Odyssey* 4.480, 4.718, 17.575).

From threshold to threshold, *odos* to *odos*, everything happens on or around the threshold. Let me recall here, in anticipation of a fuller treatment of Plato in Chapter 6, just one reference to the threshold in Plato, a passage from the *Republic* that actually brings together in the space of just a few lines the two words that, as I suggested earlier, can be heard to mark two different ways of approaching the notion of hospitality, *odos* and *hodos*, threshold and path. The passage occurs right near the beginning of the dialogue, when Socrates asks Cephalus, at whose home he is being hospitably received in the Piraeus, how he is faring in his old age:

> I enjoy talking with the very aged. For to my thinking we have to learn of them as it were from wayfarers who have preceded us on a road (*hodos*) on which we too, it may be, must some time fare—what it is like—is it rough and hard going or easy and pleasant to travel. And so now I would fain learn of you what you think of this thing, now that your time has come to it, the thing that the poets call "the threshold (*odos*) of old age." Is it a hard part of life to bear or what report have you to make of it? (*Republic* 328e)

Having just arrived at the home of Cephalus in the Piraeus, having just crossed the threshold, as it were, Socrates inquires of his host at the outset of the dialogue, still on its threshold, about the threshold of old age. It is an open question, a request for information, for testimony, that will soon lead to an ontological question, a *ti esti,* or "what is," question, a methodological question that will then orient the rest of the dialogue, namely, "What is justice?" It is a question as old as Plato, Anaximander, or Homer and a question that remains brand-new and still burning for us. Not to mention the related question, "What is hospitality?"

2

Translating Hospitality

We will speak again often of translation and hospitality; basically, it is the same problem. (*H* 1 3/21)

Derrida recalls very early on in the seminar that the theme of hospitality is related to language. Indeed, it is hard to imagine a scene of hospitality, as Derrida suggests, that would not involve some kind of explicit or virtual language, some kind of "Welcome to my home" on the part of a host and a reciprocal "Thank you" on behalf of a guest, some kind of interpretable word or gesture on the one side and the other. It is what prompts Derrida to say in the second session, "there is no hospitality without language" (*H* 1 40/65).

And yet, because being a foreigner often means first and foremost being a foreigner to the language, to the language in which rights and laws are established and hospitality is given, language poses particular challenges to hospitality. One must typically ask for hospitality in a language that is not one's own, and that requirement is often, says Derrida, the "first violence" done to the foreigner or stranger:[1]

[The foreigner] has to ask for hospitality in a language which by definition is not his own, the one imposed on him by the master of the house, the host, the king, the lord, the authorities, the nation, the State, the father, etc. This personage imposes on him translation into their own language, and that's the first act of violence. That is where the question of hospitality begins: must we ask the foreigner to understand us, to speak our language, in all the senses of this term, in all its possible extensions, before being able and so as to be able to welcome

him into our country? If he was already speaking our language, with
all that that implies, if we already shared everything that is shared with
a language, would the foreigner still be a foreigner and could we speak
of asylum or hospitality in regard to him? This is the paradox that we
are going to see become clearer. (*OH* 15–17/21; see *H* 1 80–81/116–17)[2]

The question not just of language but of translation is thus central to hospitality, and that is true both for private hospitality and hospitality at the level
of the state or the nation-state. We all know of the terrible injustices that
can occur when translators or interpreters are not made available at borders,
detention centers, immigration offices, or courts. This is sometimes simply
because of a lack of resources, but often it is the result of the expectation,
whether spoken or unspoken, that in order to receive hospitality from a state
one ought to be able to ask for it in the language of that state.[3]

As a threshold phenomenon, translation is always at the heart of the question of hospitality—and it is at the heart of Derrida's seminar and, indeed, of
his own writing. Before going any further, then, let us take a look at some of
the trickier terms to translate in Derrida's seminar, trickier to translate from
Derrida's French into other languages though also, sometimes, from French
into French. That is the case with the French *hôte*, which can, rather un-
cannily, mean both *host* and *guest*, either *host* or *guest*, depending on the
context. In order to make sure he is being understood correctly when he uses
this common French word, Derrida will often try to contextualize the term
or parse it, telling us, for example, that what he means by *hôte* in a given instance is "the one who invites" or, in another, "the one who is invited." More
frequently, however, Derrida will resort throughout the seminar to using the
English words *host* and *guest*, which are more succinct and *economical* than
those French paraphrases. In other words, to specify which of the two meanings of *hôte* he intends, Derrida will turn to English, as if the French language
required the supplement of another tongue in order to make itself understood. He writes, for example, "Comment distinguer entre un hôte (*guest*)
et un parasite?"—that is, "How are we to distinguish between a *hôte* (guest)
and a parasite?" (*OH* 59/57; see *H* 1 95/134). Or else, early on in the seminar,
"Adresser dès lors, comme un hôte à un hôte (*as a host to a guest*)" (*H* 1
8/27). We might wonder what this curious inclusion of foreign words into the
seminar, this appeal to a foreign tongue within it, this welcoming of another
language—and English, no less—tells us about translation and hospitality. At
the very least, it is one sign among others that no language is ever so airtight as
not to include other languages within it and one sign among others that when
it comes to hospitality it is often a question of trying to clarify if not stabilize

a language or a logic wherein terms and positions can easily turn into their opposite, the *hôte* into a *hôte*, that is, the host into a guest, the friend into an enemy, and so on. One is reminded here of the interest Derrida once took in the Greek word *pharmakon*, which can mean *either* remedy *or* poison, *at once* remedy *and* poison—a single word that seems to mean two very different, even contrary things.

Hence we have *hôte*, a single word that can mean two opposing things, *guest* or *host*, but then there are, as Derrida traces through Benveniste, the etymological connections between *hospes*, meaning stranger or guest, and *hostis*, which can mean stranger or guest but also enemy, a troubling affinity for Benveniste insofar as it brings hospitality as close as possible to hostility, the foreigner into a worrisome proximity with the enemy (see *H* 1 52/81, 71–72/105–6).

And then there is the French term *étranger*, which can be used to refer to someone who is completely unknown to us, a *stranger* to us, but also to someone who is from another state or nation-state, that is, a *foreigner*, someone who may be either a stranger to us or more or less known and familiar (*H* 1 52/81). In terms of translating this relatively simple word from French into English, one might be tempted simply to opt systematically for a term from the same linguistic family, namely, "stranger," so that the English reader knows that we are dealing each time with the same French word. But then what would one do in all those places where Derrida speaks of a nation's willingness or lack of willingness to grant asylum or visas to *étrangers*? In these cases, "foreigners" seems necessary, and "strangers" misleading. And then there's the fact that the phrase *à l'étranger* means something like "in foreign lands" or, more colloquially, "abroad." The English translators of the *Hospitality* seminar, Ellen Burt for year 1 and Peggy Kamuf for year 2, thus had to make difficult decisions on almost every page. As Derrida puts it in the first session of the seminar, "translation too is a phenomenon or enigmatic experience of hospitality, if not the condition of every hospitality in general" (*H* 1 8/28).

Now, in many contexts, the English *stranger* or *foreigner* and the French *étranger* are the translations of the Greek word *xenos* or *xeinos* (usually translated into Latin as, again, *hospes*), a word probably best known to English speakers—and this too is probably telling—through the term *xenophobia*. (It is notable that while the term *xenophilia* exists in English, it far less known and popular than its negative twin.) Sometimes translated as "stranger," sometimes as "foreigner," the one meaning that the term *xenos* really cannot have, as Derrida will go on to suggest, is what Levinas will call the "absolute other," for the *xenos* is almost always someone caught up in relations of kinship or guest-friendship that make him or her more or less known even in his or her strangeness or foreignness. We will see just a bit later the way in which *xenos* is related to *xenia*, that is, to relations of what is often translated as "guest-friendship." The term thus cannot really mean "absolute other," though it will retain much of the ambiguity (or ambivalence) that we saw in the French *hôte*. Here is just part of the entry on the term in the Greek–English dictionary *Liddell & Scott*:

> ξένος Ion. ξεῖνος, ὁ, *a guest* or *host*, Lat. *hospes*; either as I. *the friend*, with whom one has a treaty of hospitality; in this sense both parties are ξένοι, and the relation was hereditary. II. in Homer mostly *the guest*, as opp. to *the host*. 2. *any stranger*, as being entitled to the rights of hospitality. 3. later, ὦ ξένε, *O stranger*, was a common term of address. 4. from meaning *a stranger* ξένος came to signify *a hireling*, who entered into *foreign* service, *a mercenary soldier*, e.g., of the Greeks in Persian pay. 5. simply for βάρβαρος, a foreigner.

Host, guest, friend, foreigner: All of these can be translations of the same Greek word, an indication of the challenges that any translator of texts on hospitality inevitably faces but also, perhaps, of the strange ambivalence (or pervertibility) at the very heart of the concept of hospitality.

Hôte, étranger, xenos: Those are just some of the key terms of the seminar, some of the key terms for any rethinking of hospitality. Earlier I spoke of the *seuil* in the expression *chez Seuil*, but I did not really touch upon the *chez*. This little word is another one of those "untranslatables" (to cite the title of Barbara Cassin's dictionary) at the heart of this seminar, yet another untranslatable *chez Derrida*.[4] The translator of the first year of the seminar, Ellen Burt, writes this in the "Translator's Note" that precedes her translation:

> For reasons discussed by Derrida at length [see 153–54 and 176–77], the translation of this term central to hospitality causes difficulties. *Chez* is a preposition indicating directionality or location, and *chez moi* is most often translated as referring to the place where hospitality is offered: "at, to, or in my house, my place." *Chez* may also be extended to refer to a family or community as the "place" indicated, or even to the interiority of the self, the innermost being. It is also one manner of referring to a work, for instance, *chez Kant*, "in Kant's work." The form employing the third-person indeterminate pronoun, *chez soi*, will be translated as "at home"; where a determinate personal pronoun is involved (e.g., *chez moi*), the English formulation, "at my house, at my place," will generally be preferred to the less idiomatic "at my home." (*H* 1 xxii)

Derrida will begin the sixth session with an infinitive repeated twice—
chercher, chercher—in which we are to "hear" (because we cannot "see" it)
the word "chez," that is, the "home" or the "at home," hidden within it, the
chez hidden within *chercher*, the question of hospitality being always related
to a certain "economy," a term itself derived from *oikonomia*, which of course
does have the house, the Greek *oikos*, visible within it.[5] "Chez" is a prime example of a word with an extraordinary semantic richness in French that cannot simply be translated into English by "at home" or into German by *bei* (*H 1*
178/241). Though Derrida will remark that in speaking of the French "chez"
in this way he is not simply singing the praises of his "mother tongue," he will
never cease—both here and elsewhere—to remark on its remarkable semantic range, on the possibilities for thinking and for writing sheltered within it,
that is, *chez elle*.

This is just the beginning of a series of reflections about translation and
the difficulties of translating various French idioms, such as *la question de
l'étranger*, which we will take up in some detail later, and *pas d'hospitalité*,
a "step" (*pas*) of hospitality but also a lack or absence (*pas*) of hospitality—a
phrase that opens the fifth session of the seminar and so is yet another one
of those threshold phrases, another phrase that takes us back to the question of the threshold, back to the step or the doorstep.[6] These are thus never
gratuitous plays of or on language but always, each time, attempts to think
the phenomenon in question—in this case, "hospitality." For as we will see
later, as soon as we begin to offer hospitality to those whom we recognize, as
soon as we take that first step (*pas*), there is no (*pas*) hospitality worthy of the
name, no hospitality in the sense of an absolute hospitality to the absolutely
other. But then again, there is no (*pas*) possible hospitality for this absolute
other without taking a step (*pas*) in their direction, without turning them into
a foreigner, that is, without recognizing them to some degree. One *pas* thus
leads to or calls for another; a "step" leads to "not," and the "not" requires a
"step." Everything at stake in hospitality, in what we will later see to be the
aporia or antinomy between conditional and unconditional hospitality, is thus
already contained in the phrase *pas d'hospitalité*—a French phrase that poses
difficulties for anyone who would wish to welcome it into English or any other
language.[7]

But what is it about these words or idioms that Derrida finds so valuable? I
have already suggested that they seem to be dictated by the ambivalent nature
of the "phenomenon beyond phenomena" they seek to describe, that is, by the
very concept of "hospitality" or by the "threshold" around which this concept
turns. Beyond that, they also provide Derrida—the *philosopher* Derrida—with
a chance for thinking. Much later in the seminar, Derrida will say this about

the supposed uniqueness of the German language: "It is no accident if the privilege of the untranslatable language returns so often starting from German, although I have multiplied several remarks on the untranslatability of certain happenstances in French [*chances françaises*]" (H 1 221n43/295n1). It is thus not only the German language, as a certain Heidegger would have it, but the French that offers certain "chances" or "opportunities," certain "coups de chance" for thinking, opportunities that are offered or opened up by a series of associations and a unique economy of language that is to be found in one language rather than another. In speaking of the supposed uniqueness of the German language, Derrida is, of course, recalling Heidegger's comments about the putatively unique philosophical nature of German and Greek. One can read much of Derrida's work on the French language, his prioritizing of French idioms, for example, as at once following in Heidegger's footsteps and forging a very different path. As an attempt to undermine Heidegger's claim or to show its Greco-Germano-centrism, as it were, Derrida will tend, here and elsewhere, to privilege Latin sources, French idioms, all these "chances" for thinking hospitality in the language that is "his," the duplicity of *hôte*, for example, the semantic openness of *chez*, the fact that, in Latin, hospitality seems to be related to both guests and enemies, *hostis* (plural *hostes*) and *hospes* (plural *hospites*), words that perhaps give us a chance to think something like an originary "hostipitality."

What is untranslatable from one language to another, says Derrida in several places, is thus often not a word or phrase or sentence as such, for many difficult words, phrases, and sentences can be translated in some way, in other words, parsed, explained, from one language to another. What is untranslatable—and thus unique—is the *economy* of a word or phrase. Derrida says in an oral aside:

> One cannot translate "*Unheimliche*" because "*Unheimliche*" means at the same time "familiar and not familiar." There, I translated it. However, I needed two words in place of one, or three words. What is untranslatable is economy, it is the word, it is not the link of meaning with the German language; it is the economy in one word of two apparently contradictory meanings. (H 1 221n44/295n2)

This untranslatable economy of a word or phrase explains in part why Derrida often parses, rather than simply translates, words and phrases, offering various shades or nuances in them rather than trying to give a word-for-word translation of them. It is the idiom, the economy of the idiom, that is often not translatable. For example, the English "economy" itself, as we mentioned a moment ago, which at once does and does not fully translate the Greek *oikonomia*, since this latter maintains through its reference to the *oikos*, that is, to the "house," a relation to managing the *household*, that is, to a certain domestic sphere, that the English does not. One can thus translate *oikonomia* into English as "economy" or into French as "économie," though these single-word translations miss, at least on their surface, the "economy," precisely, of the Greek.

From one language to another then, it is a question of economy or, rather, a question of moving between different economies. This would seem to suggest — and Derrida's seminar on hospitality bears this out on every page — that language is itself, in its very structure, "hospitable" to what is outside it or at least open to reinscription and thus to the outside, to what is other than it, to the graft or, as we will see in Chapter 14, the xenograft of the other, including the other's language. Derrida thus suggests reframing or recontextualizing in a seminar on hospitality a series of claims that he will have made and repeated in numerous other circumstances and contexts since at least the time of "Signature Event Context." In that pivotal essay of 1971, he wrote:

> By structure, and in what the linguists are no doubt right to call its system, its systematicity, a language is open to incorporation, insemination or dissemination, fecundation, grafting, prosthesis, a grafting either natural or artificial in appearance, artificial insemination, etc. (*H* 1 40–41/65–66)

Questions of language and translation are thus essential to any thinking of hospitality. And yet, already in the first session of the seminar, Derrida wonders aloud whether hospitality is coextensive with language, since there would seem to be something about hospitality that requires going beyond any particular language, welcoming the other not simply in their own language but beyond language altogether.

> Inviting, receiving, asylum, lodging, go by way of the language or the address to the other. As Levinas says from another point of view, language *is* hospitality. Nevertheless, we have come to wonder whether absolute, hyperbolical, unconditional hospitality doesn't consist in suspending language, a particular determinate language, and even the address to the other. (*OH* 133–35/119; see *H* 1 119/165)

The language of hospitality that is first opened up on the threshold, that is, on the *seuil*, on the *odos*, would thus perhaps be at once the beginning and the end of hospitality as such, and the determination of the threshold in terms of one language rather than another — English, French, or Greek — is perhaps already a first sign that the threshold has already been overstepped, overlooked, determined, and thereby forgotten. Derrida says in an interview from December 1997, that is, just months after the conclusion of his two-year seminar on hospitality:

> In the political field as well as in the field of poetic or philosophical translation, the event to invent is an event of translation. Not translation in . . . univocal homogeneity, but in the meeting [*recontre*] of idioms that come to be in accord [*s'accordent*], that accept one another without renouncing as much as possible their singularity. At every moment there's a difficult choice. (S 74)

3

Masters of the House:
Hospitality and Sovereignty

> The host remains the master in the house, the country, the nation; he
> controls the threshold, he controls the borders . . . ("HJR" 69)

Very early on in his seminar on hospitality, Derrida, as head of the seminar,
as the one who, according to good pedagogical conventions, should welcome
others—his students and auditors—into it, Derrida at once *mentions* and *uses*
the language of hospitality, welcoming the members of the seminar, in both
French and in English, before then confessing that he does not yet know what
hospitality is:

> *"We do not know what hospitality is."* This is a phrase I address to you
> in French, in my language, at home [*chez moi*], so as to begin and as
> if to wish you welcome into this seminar where I take the floor first, in
> my language, which seems to assume that I am here *at home*, master
> of my home, that I receive you, invite, accept or welcome you, allow
> you to come and pass the threshold, while saying to you "welcome."
> (H 1 7/27)

Derrida says, notice, that the language and the context would all suggest,
would lead anyone to "assume," that he is *chez lui*, at home, as leader or master of the seminar. But this is, Derrida is suggesting, just a presupposition, an
assumption, because it may be that when we come to know a little bit more
about hospitality we will understand that we are always at home in the home
of the other and that the other is always at home in our home.

And yet that presupposition—perhaps even that phantasm, as we will later
suggest—remains and cannot be so easily ignored or dismissed. As we heard

Derrida say in the preceding chapter, "[The foreigner] has to ask for hospitality in a language which by definition is not his own, the one imposed on him by the master of the house, the host, the king, the lord, the authorities, the nation, the State, the father, etc." (*OH* 15/21; see *H* 1 80/116). It is notable the way Derrida here assembles a series of terms into a kind of configuration: master of the house, host, king, lord, nation, state, father. These are obviously not all the same thing. But because words mean nothing on their own, nothing outside of some context, nothing outside of sentences — as Derrida liked to recall J. L. Austin saying — then one can begin to understand the term "host" only by marking it or surrounding it with other terms that are structurally bound to it in Western philosophy, literature, etymologies, and everyday language, terms having to do with power in the form of, for example, patriarchy, lordship, nation-state sovereignty, and so on. We will see Derrida doing this throughout the seminar, refraining from giving some straightforward definition at the outset of his investigation or analysis but instead situating a word within a semantic field or skein that will help us understand certain aspects of it. Because there is no center or core to such a semantic field, because each term defines and is defined by all the others to which it is linked, there is no way to ask about hospitality except by beginning somewhere in language, that is, always from a place or a threshold that has meaning only because of the terms around it.

According to a certain tradition and history of hospitality — the one that Derrida is trying to rethink if not "deconstruct" — the position of the host is always identified with that of the father, the king or the lord, the state or the nation. In other words, it is indissociable from a certain notion of power or sovereignty, from the sovereign power to grant hospitality or not, a power grounded in the ability of a self to return to itself in order to say "I" or "I can." In *Hospitality* and elsewhere, this configuration of identity, self-identity, sameness, power, capacity, the power or capacity to say "I," to decide and to act, and so on is called by Derrida, with a kind of shorthand, "ipseity."

Ipseity would thus itself be a threshold notion, since it is always from the threshold that hospitality is offered and since it is always on or at the threshold that the power to offer hospitality is determined. Derrida says during the first session of the seminar, linking ipseity once again to the notion of the threshold, to the *seuil*, and to the notion of sameness or self-sameness at the root of identity itself:

> So, here is a *first threshold*, on the threshold of the threshold that is
> the place of hospitality. The question of hospitality is then also the
> question of ipseity, and it proclaims itself such; Benveniste, too, in his

way, will help us to confirm it from language, the *ut pote* and what he calls the "mysterious *-pse* of *ipse*." . . . The first step toward the threshold concerns, then, the strange link, in its etymological-institutional figure, between hospitality offered, the mastery of power, and ipseity *itself*, being *oneself*, identity *itself* as identity to *oneself* [*l'ipséité* même, *l'être soi*-même, *l'identité* même *comme identité à soi*-même]. It is the little word *"même"* [same] that should capture our whole attention here. (*H* 1 33–34/56–57)

It has often been said that Derrida, often in association with Heidegger, carried out a critique or a deconstruction of the "metaphysics of presence." What this passage from *Hospitality* makes clear is that Derrida's aim was also, or indeed was primarily, a deconstruction of the *metaphysics of ipseity*, that is, the metaphysics of power and self-identity, of ownness, propriety, and self-sameness. That metaphysics is on full display in traditional notions and analyses of hospitality, and it is confirmed by Benveniste's analyses in *The Dictionary of Indo-European Concepts and Society*. Derrida's claim early on in the seminar that hospitality always involves a law of the house, of the master, an *oikonomia*, once again, is motivated in large part by the etymological work of Benveniste, even if it will be verified and confirmed by an entire literary and philosophical tradition (see *H* 1 4/23). Derrida writes near the end of the first session of the seminar, turning here explicitly to Benveniste's analysis of the lexicon of "hospitality" in his article on the topic in *The Dictionary of Indo-European Concepts and Society*, book 1, *Economy*:

> The "basic term," then, is the Latin *hospes*, which term, Benveniste recalls, is divided in two, into two distinct elements, he says, which "finally link up": *hosti-pet-s* . . . *Pet-* alternates with *pot-*, which means "master," so that *hospes* would signify, notes Benveniste, "the guest-master." (*H* 1 22/44)

Hospitality is thus related, according to Benveniste, to a certain notion of sovereignty and power, of *mastery*, of being master over a house, having the power and ability to invite, to offer hospitality. As Derrida writes, "the host, the one who offers hospitality, must be master at his house, he (in the masculine, first of all) must be assured of sovereignty over the space and the goods that he offers or opens to the other as stranger or foreigner" (*H* 1 23/45).

A certain configuration thus begins to come into view: The Latin *hostes* leads back to *hosti-pets*, from *hostis* (both guest and enemy) and *pets*, which is related to *despotès*, the master of the house, and so to mastery and sovereignty more generally. It is the master of the house who offers hospitality: This seems to be a law of hospitality. The law of hospitality would always seem to be a hospitality of laws, laws laid down, in the first instance, by the master of the house, who would always implicitly say to his guest: "'Make yourself at home' but on condition that you observe the rules of hospitality, that is to say, respect the being at home of my home, the being oneself of what I am" (*H 1* 23/45). If hospitality is related to mastery, to power, to sovereign power, then it begins, and precisely because of this power and these conditions, to limit itself right from the outset, right on the threshold. It limits itself because of the conditions that are set upon it by this mastery, turning it into something other than hospitality, something with an edge, perhaps, of hostility, hostility born of resentment.

Derrida concludes his brief reading of Benveniste in the first session by recalling yet again the relationship between sovereignty and ipseity. He recalls that the power of the host, of the master, is, in the end, nothing other than *ipseity*:

> We shall see how power (the despotic sovereignty and virile mastery of the master of the house) is nothing other than *ipseity* itself, the same-ness of the oneself, to say nothing of the subject, which is a stabilizing and despotic bid to raise the stakes of ipseity, of self-being or the *Selbst*. (*H 1* 25/48; see also 33/56)

As traditionally understood, hospitality is thus dominated by the "conjugal, paternal or phallogocentric model" that determines the one who offers hospitality as the father, the familiar despot, the husband, the boss, the master of the house—all those who, from Sophocles, as we will see, to Klossowski—lay down the laws of hospitality.

It is this notion of ipseity, ipseity in its relation to sovereignty, that will end up informing and motivating much of Derrida's thinking on the question of hospitality. As understood by him, ipseity is even more radical than egoicity, *ipse* being more radical than the *ego* (see *H 1* 38–39/63). Derrida will thus follow, again with the help of Benveniste, the Latin filiation of *même*—*metipse*, *ipse*, etc.—in order to fill out this configuration of *ipse*, power, and hospitality, that is, sameness, identity, self-identity, power, and hospitality, for example, the notion of a host who has the power or the ability to invite and who will invite only under certain conditions—for example, only under the condition that hospitality will one day be returned in kind, or only under the condition that the one invited is sufficiently "like" or the "same" as the one doing the inviting to be considered capable of offering hospitality in return. At this level, *ipseity*, understood as the minimal condition for granting hospitality, thus seems always to involve a certain "pulsion de pouvoir," a power drive, a *Bemächtigungstrieb* (*H 1* 39/63–64).

With that Freudian notion of the *Bemächtigungstrieb* no doubt in the back of his mind, informing his reading, Derrida finds in Benveniste a persistent etymological relationship between mastery and identity—a relationship that sometimes seems to surprise Benveniste himself (see *H* 1 41–42/67). It is thus while reading Benveniste that Derrida opens up a long parenthetical remark about this relation between identity and power: everything from the Kantian/ Husserlian "I can" to the relationship between identity, power, and possibility in Maine de Biran, Heidegger, and, especially, Hegel, in the master-slave dialectic (see *H* 1 43–45/68–71). Derrida then goes on to show the ways in which thinkers as diverse as Bataille, Sartre, and Lacan were all marked by this Hegelian analysis of sovereignty (see *H* 1 46/72). All this is done in an attempt to argue, to show, that Benveniste should not have been so surprised to find the close relationship between "mastery" and "identity." Not only is it not surprising; it is a regular and reoccurring association in Western philosophy, a dominant thread or throughline at the level of both language and conceptual analysis.

There is no hospitality without finitude, says Derrida, that is, no hospitality without the necessity of some limitation and selection, some filtering, on the part of the one offering hospitality. As Derrida adds in an aside: "By definition, between infinite beings, there is no hospitality, the *hôte* in both meanings of the term (host and guest) must be finite" (*H* 1 94n30/132n2). But this also means that there is no hospitality without power or sovereignty, even if power or sovereignty always tends toward the unconditional. There is no hospitality without the power of a host to choose and thereby limit his guests.

> Paradoxical and corrupting law: it depends on this constant collusion between traditional hospitality, hospitality in the ordinary sense, and power. This collusion is also power in its *finitude*, which is to say the necessity, for the host, for the one who receives, of choosing, electing, filtering, selecting their invitees, visitors, or guests, those to whom they decide to grant asylum, the right of visiting, or hospitality. No hospitality, in the classic sense, without sovereignty of oneself over one's home, but since there is also no hospitality without finitude, sovereignty can only be exercised by filtering, choosing, and thus by excluding and doing violence. Injustice, a certain injustice, and even a certain perjury, begins right away, from the very threshold of the right to hospitality. (*OH* 55/53; see *H* 1 94/132)

Hospitality is, therefore, always linked to the power of a host and to the necessity of him choosing, electing, filtering, and selecting his guests—in short, subjecting them to the threshing or the thrashing that, as we saw, takes place always on or at the threshold.[1] There is no hospitality in the classic sense of the term without the sovereignty of the self over "one's home," no hospitality without finitude, selection, and, thus, violence. We said earlier that hospitality, through this very identification of mastery and identity, begins to limit itself right from the threshold. This also seems to mean that a certain injustice begins always at the threshold as well. And that would be the case in both private hospitality and that form of public hospitality we call immigration or the right to visit; there is no immigration without finitude, selection, and, thus, violence. In the third session, Derrida recalls the relationship between the threshold, power, and *ipseity*:

> It is that a hospitality regulated by right, a hospitality normed by a system of norms and rules that come to confirm the propriety and power of the host, and first of all his ipseity, a hospitality getting determined precisely on the basis of that which determines, namely, the limit of the threshold, the at-home, where the "make yourself at home" remains the "as if" of a fiction in which, above all, no one ought to believe, a hospitality contained within the circle of duty and right and statutory obligations, such a hospitality is doubtless determined, hence apparently concrete and actual, but it is so well limited by its de-termination that it ends where it begins; its actuality ruins it, so to speak. In its very positivity, then, it ruins itself. (*H* 1 56/86–87)

It is not long after this important passage, which we will have occasion to look at again with another objective in view in Chapter 8, that Derrida adds a long parenthetical remark on the *Beiträge*, one of the texts of Heidegger's that Derrida rarely mentions but the one where, according to some, Heidegger seems closest to Derrida, even though, as we will hear, Derrida himself will pose the same questions to Heidegger here as he does elsewhere, that is, questions concerning selfhood or self-identity, property or propriety, *Selbstheit* or *Eigentlichkeit*. Derrida writes—let me note it again—parenthetically:

> (. . . in the *Beiträge zur Philosophie* (*vom Ereignis*), [I don't know how to translate that: *Contributions to Philosophy* (*Of the Event*)], in those rich working texts published in Heidegger's centenary year and dating from the end of the '30s [1936 . . .], Heidegger distinguishes *Selbstheit*—which one could translate by "ipseity," I think, the self, oneself-ness—from egoity, from the I. He says that *Selbstheit* is more originary [*ursprünglicher*] than every I and you and we. The first and second persons [I, you, we] are only derived, constituted forms, effects of ipseity, hence, particular forms of ipseity like person and subject. And these Heideggerian propositions appear in passages [§ 197, particularly, p. 320] where *Selbstheit* and the self-relation of ipseity

are analyzed as experiences of the proper, property and appropriation [*Eigen-tum, Eignung, Zueignung, Übereignung, Eignung im Ereignis,* etc.]—after a passage, and here we ought to linger over it at length, where the relations of *Dasein* with the notion of people [*Volk*] are defined in a brief, but dense and difficult way.) (*H* 1 60/91–92)[2]

Hospitality is therefore offered on the basis of a selfhood, a self-identity or a self-relation, that comes before, that would be more basic than, the self or the ego. Hospitality offered on the basis of such selfhood or self-identity, such mastery or ipseity, is thus *already* selective, filtering, limited, and ultimately unjust. But this does not mean that at its most basic, fundamental level an *ipseity* is closed in upon itself and closed off to the other, closed up without any original relation to an other or to the outside. On the contrary, Derrida will argue later in the seminar that I am an *ipse* only on the basis of this other in me (see *H* 1 130–31/180), which means that even before there is any organized hospitality—and thus selection—the other is already there, in me, in me before any welcoming *on my part*. As Derrida will say even later in the seminar, hospitality is offered out of a gesture that is *at once* narcissistic and antinarcissistic (*H* 1 198/265). Hence the *"il faut"* must be understood as preceding ipseity, perhaps in the same way that, as we will soon see, the "question coming from the foreigner or the stranger" precedes any question "about" the foreigner or stranger or any question posed "to" them.

This relationship between hospitality and power suggests that we are already, in anticipation of a more formal analysis of Derrida's more formal articulation of hospitality, sketching out a relationship between two kinds of hospitality, that is, between a conditional—that is, a selective, filtering—hospitality that is always related to the power and authority of a host and an unconditional hospitality that is offered beyond or before that selective or filtering power. We are also developing here not only two kinds of hospitality (conditional and unconditional) but also two valences of unconditionality, one related to the power and sovereignty of the one offering hospitality and one related to the arrival or the coming of a guest who has not even been invited by a host. As Derrida says in "Fichus," from 2002:

It is from this possibility of the impossible, and from what would have to be done so as to try to think it differently, to think thinking differently, through an unconditionality without indivisible sovereignty, outside what has dominated our metaphysical tradition, that I try in my own way to draw some ethical, juridical, and political consequences, whether it's to do with the idea of time, or the gift, or hospitality, or forgiveness, or the decision—or the democracy to come. ("F" 168/20–21)

It is a point Derrida will make right around the same time, yet again with reference to the "democracy to come," at the beginning of *Rogues*:

> When it comes to reason and democracy, when it comes to a demo-
> cratic reason, it would be necessary to distinguish "sovereignty" (which
> is always in principle indivisible) from "unconditionality." Both of
> these escape absolutely, like the absolute itself, all relativism. (*R* xiv/13)

If it is permissible to transfer this logic from *Rogues* into the register that is here ours, then it might be said that, when it comes to hospitality, and perhaps even to cosmopolitical hospitality, it is necessary to distinguish sovereignty, the sovereignty of the host (which is in principle indivisible), from unconditionality, that is, from the unconditional demand put upon the host by the guest, who is perhaps so unknown or so unconditioned that he or she or it cannot even be recognized as a guest, certainly not as "my" guest.

4

Xenos and Xenia (Homeric Hospitality 2)

. . . and from the threshold of the house, to be the first to speak in one's own language as master at home and to wish "welcome" [in English in original]. (*H* 1 8/27)

The *xenos* is a guest, or a stranger who should be treated as a guest, the ambivalence of this word *xenos* marking out, it would seem, at once the promise and the challenge of hospitality. As we have seen, *xenos* (sometimes spelled *xeinos*) means both guest and stranger—guest, though also friend or foreigner and, potentially, enemy. In the *Iliad*, for example, Agamemnon says that Tydeus once came as a guest (*xenos*) to Mycenae (4.377), that is, he seems to be saying, as a welcomed guest, though the ambivalence of the word *xenos* is evoked just a few lines later when Agamemnon says that when Diomedes once traveled to Thebes he had no fear *even though* he was a *xenos*, i.e., a stranger. Like the term *philos*, that is, friend, *xenos*, which can mean not only stranger or guest but friend or guest-friend, seems always to express or to mark some relationship of proximity or distance, of proximity reestablished or distance eclipsed. That is clear in Homer's very use of the name *xenos*, though it becomes even clearer in his depiction of the more formal, ritualized relations known as *xenia* or guest-friendship.

As Derrida suggests in large part through his reading of Benveniste, the question of the *xenos* must always be asked in relationship to the question of *xenia*, which is always a collective agreement or alliance, a pact of hospitality that is never simply between individuals but always between families, clans, or groups (see *OH* 29/31–33, *H* 1 85/122). In *xenia*, one agrees to offer hospitality not just to one individual but to an entire family, sometimes from one generation to the next. In such cases, hospitality is at once extended—and thereby limited—to a *particular* family, with a lineage, a patronym, and so on. One thus offers hospitality to more than the individual but still only to those with recognizable names or lineages (see *OH* 23–25/27–29, *H* 1 83/120). This is the difference, as we suggested earlier, between the *xenos* and the *autre absolu*, the absolute other, to whom we might offer hospitality regardless of their name, or before their name, before even asking their name, and thus regardless of their origin or their identity, their family lineage, language, and so on.

According to Benveniste, *xenia* indicates relations linking men by a past that implies precise obligations that carry on to their *descendants*. What is important here, for Derrida, is the "reciprocity" of rights *and* obligations between the parties, a reciprocity that engages families and generations (see *OH* 21–23/25–27, *H* 1 82–83/119). Derrida comments: "The right to hospitality commits a household, a line of descent, a family, a familial or ethnic group receiving a familial or ethnic group" (*OH* 23/27; see *H* 1 83/120). And it seems that the name alone is enough to do this, an individual's name, which always brings along with it a lineage and a history. As Derrida very simply puts it: "A proper name is never purely individual" (*OH* 23/27; see *H* 1 83/120). In other words, a proper name is never simply proper to the one who bears it; it carries a whole network of familial and other relations.

While Derrida does not refer to this example, it might be useful to recall here the classic scene of guest-friendship, of *xenia*, in the sixth book of the *Iliad*, a scene that, because it ends with a sort of blindness or madness, could have provided Derrida in the seminar with yet another transition to Oedipus (see Chapter 5).

In the midst of a raging battle between the Greeks and the Trojans, the spotlight shines down upon and isolates, as it were, two warriors, Glaucus, a Trojan ally, and Diomedes, a Greek, for a scene of guest-friendship that will conclude with an exchange of armor and a renewal of that guest-friendship.[1] The two warriors come together in the sort of no-man's-land between the ranks of the Trojans and the Greeks. They come together to confront each other, to fight to the death, but before doing so, before exchanging blows, they decide to exchange lineages:

> Glaucus, son of Hippolochus, and the son of Tydeus [that is, Diomedes] came together in the space between the two hosts, eager to do battle. And when the twain were now come near as they advanced one against the other, Diomedes, good at the war-cry, was first to speak, saying: "Who art thou, mighty one, among mortal men? For never have

I seen thee in battle where men win glory until this day, but now hast
thou come forth far in advance of all in thy hardihood, in that thou
abidest my far-shadowing spear. Unhappy are they whose children
face my might. But if thou art one of the immortals come down from
heaven, then will I not fight with the heavenly gods." (*Iliad* 6.119–31)

Diomedes thus asks for a name, an identity, a lineage, in order to know
whether he should slay the one facing him, though also, no doubt, in order to
fill out his boast should he slay him. But what he gets in return is something
rather unexpected.

Then spake to him the glorious son of Hippolochus [Glaucus]:
"Great-souled son of Tydeus, wherefore inquirest thou of my lineage?
Even as are the generations of leaves, such are those also of men. As
for the leaves, the wind scattereth some upon the earth, but the forest,
as it bourgeons, putteth forth others when the season of spring is come;
even so of men one generation springeth up and another passeth away.
Howbeit, if you wilt, hear this also, that thou may know well my lineage; and many there be that know it. There is a city . . . (6.144–55)

It is thus just after this comparison between human generations and the suc-
cession of the seasons—already a suggestion, it seems, that guest-friendship
is what links generations—that Glaucus goes on to recount his lineage, including the exploits of his ancestor Bellerophon, who once received guest-
friendship from an ancestor of Diomedes (6.144–55). Glaucus concludes some
fifty lines later: "This is the lineage and the blood whereof I avow me sprung"
(6.211), and the poet continues:

So spake he, and Diomedes, good at the war-cry, waxed glad. He
planted his spear in the bounteous earth, and with gentle words spake
to the shepherd of the host: "Verily now art thou a friend [*xeinos*]
of my father's house from of old: for goodly Oeneus on a time entertained peerless Bellerophon in his halls, and kept him twenty
days; and moreover they gave one to the other fair gifts of friendship
[*xeinēia*]. Oeneus gave a belt bright with scarlet, and Bellerophon
a double cup of gold which I left in my palace as I came hither. . . .
Therefore now am I a dear guest-friend [*xeinos philos*] to thee in the
midst of Argos, and thou to me in Lycia, whenso I journey to the land
of that folk. So let us shun one another's spears even amid the throng;
full many there be for me to slay, both Trojans and famed allies,
whomsoever a god shall grant me and my feet overtake; and many

Achaeans again for thee to slay whomsoever thou canst. And let us
make exchange of armor, each with the other, that these men too may
know that we declare ourselves to be friends [*xeinoi*] from our fathers'
days. (6.212–31)

From both sides of the confrontation, on the part of both a Trojan ally and
a Greek, we have the inscription of a previously anonymous other into language, and into history, by means of a name and, thus, a lineage.

After the exchange of lineages and the recognition of a guest-friendship
that goes back generations, the two warriors swear not to fight each other and
prepare to renew their ancient pact through an exchange of armor. This is
done both for themselves and their families and for those who will bear witness to their guest-friendship. But then there's this:

> When they had thus spoken, the twain leapt down from their chariots
> and clasped each other's hands and pledged their faith. And then from
> Glaucus did Zeus, son of Cronos, take away his wits, seeing he made
> exchange of armor with Diomedes, son of Tydeus, giving golden for
> bronze, the worth of an hundred oxen for the worth of nine. (6.232–36)

The two warriors, having come together to exchange lineages in this no-man's-
land between the two armies, jump down from their chariots to exchange
armor, like soccer players trading jerseys after a game, only in this case one jer-
sey is a whole lot more valuable than the other. They thus declare themselves
to be "friends [*xeinoi*]" (6.231), friends of old, as it were, and they proceed to
exchange armor, but Zeus takes away Glaucus's good sense, his sense of eq-
uitable exchange, causing him to give away golden armor for bronze, that is,
armor worth more than ten times the armor he receives in return (6.241–44). It
is as if Homer wanted to illustrate not only the way guest-friendship links generations but also the way it requires a kind of leap of faith between those who
engage in it, a commitment beyond rational or reasonable exchange, in short,
a kind of madness. And it is as if he wanted to show that such guest-friendship
is never simply given but must be maintained and that it always risks falling
apart. In book 17 of the *Iliad*, the very same Glaucus chides Hector, calling
him "heartless," for not protecting Sarpedon, who "was at once thy guest [*xe-
inon*] and thy comrade" (17.150).

Before leaving this classic scene of guest-friendship from the *Iliad*, it will
be worth recalling Socrates's equally famous invocation of it in the *Symposium*, since it illustrates something about the philosophical reinscription and
transformation of the codes of hospitality. It comes in the midst of Alcibiades's
encomium of Socrates and his tale of how he once attempted to seduce him

by giving him what he thought to be the object of Socrates's desires, namely, himself, or, rather, his body. This, says Alcibiades, led to Socrates's saying with his characteristic irony that Alcibiades was actually trying to deceive him, trying to get him to trade his spiritual wisdom for Alcibiades's physical body, that is, in effect, to exchange gold armor for mere bronze:

> My dear Alcibiades, I daresay you are not really a dolt, if what you say of me is the actual truth, and there is a certain power in me that could help you to be better; for then what a stupendous beauty you must see in me, vastly superior to your comeliness! And if on espying this you are trying for a mutual exchange of beauty for beauty, it is no slight advantage you are counting on—you are trying to get genuine in return for reputed beauties, and in fact are designing to fetch off the old bargain of gold for bronze. (*Symposium* 218e–219a)

It is in this way that Plato's Socrates at once appropriates and transforms the Homeric tradition, in this case the tradition of guest-friendship, turning the exchange between two warriors in the *Iliad* into a philosophical exchange, one in which Socrates would be getting the short end of the stick were he to accept the mad exchange of spiritual goods for physical ones, real goods for merely apparent ones. In the wake of the *Symposium*, philosophical guest-friendship would become the only guest-friendship worthy of the name, that is, the only true and valuable form of guest-friendship, a *xenia* defined and oriented, it seems, by a very different system of values and, thus, a very different kind of reciprocity, no longer armor for armor but the body that goes in that armor for the soul that is in that body.

5

On Dying Abroad: Oedipus (on the Threshold) at Colonus

> We will find this care with seeing and not seeing, the "in view of not seeing," in a certain Oedipus leaning on Antigone at the moment when he presents himself as a foreigner and addresses foreigners, at the threshold of the town, who address him as a foreigner. They all call one another "foreigner" [xenos]. (H 1 37/62)

For Derrida, *Oedipus at Colonus* is the exemplary story of a stranger arriving in a strange land to ask for hospitality from strangers. That strange land is, of course, Colonus, a district on the outskirts of Athens, under the control of Theseus, the king of Athens. Oedipus will be, in Derrida's reading, exemplary in some sense of all strangers or foreigners, all guests, residing somewhere between the sacred and the profane, the divine and the human, already on the threshold, as it were, between these distinctions (OH 35/37; see H 1 86–87/124). The story of Oedipus will also, of course, set up the whole question of sanctuary cities or cities of refuge that will be at the center of a later session in the seminar and Derrida's text on cosmopolitanism.

Because Sophocles's play will be such an important text for Derrida in the seminar, we would do well to read it briefly on our own, informed, of course, by Derrida, but with an eye for other themes. For example, since we have been following the figure of the threshold, the *odos*, in Derrida and the texts he reads, we will see in this seminal text for Derrida on hospitality at least two thresholds, two uses of the word *odos* that mark more or less the beginning and the end of the play, Oedipus's salvation and the salvation of Athens near the beginning of the play and Oedipus's death at the end.

As the play opens, Oedipus, old and blind, asks Antigone where they are.

Strangers, outsiders, *xenoi* (13), says Oedipus, they have been wandering, suffering, and are seeking refuge. They are near Athens, Antigone tells her father, but they must question a passing stranger, a *xenos* as well in Sophocles's Greek, to find out exactly where they are (33). It is thus *xenoi* (plural) asking a *xenos* (singular), strangers wandering in a foreign land who must ask a stranger, where they are.

This *xenos* from near Athens, this stranger to Antigone and Oedipus, tells them they are on holy ground, in a sacred grove dedicated to the Eumenides (42). These are, of course, the same goddesses celebrated at the end of Aeschylus's *Oresteia* when Orestes is acquitted of the murder of his mother, Clytemnestra, who had killed Orestes's father, Agamemnon, and the Furies, the gods of blood and vengeance, are transformed into the Eumenides, the Kindly Ones. Oedipus asks that he be received in this place as the "outlaw" that he is as they stand on the threshold, the *odos*, of the grove or sanctuary of the Eumenides (56) (see *OH* 37/39; *H* 1 88/126).[1] This is, as I suggested earlier, the first of two thresholds that seem to mark the beginning and the end of the play, its initial dilemma and its resolution.

When the Stranger tells Oedipus that the place, Colonus, is ruled by Theseus, king of Athens, Oedipus says that he can be of some good to Athens. He wants Theseus to be summoned, for he was once promised "haven in a foreign land" (90) and wishes to plead his case before Theseus and offer himself as Athens's protector, its savior or salvation. It is thus the migrant, the stranger, the foreigner, someone coming from the outside, who promises to be able to save or protect Athens so long as he himself is protected. "Pity this dishonored shade," he says, "The ghost of him who once was Oedipus" (109–10).

Worried that Oedipus may defile the precinct of the Eumenides, the Chorus asks Antigone to guide Oedipus away from the grove: "In a strange land strange thou art [*xeinos epi xenēs*]" (187). Oedipus explains his predicament to the Athenian Chorus by echoing their own language, returning the word stranger for stranger, *xenos* for *xenos*: "Strangers [*xenoi*], I have no country"; banished from Thebes, he has no state, no *polis*, of his own (208). After learning that he is indeed the "hapless Oedipus" (221), the Chorus worries that Oedipus will be a curse rather than a blessing upon their land. But Antigone defends her father, saying that while he is "not innocent," since he did kill his father and sleep with his mother, he did so "with no ill intent."

We will see Derrida much later in the seminar take up a Talmudic commentary by Levinas on this very thing, cities of refuge for those who are guilty of involuntary murder, that is, refuge for those who are not free of guilt or responsibility but who did not *intend* to do what they did. It is a defense that would have been resonant with a Greek audience as well. Since we have been looking for even earlier traces of Greek hospitality, guest-friendship, and so on in Homer, we would do well to recall that, in book 23 of the *Iliad*, Patroclus, after having been slain by Hector, comes to Achilles in the form of a spirit or phantom to recall how Achilles's father, Peleus, had received him and given him refuge after he had killed someone as a child. "Menoetius brought me, being yet a little lad, from Opoeis to your country, by reason of grievous man-slaying, on the day when I slew Amphidamus's son in my folly, though I willed it not, in wrath over the dice. Then the knight Peleus received me into his house and reared me with kindly care and named me thy squire" (*Iliad* 23.86–90). We hear a similar tale from Phoenix in book 9. Having been induced by his mother to sleep with his father's concubine as a way for the mother to take vengeance upon her husband, Phoenix had to flee his native land to escape his father's wrath, and when he "came to deep-soiled Phthia," King Peleus, he says, "received me with a ready heart, and cherished me as a father cherisheth his only son and well-beloved, that is heir to great possessions" (9.478–83). Hence the two people closest to Achilles, the two men most beloved by him, at once back home in Phthia and on the shores of Troy, were exiled from their own city-states, where they were reviled because of their actions—their not wholly intentional actions—by their townspeople and offered refuge as suppliants in a foreign city.

Like Patroclus and Phoenix, then, Oedipus pleads for help in a foreign land. He pleads, in effect, for refuge, for sanctuary. "Athens is held of States the most devout," he says, "Athens alone gives hospitality/And shelters the vexed stranger [*xenos*], so men say" (260). Oedipus says he has come to Athens as a suppliant (282), and he asks that their "chief," Theseus, be informed of his request (295). He makes his plea for a sort of reciprocal suppliance or hos-pitality whereby the one who helps others will eventually himself be helped by those others: "Who serves his neighbor serves himself," as Oedipus simply puts it (308).

Ismene, Oedipus's other daughter, now arrives, with news that her two brothers, Oedipus's sons, Eteocles and Polyneices, are vying for power in Thebes (370). She reports having heard an oracle that Oedipus's body, living or dead, will be a boon, a salvation, for the city that has it (389–90). Once again, the cursed foreigner, the stranger, can become a blessing, the outcast the "deliverer" or "savior" of the state (460). This is why Creon wants Oedipus to return to Thebes and be buried there.

After libations have been made to the Eumenides, Oedipus initially resists revealing his accursed past to the Chorus, invoking the name or the principle of hospitality: "In the name of your hospitality [*xenias*], don't ruthlessly open up what I have suffered" (515). Finally, Oedipus reveals his identity and admits his deeds; he is indeed the father of his sisters and the slayer of his own father, but, like Antigone earlier, he defends himself against having done these deeds with willful intent (533–45).[2]

It is then that Theseus enters (551), Theseus who realizes who Oedipus is and who recalls that he too was raised in exile, a foreigner in foreign lands [*xenos . . . xenēs*]—that same phrase from earlier being more or less repeated here. Oedipus tells Theseus, just as he had told the Chorus, that Athens will benefit from him when he is dead and buried (582). Again—for it cannot be repeated too often—it is not the abilities of this foreigner, his skills, his economic or cultural capital, and so on, that will help the host country but the blessings conferred by his dead, buried body. It is the body of the migrant or the stranger, the body of the one to whom hospitality is given, that will protect and save the host country. Oedipus will not be, he says, an "unprofitable" guest (625), and he reminds Theseus that he wishes to "claim the hospitality/To which by mutual contract we stand pledged" (632). For there is or has been an implicit agreement, a prior contract of guest-friendship, between them, perhaps not unlike the one we saw between the ancestors of Diomedes and Glaucus in the *Iliad*. There is some prior, reciprocal agreement between them or their cities, and Oedipus is now asking Theseus to respect it, Theseus who, as king, as sovereign, is the only one *able* to offer hospitality in this context, the only one who, as host, will have the *power* to offer hospitality or refuge to Oedipus the *xenos* (564–65; see *OH* 41–43/41–43, *H 1* 89/126). Theseus says that because Oedipus has come to him as a suppliant he will grant him "the full right of citizen" if he so wishes. Oedipus can thus either stay in Colonus or go to Athens with Theseus. When Oedipus chooses the former, Theseus vows to protect him and his daughters, even against Creon, who wishes to bring them back to Thebes by force (730ff.). Antigone calls Theseus her "savior," using the same word that Oedipus had used to describe what he could be for Athens (1118).

After Theseus has proven himself worthy of his word, protecting Oedipus and his daughters from Creon, Oedipus learns that his son Polyneices, who has been banished from Thebes by his brother, has come to Athens to convince his father to return to Thebes. Oedipus will remain impervious to Polyneices's pleas, recalling that it was Polyneices who, when in power, exiled Oedipus from Thebes and made him "cityless [*apolin*]." Oedipus says to Polyneices, with a sort of irony that reflects back on what Oedipus himself once did: "I shall think of thee/As of my murderer" (1361). Oedipus then curses his sons (1380), saying that Polyneices and Eteocles are "no sons of mine," and he prophesies that Polyneices will not return home but will die "by a kinsman's hand" (1388).

Oedipus soon hears thunder, lightning bolts from Zeus's "unconquered hand" (1515), and realizes that "the predestined end has come" (1471). He himself will now show Theseus where he will die and be buried. Only Theseus will know this secret, which will then be handed down from heir to heir (1517–35). Leading the way after having been for so long led, prohibiting his daughters, who were earlier described as his "crutches," from even touching him, Oedipus says to Theseus: "Blessing on thee, dearest friend, / On thee and on thy land and followers!" (1552). And the Chorus follows this up by saying, "speed this stranger [*xenon*] to the gloom" (1561).

The Messenger then arrives to tell of Oedipus's final moments and mysterious or mystical departure (1580). He recalls that Oedipus, now without a guide, guided them all and that, having reached "the threshold [*odos*] with its brazen stairs" (1588), he made a libation as it thundered around them. Here, then, is the second threshold, near the end of the play, which no one but Oedipus will really be able to cross. Just as a reference to a threshold, an *odos*, marked the beginning of the play as Oedipus crossed over into the sanctuary of the Eumenides, a second *odos*, another threshold, here marks the end of the play, like a closing parenthesis for the one opened earlier, as Oedipus, still blind but now leading Theseus, descends into his secret tomb. It was "an end most marvelous," says the Messenger, as Theseus is left standing all alone, "shading his eyes as from some awful sight" (1650).

Oedipus thus died, as he wished, "in a foreign land [*epi xenas*]" (1705), just as, one might want to recall, he had been raised in a foreign land, that is, in Corinth rather than Thebes. This will be one of the great themes of the *Hospitality* seminar — dying in a foreign land as opposed to at home or in one's homeland, dying away from home after having received refuge or hospitality in a foreign land.

Near the end of the play, Antigone says she wishes to see Oedipus's tomb, or rather the place where he died, for she herself wishes to die there (1723ff.). But Theseus tells her that she and Ismene can never see their father's tomb, that it must remain hidden, secret, to all but Theseus (1768). Hence the daughters come to a threshold, as it were, that they cannot cross, a threshold between life and death, or between what they are able to know and what they cannot. Unable to cross over with him, unable fully to mourn their father who has disappeared, they will return to Thebes, their homeland, while their father remains in a tomb in a foreign land that they can never see or visit. That is what it means, perhaps, to be or to die a stranger in a foreign land, a *xenos* in a land of *xenoi*.

The story of *Oedipus at Colonus* provides Derrida with, on the one hand, a great example of conditional hospitality, as an exchange of oaths comes to link the two strangers or foreigners, and as the one being offered safety and hospitality promises to provide salvation to the land in which he is being received. And yet because this promise of salvation takes place beyond life, on the part of someone who has been banished from his own city as an outlaw, a legendary outlaw, there is something unconditional and hardly economic about this hospitality. Beyond life, beyond sight and light for the blind Oedipus, and perhaps beyond reason or reasonable exchange for Theseus, hospitality is here a little bit blind and, no doubt, a little bit mad.

Derrida turns to *Oedipus at Colonus* in order to try to displace the question of hospitality from birth and birthrights, hospitality given or refused on the basis of blood, family, or fatherland, the stranger or the foreigner being a stranger or foreigner by birth, to death and mourning, to hospitality being granted on the basis of the place of one's ancestors' death and burial (see *OH* 85–87/81, *H* 1 105/149). From birth to death: Derrida does something similar with regard to friendship in *Politics of Friendship*: He underscores the fact that many of the great texts on friendship in the Western tradition were born not out of some shared origin or proximity in life but out of mourning, from Achilles mourning Patroclus to Montaigne morning Etienne de la Boétie or Maurice Blanchot mourning George Bataille. In the case of both hospitality and friendship, what Derrida wishes to highlight is thus death, absence, and distance rather than life, presence, and proximity, in short, mourning rather than birth or survival (see *H* 1 135/185–86).[3]

Mourning too, then, is a major theme in this seminar on hospitality, which begins by recalling—indeed, this is its opening word, a word spoken once again right on the threshold—the very recent death of Gilles Deleuze (see *H* 1 1/19). Derrida begins the fourth session as well with a rather long homage to the former French president François Mitterrand, who had just died, following it up the next week, in the midst of his reading of *Oedipus at Colonus*—the story of a man born to one family (in Thebes) but raised by another (in Corinth), who eventually became king of Thebes but would be buried in Colonus—with a long parenthesis on the funeral of Mitterrand that had taken place just a few days before (on January 11, 1996), a funeral that consisted of both a public ceremony at Notre Dame Cathedral in Paris, the city where Mitterrand had lived for many years, including when he was president, and a more private memorial and burial in Jarnac, his hometown (*OH* 93–95/87; see *H* 1 107/151–52).[4] This homage also gave Derrida the chance to recall Mitterrand's public support for foreigners and noncitizens to vote in municipal elections and, of course, his support for philosophy, including the fundamental role Mitterrand played in establishing the International College of Philosophy in Paris in 1983 (*H* 1 76–77n1/111–12n1).

But it is especially through his reading of *Oedipus at Colonus* that Derrida will develop a discourse on the relationship between hospitality and mourning. Derrida earlier in the seminar sets up this question by asking how one can make oneself replaceable so as not to weigh too heavily on the other (see *H* 1 36/60). In other words, how can the irreplaceable make itself replaceable so as to allow for mourning?

As we have seen, Oedipus undergoes a strange experience of hospitality and, in Derrida's words, "illustrates this strange law of hospitality: you die abroad and not always at all as you would have wanted it" (*OH* 93/85; see *H* 1 107/151). As for Antigone, she must endure not knowing where her father's final resting place is, for Oedipus has Theseus swear that he will not divulge the place of his tomb. It is as if, says Derrida, Oedipus wanted to leave without leaving an "address" for the mourning of his loved ones, as if he wanted to "deprive them of their mourning," to make them *faire leur deuil du deuil*. Derrida then adds: "Do we know of a more generous and poisoned form of the gift?" (*OH* 93/85–87; see *H* 1 107/151). Everything is contained in this last question. Oedipus wants to spare his daughters their mourning, but by sparing them that mourning he also deprives them of it, making their mourning all the worse, an interminable mourning or, worse still, since all mourning is interminable, an endlessly ambiguous mourning.

The two daughters, Antigone and Ismene, thus lament that their father has died in a foreign land and that he has died without a determinable place, without a place for a localized and circumscribed mourning, without a *topos* for mourning. The daughters must therefore lament being unable to lament, mourn the mourning of which they have been deprived. They are thus doomed to "an infinite mourning defying all work, beyond any possible work of mourning" (*OH* 111/101; see *H* 1 112–13/157–58). What Antigone bemoans, suggests Derrida, is thus perhaps less her father than the mourning of which she has been deprived. Because Oedipus's death has no "place" for her, there can be no mourning, no "normal mourning," for him (*OH* 111/101; see *H* 1 112–13/157–58).[5]

Oedipus wants to choose *himself* the place of his final resting place. He wishes to hold his own funeral ceremony, as it were. And yet he has to tell Theseus the secret of his tomb, which he divulges only on the edge—on the threshold—of that tomb (see *OH* 97/89, *H* 1 108/152). It is a secret that Theseus must keep "forever" and tell only his successor, his heir, who will do the same in turn. What *saves* the city, what assures the public health of the city, what maintains the tradition, is thus the transmission of a secret come from a foreign land, from abroad, a secret that, as Derrida emphasizes, can also sound very much like a threat: Do not forget me, do not forget the secret—and do not divulge it either—for if you do the blessing that my secret tomb is to Athens will become a curse (see *OH* 99/91, *H* 1 108–9/152–53). Hence Athens, or Theseus, the host of Oedipus, risks becoming—as in Levinas—hostage to his guest, hostage to his oath, and not only him but his descendants—yet further proof, as if any more were needed, of the pervertible law of hospitality.

In the discussion session that follows the fifth session, Derrida suggests that the originary mourning he is speaking of in *Oedipus at Colonus*, not unlike the mourning at the basis of friendship in *Politics of Friendship* or *The Work of Mourning*, is not a mourning that comes only after the death of a friend or loved one but a mourning that is constitutive of our very relation with that friend or loved one, indeed a mourning that is constitutive of the very identity of the one who will mourn. Derrida speaks of an "originary mourning" for an other who is already within me, already constitutive, as it were, not only of my subjectivity, of my ego, but, even more basically, of my ipseity. It is an "originary mourning"—perhaps not unlike, as we will see, an absolute or unconditional hospitality—that precedes even my *ability* to mourn, indeed even my ability to say "me":

> Let us leave aside the pathos of mourning and the tears and sadness, etc.—let us call mourning simply the fact that there is something of the other that lives or dies without me in me, and that is in me without me, and so is greater than me in me. This mourning does not happen to *ipse*, it is that without which there would be no ipseity, no self-relation. I maintain that self-relation presupposes this foreignerness that we are here calling mourning, outside of all tears, all melancholic pathos; I maintain the word "mourning" where what one mourns is re-appropriation. The other—that is what I cannot and must not reappropriate to myself, even if I carry it within me, as experiences of mourning described for example by Freud and others attest, even if I carry the other in me and so in my body, in a place in my body, it is a place that is in me outside me, and that I cannot appropriate to myself, that I cannot get my hands on, which I do not have at my disposal. I do not have it at my disposal, so it is my law. When I spoke of the absolute law of hospitality, distinct from the laws of hospitality, I was thinking of this law of the other that commands me not because I decide that it is good to obey it, but that commands me because I am *ipse*, I can say "*ipse*," "myself," only where this law commands me, is there ahead of me in a certain manner. (*H* 1 130–31/180–81)

Originary mourning would thus have to do with an unappropriable, unassimilable, undialectizable other within, an other that, as Derrida says psychoanalysis teaches us, "dislodges" the ego from its authority, from its chez-soi, removes it from its home and submits it to other agencies or powers (*H 1* 205n1/275n1). This is not, to cite *Totality and Infinity*, the subject as "host" but, better, as we read in *Otherwise Than Being*, the subject as "hostage," my ipseity besieged by an alterity before any attempt on my part to invite another or offer hospitality to another.

Originary mourning would thus have to do with an alterity or an "enclave"—another major theme in the seminar—of the other within, but an "enclave" without which there would be no "within" in the first place. As Derrida argues two sessions after his reading of Oedipus:

> The question of hospitality will often be posed according to the logic of the enclave, that is, of a place, an external territory enclosed in an interior, an exteriority included (and that is why we speak so often of mourning, a mourning, or a mourning of mourning, which speaks or is expressed in this topography of a pocket of resistance enclosed within a space . . .) (*H 1* 185/249–50)

The death of the other would thus come first: It would come before my own death, though also before my very identity, as constitutive of my identity. We can begin to see all the consequences such an originary mourning might have on a thinking of hospitality. While hospitality is usually thought in relation to birth, birthrights, autochthony, and so on, and thus the rights of citizenship in relation to birth, Derrida will try to think it from the side of death, and thus mourning, and everything that comes with it: lack of presence, lack of identification, impossible mourning, an originary dispossession, and so on. It is to think hospitality not first and foremost in relation to being born at home but in relation to dying abroad, dying *à étranger*.[6]

6

Plato's *Xenoi*

> . . . and this begins everywhere an inside gets constituted, everywhere
> the line of a threshold, a *limen* separates an interiority from an
> outside . . . (*H* 1 52/81)

We began in the introduction by noting Derrida's tendency to go back into
the history of philosophy and literature for help or orientation in thinking the
concept or theme or subject he is investigating. One cannot simply begin in
what one might think to be a neutral way with a question such as "What is
hospitality?" without already relying upon certain classic gestures in the history of philosophy, beginning with the *ti esti* or "What is?" question. Hence
Derrida's return to Plato.

In texts such as "Plato's Pharmacy" and "Khōra," Derrida gives powerful
and original readings of Plato, the first of these on the role of writing in Plato,
in all of Plato, and the second on the role of the *khōra* in the *Timaeus*. In the
Hospitality seminar, Derrida much more simply and straightforwardly follows
Plato's use of the word *xenos* in several Platonic dialogues, such as *Apology*,
Crito, *Sophist*, and *Statesman*, in order make a point about how Plato inscribes
the stranger or foreigner in his dialogues but also, and more importantly, in
order to set up a problem concerning hospitality that will be pursued more
fully through other sources and texts. In other words, the reading of Plato has
a more strategic value here and is not meant to be a reading of Plato per se or
for its own sake.

In Plato, then, the term *xenos*, "stranger" or "foreigner," appears in many
different places and contexts. It is, first of all, the name of a central character of
the *Sophist* and *Statesman*, a character who seems to assume something like

the central position of Socrates in the early dialogues or the Athenian in the
Laws. In these dialogues, the central character—the questioning character—
is the so-called Eleatic Stranger, that is, the Stranger from Elea, the place
where Parmenides lived and taught. It is through this Eleatic Stranger that,
in the *Sophist*, the so-called parricidal question will eventually get posed, that
is, the question regarding the Parmenidean thesis that Being is one and that
only it can be understood or spoken about, while Non-Being, which is not,
can be neither understood nor spoken about. Derrida will wish to attribute a
sort of exemplarity to this moment in the *Sophist*, the Stranger being the one
who questions or disturbs the authority of the father, the power of the one who
offers hospitality, that is, the master of the house. Derrida is thus interested in
teasing out and examining a sort of "family scene" in the dialogue, in this case
that of Parmenides and his "son" or disciple, the Eleatic Stranger, who is willing to pose the question of Non-Being in a way that the father, Parmenides,
would have never allowed. While the Stranger will protest—no doubt already
in recognition of his transgression—that he should not be considered a parri-
cide, the claim that Non-Being in a certain sense "is" cannot but contest the
authority of the father (*OH* 7/13; see *H* 1 77–78/112–13). The *Sophist* is thus
used by Derrida to raise the question of the relationship, once again, between
hospitality and mastery or power, as well as paternity, and the question of
whether hospitality can be approached by means of the *ti esti* question or the
question of Being.[1]

There are, however, other resonances or aspects of hospitality in relationship to the stranger, the Eleatic Stranger, that Derrida does not mention but
that are worthy of our attention. For example, in our earlier look at hospitality
in Homer, I left out one important aspect of hospitality, namely, the fact that a
certain virtual or spectral relationship between humans and the gods appears
to haunt every relationship of human hospitality. We mentioned that Zeus is
the god of hospitality and of supplication, but we did not talk about the fact
that, in the *Iliad*, the *Odyssey*, and the *Homeric Hymns* hospitality is granted
to strangers in part because one never knows if one is entertaining a human
being or a god or goddess in disguise.[2] This notion is central to the opening
of the *Sophist* as Socrates responds to Theodorus's mentioning of a stranger,
a *xenos*, from Elea whom he and Theaetetus have brought along with them:

> Are you not unwittingly bringing, as Homer says, some god, and no
> mere stranger, Theodorus? He says that the gods, and especially the
> god of strangers, enter into companionship with men who have a
> share of due reverence and that they behold the deeds, both violent
> and righteous, of mankind. So perhaps this companion of yours may

be one of the higher powers, who comes to watch over and refute us because we are worthless in argument—a kind of god of refutation. (*Sophist* 216a–b)

Socrates's somewhat playful reference here would seem to be to a passage in the *Odyssey* in which the poet is reminding his audience of the dangers of not providing hospitality to the stranger. The passage comes from book 17, just after Antinous, the harshest and cruelest of all of Penelope's suitors, has just struck Odysseus, disguised as a stranger and beggar. Having witnessed the outrage, the other suitors say to the perpetrator of it:

> Antinous, thou didst not well to strike the wretched wanderer.
> Doomed man that thou art, what if haply he be some god come down
> from heaven! Aye, and the gods in the guise of strangers from afar put
> on all manner of shapes, and visit the cities, beholding the violence
> and the righteousness of men. (*Odyssey* 17.485–87)

That is the Homeric passage that Socrates seems to be alluding to at the beginning of the *Sophist* when he meets the Eleatic Stranger. But notice how Plato will, again, appropriate this Homeric passage and turn it in the direction of philosophy. After Socrates has playfully questioned whether the Eleatic Stranger might just be a god, Theodorus, the one who has invited him, says that the man, the stranger, is not a god, though he is indeed "divine," for he, Theodorus, "give[s] that epithet to all philosophers" (*Sophist* 216c). To which Socrates responds:

> And rightly, my friend. However, I fancy it is not much easier, if I may
> say so, to recognize this class, than that of the gods. For these men—
> I mean those who are not feignedly but really philosophers—appear
> disguised in all sorts of shapes, thanks to the ignorance of the rest of
> mankind, and visit the cities, beholding from above the life of those
> below, and they seem to some to be of no worth and to others to be
> worth everything. And sometimes they appear disguised as statesmen
> and sometimes as sophists, and sometimes they may give some people
> the impression that they are altogether mad. (*Sophist* 216c–d)

Just as a god might come to visit humans in disguise, so might a philosopher— a true philosopher, perhaps like Socrates, Plato might have wanted us to hear—remain disguised and unrecognized by ordinary human beings. This will then set up the question of how to distinguish the philosopher from the sophist or the statesman, the answer being that the true sophist or the true statesman, beyond all the appearances and disguises, is indistinguishable from the philosopher inasmuch as he follows the truth.

It is thus also worth recalling here that, in the second book of the *Republic*, it is precisely such passages in Homer regarding the gods changing shapes that are deemed inappropriate for the young guardians of the state to hear, inappropriate because they are morally damaging but also because they are *untrue*. Socrates there argues that gods would not and could not change shapes in that way:

> Do you think that God is a wizard and capable of manifesting himself by design, now in one aspect, now in another, at one time himself changing and altering his shape in many transformations and at another deceiving us and causing us to believe such things about him; or that he is simple and less likely than anything else to depart from his own form? (*Republic* 380d)

Socrates here seems to be replacing what the poets, and principally Homer, say about the gods with what reason itself would say about them. Because the gods are good and fair, they would not want to depart from that original state and so would not alter either their inner essence or their outer appearance. "It is impossible then," Socrates concludes, "even for a god to wish to alter himself, but, as it appears, each of them being the fairest and best possible abides for ever simply in his own form" (*Republic* 381c). Socrates goes on to cite the very passage from the *Odyssey* that is cited in the *Sophist* (216b–c): "No poet then, my good friend, must be allowed to tell us that 'the gods, in the likeness of strangers [*xeinoisin*], / Many disguises assume as they visit the cities of mortals'" (*Republic* 381d). Mothers "under the influence" of these poets, says Socrates, must thus not "terrify their children with harmful tales, how that there are certain gods whose apparitions haunt the night in the likeness of many strangers [*xenois*] from all manner of lands, lest while they speak evil of the gods they at the same time make cowards of the children" (*Republic* 381e). Again, these stories are not only harmful to children, as Socrates argues; they are also untrue, since they do not reflect what the gods are most likely to be and what it would be most reasonable for them to do.

But what does this mean for the history of hospitality, beginning with Homer? Socrates seems to be rejecting one of the major premises of Greek hospitality, namely, that the *xenos* could always be a god in disguise. What happens when that premise gets questioned? And what happens when the philosophical ideal or telos for understanding the nature of a god is an unchanging form? Should we, in the wake of that expressed ideal, purge the language of hospitality of all those ambiguous or ambivalent words that seem to plague it, beginning with *xenos*, which, as we have seen, can mean stranger, guest, or friend, or the French *hôte*, which can mean guest or host? Should we clarify or purify our language? Run it through some kind of threshing machine in order to purge it of all these deceptive words? If we do not, how will we ever get a clear definition of what hospitality *is* in its singular essence? By evoking this philosophical and literary past, by recalling those etymologies, is not Derrida perpetuating the kind of confusion caused by those poets or those mothers who repeat their tales and who suggest that, for example, the guest at my door may be not just another human refugee from a foreign land asking for asylum but a god in disguise? Should we be able to see or to know who is at our door in order to offer hospitality, or should hospitality always be given out of a certain madness or, even, a certain ignorance and blindness?[3]

After recalling that the Stranger from Elea also appears in Plato's *Statesman*, where what is at issue is the nature of the statesman and of politics more generally, Derrida reminds us that in the *Apology* it is none other than Socrates, the very thinker who in the *Crito* says he left Athens less frequently than the crippled or the blind (*Crito* 53a), who presents himself as a stranger, a *xenos*, to Athens (see *OH* 13/19, *H* 1 80/116). This happens during his trial, as Socrates insists that he will speak the truth in a straightforward way, being foreign to the ways of the law court, foreign to its rhetoric and persuasive language.[4] Socrates there asks the Athenians to treat him *as a xenos* because of his age and inability to speak the language of the court. He thus asks them to accept him and his language, a language that is at once more philosophical and less refined than that of the court, as if he were a foreigner in the literal sense to Athens (see *OH* 21/25, *H* 1 82/118–19). The passage thus recalls in passing that foreigners *had* certain rights in Athens and were allowed to defend themselves in their own language, their own dialect. Socrates thus asks in effect that the rights commonly accorded to a literal *xenos* be accorded to him, a citizen of Athens who is a *xenos* to the ways of the court (see *OH* 17–21/23–25, *H* 1 80–83/117–19). Cited by Derrida in this way, in this context, Socrates in the *Apology* recalls the very real contemporary problem of being a foreigner in or to the judicial system, not knowing how to speak the language of the court or of the city or country in which one is being tried. The brief reading of the *Apology* will thus be used to raise the question of language and translation in relation to hospitality that we spoke of earlier, particularly with regard to the judicial system.

In the *Crito*, it is Socrates once again who is placed in the position of the stranger or the foreigner, the position of the one being questioned, that is to say, being posed a series of rhetorical questions by the laws of Athens in his extended *prosopopoeia* of them (see *OH* 31–33/33–35, *H* 1 85–86/122–24).

Socrates is being questioned by the laws as he contemplates leaving Athens and becoming himself a foreigner or an exile to Athens. Still in prison after his trial and awaiting his execution, Socrates places himself, rhetorically at least, on the border of Athens, as Crito tries to persuade him to flee the city. He is not unlike Oedipus in this way, on the border or the fringe, on the threshold, of the city, being urged by Crito to become an "outlaw" by disobeying the laws of the city in fleeing the city and its punishment (see *OH* 33–35/35–37, *H* 1 86/124).

Derrida motivates his return to Plato through these references to the Xenos from Elea in *Sophist* and *Statesman* and the figure of Socrates as a *xenos* to or in Athens in *Apology* and *Crito*. But there is one more dialogue alluded to in the *Hospitality* seminar that deserves special mention, and it should come as no surprise. Derrida says during the very first session of the seminar:

> You sense already that this whole seminar on hospitality will be a sem-
> inar on what "receive" might mean, as a postscript to Plato's *Timaeus*,
> in which *khōra*, place, is that which receives (*endekhomai, ende-*
> *khomenon*), the receptacle (*dekhomenon*, which can signify also "it is
> acceptable, permitted, possible." (*H* 1 9/29; see *Timaeus* 20c)

Much could be made of this passing reference to *khōra* as a place of receptiv-ity and thus, in a certain sense, as a place of hospitality.[5] It might suggest that the ultimate hospitality consists not in giving anything in particular but, more simply, in "giving space," that is, in making space or giving place for an other to appear. That is, in many ways, the central premise of Derrida's little book *Khōra* devoted to the *Timaeus*.

But it is in the *Laws* that we find Plato's most explicit and developed treat-ment of hospitality, in the form, for example, of regulations established for the receiving of exiles and the harboring and sheltering of foreigners (see *Laws* 955b). Let me thus conclude this brief reading of hospitality in Plato by looking at the comparison in the *Laws* between the innkeeper—and one will recall that Kant's *Perpetual Peace* begins with an innkeeper—and *khōra*, or at least between the innkeeper and some of the defining attributes of *khōra*, namely, as a mother or nurse, a provider of nourishment and shelter. For that is precisely how the Athenian of the *Laws* describes the trade of an innkeeper when it is plied or practiced in its best or most noble and uncorrupted form. Using language that cannot but remind one of *khōra*, the Athenian there ar-gues—through a sort of thought experiment—that if they were able to get the very best men and women to take up this trade and become innkeepers for a time, one would see that they can be most noble and that, when "free from corruption," they deserve to be paid the honor of a "mother or a nurse [*mētros an kai trophou*]."[6] Like a mother or a nurse, says the Athenian, the innkeeper is able to provide nourishment and protection to travelers—to wanderers—in need. But that is not what usually happens. Instead of offering friendly gifts and "entertainment [*xenia*]"—*xenia*, again—to travelers in distress, innkeepers often hold their guests hostage, the Athenian complains, engaging in a sort of price gouging, "demanding very high sums of unjust and unclean ransom-money." That is why innkeepers have such a bad reputation and why a lawgiver must provide some "medicine [*pharmakon*]," some remedy, against such abuses (*Laws* 919a–b). In the city for which the Athenian is legislating, the profession of the innkeeper must thus be treated as a noble one. In the city of the *Laws*, the inn, like *khōra*, would be a place of hospitality or receptivity, a place where wanderers and travelers, where *xenoi* of all kinds, would be given shelter and nourishment, and, perhaps first of all, a place or a space simply to appear, to become phenomenal without abuse.

But is that actually possible once one has crossed over the threshold? Is not the possibility of perversion an unavoidable threshold phenomenon when it comes to hospitality?

PART II
The "Concept" of Hospitality

7

Stranger Things

We had paused before two limits: two *limina* or preliminaries. The two thresholds or two doors that we proposed to approach . . . were first that of the *foreigner* (*l'étranger*) . . . then that of the enemy (*hostis*), namely, in appearance the contrary of the *hospes*, the host, but in truth one whose affinity with the *hospes* remains very troubling. (*H 1* 52/81)

Derrida begins the fourth session of *Hospitality* 1—a session dated January 10, 1996, one of the two sessions revised and published in *Of Hospitality*—with a question, or at least with reference to a question. The question is placed right on the threshold of the session as if to underscore that the threshold is the place of the question, the place where the question is posed and where it is itself questioned, whether with regard to hospitality or justice anything else. In the case of hospitality, it is the place where one might pose a question such as "*Qui êtes-vous?*" "Who are you?" or, if I may immodestly recall Derrida's first question to me in the fall of 1988, "*Alors, qui êtes-vous?*" "So, who are you exactly?"[1]

Derrida sums up all these aspects of the question of hospitality in the very *economical* translatable/untranslatable French phrase *question de l'étranger* or, later, *la question de l'étranger* (*OH* 3/11; see *H 1* 76–77/112).[2] It is a question, or a phrase about a question, that is just as liminal and elliptical as the phrase we looked at earlier that opens the following session, *pas d'hospitalité*.[3] It is deceptively simple yet already divided, with multiple senses and multiple addressees. It is unclear how to hear this phrase already in French, though it poses a particular challenge to translation, which, as we have already seen, is not just some academic question but perhaps already the very question of hospitality itself. Do we address or question the one who is asking for hospitality in their language, or in ours, or in no language at all?

Question de l'étranger, then. The first question one might ask is whether to translate *étranger* here as "stranger," perhaps as "outsider," or as "foreigner"? Without any further context, there on the threshold, it is impossible to decide. But Derrida's quick addition of the phrase *venue de l'étranger*, that is, "come from abroad" or from "foreign lands," gives the phrase a more political cast and so tips the scale in favor of "foreigner." "Question of the *foreigner*," then: That is clearly the best translation here, though the choice is hardly anodyne or innocent.

The session thus begins, there on its threshold, without any further context, with the phrase "the question of the foreigner," a threshold phrase that immediately divides into at least five different valences:

First, the question of the foreigner is a question *about* the foreigner, a question we can pose about the foreigner in general, about what "foreigner" means in its essence, what is essentially foreign about the foreigner, and so on. "What is the foreigner?" or "What is a foreigner?" "*Qu'est-ce qu'un étranger?*"; *ti esti ho xenos?* In this case, the foreigner is the object of a questioning or an interrogation, on the way to becoming the subject of a thesis or definition if not a program. The foreigner is here the object of a question that would, in the best of cases, yield some knowledge, the object of that famous *ti esti* or "what is" question, the philosophical question par excellence, a question inaugurated, as we all know, by Plato or Plato's Socrates when he asks, as in the *Republic*, for example, "what is justice?" The question of the foreigner would thus be the question of what *defines* the foreigner, what a foreigner is in his or her essence. It is an ontological or epistemological question about the being or essence of the foreigner.

Second, "the question of the foreigner" might also be heard not as a definitional question but, more practically, more ethico-politically, as a question about what to do with the foreigner. Are we going to put the foreigner on a plane back to their native Haiti—or Mexico or Honduras—or are we going to grant them a visa, or at least a temporary stay in order for them to explain their situation, the economic or political dangers they would face if forced to return to their country of origin. In a word, just what should our immigration policy, our policy on public hospitality, be?

But then, third, related to this more explicitly ethical or political question *about* the foreigner, "the question of the foreigner" might be heard as the question one poses *to* the foreigner: For example, "Who are you? Where are you from, and what do you want? What language do you speak? And why are you asking for asylum or sanctuary or hospitality here? What are your intentions in coming here, and what kind of claim are you making on us?" And of course, all the questions of translation, questions of what language one should use to address the foreigner or stranger, emerge most forcefully here.

Fourth, the question of the foreigner can be heard to mean the question that comes *from* the foreigner, subjective genitive this time rather than objective genitive, a question that comes from a foreigner who has perhaps come *de l'étranger*, that is, from abroad or from foreign lands. Unlike the first two valences, where the question was asked *of* the foreigner, *about* the foreigner, by, say, the philosopher or the immigration official, by some subject at home, in power, a subject who is able and willing to ask the question, or the third, where the question was posed by some subject in power *to* the foreigner, the question comes this time *from* the foreigner. It is a question come *from* the foreigner that is now posed *to* the inquiring subject or the one who is or who is assumed to be at home and in a position to offer hospitality—or not.

But this fourth question may *itself* be heard in at least two ways. It may be heard as a question or an appeal addressed to a host by a foreigner asking for entry or asylum, an ethical or political question that is, again, typically posed on the threshold, a question like "May I come in?" or "Will you grant me asylum in your country?" As such, it is a question that could elicit any number of responses from the master of the house or the sovereign nation, everything from total acceptance to outright denial, with everything in between.

But this question of the *étranger*, of the "foreigner," or perhaps better here of the "stranger," or even the "absolute other," may also be heard, and this would be the fifth and final sense, as that which puts the host himself into question, a putting or calling into question, as in Levinas, of the very *ability* of the host to ask or even to answer questions from a position of power and authority. Posing the first question, the foreigner or the stranger or the other puts the host in question, calls his power—including his power to ask questions—into question, his power to ask an ontological question (as in meaning 1) or even an ethico-political question (as in meanings 2 and 3). While the first question is thus, we could say, more ontological or epistemological and the second, third, and fourth more political or sociopolitical, this fifth question— which is less a question than a putting-into-question—is essentially ethical.

The five senses of "the question of the foreigner" or "the question of the stranger" thus take us from the host being assured of his sovereignty to being put into question. We move in five steps, five *pas*, as it were, through this singularly economic phrase, this phrase pronounced on the threshold of the fourth session of the seminar, from Plato to Levinas, from the *ti esti* question asked of the foreigner to the other who puts the questioner in question—this fifth step bringing us back to the beginning or even to before the beginning, to ethics as first philosophy, a fifth sense of the question that in some sense must always come first.[4]

All this then raises, of course, the whole question of the question in philosophy. Is *questioning* the primary mode of engagement or inquiry in philosophy, or is there another mode of engagement that precedes the question? This is the question that will occupy Derrida in many places, including, of course, *Of Spirit*, whose subtitle is "Heidegger and the Question."[5] Is there a mode of language, Derrida asks of Heidegger, that would come before the question, before the *ti esti* question but also before any question whatsoever? The question of the threshold brings us, it seems, to the threshold of the question, and both lead us back to the question of hospitality, the question of the "concept" of hospitality, though also, as we have already suggested, the question of the very nature or essence of the "concept."

8

Conditional and Unconditional Hospitality

> These two thresholds, in many respects, form only one; and we are going to realize very quickly that we must treat the questions of the enemy and the foreigner simultaneously. (*H 1* 52/81)

We are now prepared to take up Derrida's more formal analysis of and distinction between two kinds or two regimes of hospitality, both of which must be considered if we are to think hospitality "itself."[1] The two regimes are given various names throughout the seminar, but the two that names that run throughout and that perhaps best describe them are "conditional" and "unconditional" hospitality. In what follows, I will try to gather together the attributes of each of these two kinds of hospitality, both because it will help illuminate Derrida's approach to hospitality specifically and because it will allow us to see certain recurring figures, themes, and terms, a similar configuration or structure, in Derrida's analyses of hospitality, the gift, forgiveness, the secret, and so on.

To introduce this more formal relation between an unconditional and a conditional hospitality, let me begin with a very informal anecdote, one inspired by a common expression that Derrida recalls throughout the seminar and that he calls at one point a sort of "fiction." The expression is *Faites comme chez vous*, which has equivalents in many other languages, "mi casa es su casa," "make yourself at home," and so on (*H 1* 10n22, 23–24, 56/30n11, 46, 86). Derrida calls it a "fiction" because it would seem that no host ever *really* invites a guest to make themselves at home in that way, that is, to treat the home of the host as *their own*. Well, when speaking not long ago with an Algerian academic about Derrida's seminar on hospitality, I was told that there is an equally common iteration of this very common Algerian expression that makes the fiction of the expression explicit through a sort of joke. The saying goes, *Faites comme chez vous—mais restez pas trop longtemps*, in other words, "Make yourselves at home, but don't stay too long, don't overstay your welcome," or even, "Make yourselves at home—but when did you say you were leaving again?" As we will see, this expression illustrates perfectly the problems—though also, perhaps, the promise and the prospects—at the heart of the relationship between unconditional hospitality (make yourselves at home, treat this as your home, treat it as if it really were yours) and conditional hospitality (don't forget that your stay here is temporary, that you must treat my home as you would your home, without ever forgetting that this is in the end *my* home).

There are several extended passages in the *Hospitality* seminar that attempt to articulate the relationship between conditional and unconditional hospitality. Each iteration adds something different or new to our understanding of the two kinds of hospitality and of the complicated relation between them. I would like to look here, at least to begin, at just one such iteration, the very first one in the seminar. It is found in the third session, on the heels of an extended analysis of both the restrictions that Kant puts on hospitality in *Perpetual Peace* and the way in which the stranger or foreigner in Hegel is always determined in the family, in civil society, and in the nation-state by means of customs and mores, rights and laws. It is in light of these restrictions or determinations that Derrida begins to develop what he will call "conditional" hospitality. Let us work slowly through this passage, the first of its kind in the seminar, in order to begin to draw up a table of terms and attributes, as it were, between conditional and unconditional hospitality. Once we do that, we can then consider the dangers inherent in both hospitalities, the double danger or the double pervertibility of both the conditional and the unconditional. The passage comes just before the two sessions included, in revised form, in the *Of Hospitality* volume published with Anne Dufourmantelle. It's a passage in three paragraphs, the first rather long:

> A. *First*. Here is a consequence that I will dub radical, extreme, hyperbolic, and that you have already glimpsed in certain propositions I ventured in the previous sessions. It is that a hospitality regulated by right, a hospitality normed by a system of norms and rules that come to confirm the propriety and power of the host, and first of all his ipseity, a hospitality that gets determined precisely on the basis of that which determines, namely, the limit of the threshold, the at-home, where the "make yourself at home" remains the "as if" of a fiction in which,

above all, no one ought to believe, a hospitality contained within the circle of duty and right and statutory obligations, such a hospitality is doubtless determined, hence apparently concrete and actual, but it is so well limited by its de-termination that it ends where it begins; its actuality ruins it, so to speak. In its very positivity, then, it ruins itself. Such a hospitality is finite and thus on the point of converting itself into its opposite; of treating as an enemy, then, as a virtual enemy but also, unconsciously, as a real enemy, whomever it welcomes, whether man or woman. (*H 1* 56/86–87)

Derrida begins here by speaking of the "radical," "extreme," or "hyperbolic" consequence of what he has just worked through in Kant and Hegel, these attributes "radical," "extreme," and "hyperbolic" being the very ones that will soon characterize unconditional hospitality itself. We will return to this "consequence" in a moment, but let us look first at the two kinds or types of hospitality that Derrida tries to distinguish here by asking of this passage—as Derrida was inclined to do when reading others—*où passe la ligne de partage ici*, that is, where is the line being drawn, where is the line of division being marked out between the two kinds of hospitality, and what terms are being used to characterize that division or that dividing line, that is, the threshold where the two hospitalities are at once linked and distinguished?

First, there is what Derrida calls "a hospitality regulated by right," a hospitality of "norms" and "rules" that "confirm the propriety and power of the host, and first of all his ipseity," a hospitality on the side, then, of that configuration of power, identity, and selfhood we looked at in Chapter 4 and that goes under the name *ipseity*. This is a hospitality determined by the *fiction* of a "make yourself at home," a fiction, as we said, because no host ever really asks a guest to treat the host's home as their own. This is, says Derrida, a "hospitality contained within the circle of duty and right and statutory obligations," and to help explain this notion of a "circle"—this "circle of exchange"—Derrida refers to his previous work on the gift in *Given Time*. A bit later in this passage, he will speak of conditional hospitality as one that "protects itself" or that keeps itself "within the limits of right and duty, of debt," a hospitality restricted to a "circle of exchange, gift and counter-gift." We could thus say that conditional hospitality is, in a word, an "economic hospitality," a hospitality controlled and contained within what Derrida calls "the economy of a circle" (*OH* 135/119; see *H 1* 119–20/165; phrase added to *OH*).

Now such a hospitality, such a limited, conditioned or conditional, economic hospitality, is, says Derrida, "determined," and thus "apparently concrete and actual"—and that all seems good and positive—but it is so determined, so limited, that, Derrida goes on to say, it "ends where it begins; its actuality ruins it, so to speak." It is, therefore, the determined and seemingly "actual" nature of conditional hospitality that ruins or undermines hospitality itself. Positively determined, it is no longer really the hospitality it was supposed to be. For by protecting and limiting itself in this way, it begins to undo or to ruin the very hospitality that those protections and limitations were meant to preserve or to guarantee. Determined by that circle of exchange, of gift and counter-gift, conditional hospitality begins to ruin the very hospitality it first makes possible. This is thus a "finite" hospitality that is always on the verge of turning into its opposite or its contrary, a hospitality where the guest is treated as an enemy, as a virtual or real enemy.

It is just after this first attempt to define or to describe this limited, finite hospitality, this attempt to describe and, as one might hear, *criticize* this conditional and conditioned hospitality, that Derrida voices what he will call a commonsense objection to this criticism. It runs like this: Well, "such hospitality is better than nothing" (H 1 56/87). Better than nothing, perhaps, but Derrida recalls that such so-called hospitality, such determined, finite, limited, conditioned and conditional, supposedly actual hospitality, "is not hospitable to the other as other, to the newcomer [*arrivant*]" (H 1 56/87). It is *called* a "determined" hospitality because it is supposedly concrete, actual, but also because it is offered to a determined or determinate other, to a particular other, that is, to a foreigner who has been selected, filtered, a foreigner whom the host can identify and, more often than not, identify with, and whom the host can thus always reject and send out of their home or country if they do not abide by their rules. It is in this way that the conditional reception of the guest is haunted by the possibility of that guest becoming an enemy. For it is not just that the welcomed guest might one day, at some point in time, become an enemy. It is, rather, that the very reception of such a guest is structurally conditioned from the outset, already from the threshold, by the *possibility* of that guest becoming an enemy, thereby making the guest a virtual enemy right from the start, from the very moment of their reception.

So that's conditional hospitality, a hospitality of laws and limitations, a determined and actual, real, effective hospitality but a hospitality that, says Derrida, is "too hospitable to its opposite," the welcoming of the foreigner turning so easily into their rejection or their persecution, or rather, their welcoming being haunted already from the threshold by the possibility of their rejection or their oppression. It is a hospitality that limits those who can enter, and it treats those who have already entered as guests who could turn into enemies, whether enemies of the household or enemies of the state, at the turn of a dime, or with the turn of the next elections.

But then there is, as its "opposite," Derrida goes on say, a "pure hospitality," a "perhaps impossible hospitality," an "infinite hospitality," one where, when "faced with the singularity of each other who is received, renounces every prerogative, indeed every inviolability of ipseity, every power, if you prefer." This pure, infinite, unconditional hospitality initially sounds like the kind of hospitality Derrida will prefer to the conditional one, a "good" hospitality that might be opposed to that "bad" conditioned, self-ruining hospitality. And yet this unconditional hospitality is also called "a perhaps impossible hospitality" not just because it is utopic and so cannot be realized, made effective, concrete, actual, and so on but because it is beyond the *power* or *possibilities* of the one who would offer it. It is a hospitality that precedes, like that final valence of the question of the stranger or foreigner that we spoke of in the previous chapter, the power or ipseity or even the identity of the host. As Derrida writes, "It is an infinite hospitality in which the host who receives would . . . become the invitee delivered over to the invitee, the guest of the guest, if not their hostage" (*H* 1 57/87). This last claim, an echo of Levinas's suggestion that the subject is not only a *host* but also, in *Otherwise Than Being*, a *hostage*, puts us on guard against thinking that this kind of infinite, pure, unconditional hospitality is the kind of hospitality we should be seeking and aiming for *unconditionally*, even though we know from the outset that we will always have to settle for what is just a conditional, economic, law-bound hospitality and that that is, in the end, "better than nothing."[2] Derrida continues:

> The commonsense objection one cannot avoid making at the idea or movement of this absolute hospitality must not be disregarded. For, like that other hospitality, the one that protects itself within the limits of right and duty, of debt, then, and the circle of exchange, gift and counter-gift, like that everyday, economic hospitality, the absolute hospitality of which I am now speaking risks turning into its opposite [*contraire*], creating a situation in which no one receives anyone or gives anything, especially not a determinable place, to an identifiable person. This absolute hospitality, then, can open a savage space of pure violence that would cause it to lose right down to its meaning, its appearance, its phenomenality of hospitality (of course, it is the same logic as that of the gift, which I tried to formalize in *Given Time*). According to the hypothesis of this absolute hospitality, it would no longer be known who gives hospitality to whom, and as a result, nothing, no norm, no third party, no rule, no contract could prevent the *hôte* (host or guest [in English]) from becoming the worst enemy, from becoming or being it already. We must not disregard this risk, nor

must we then despise those who want to set the backfires or establish the safeguards (*garde-fous*) of right against this madness of absolute hospitality. But what I believe that we cannot not try to think, think and live, and endure, is that the possibility of inversion, hence, of perversion, has to remain open in both cases in order that a hospitality might be possible. (*H* 1 57/87–88)

While unconditional hospitality might have looked like an unconditional ideal, a goal or telos toward which we must aim but that we can never attain, things are more complicated than that. It is true, however, that Derrida multiplies what would seem to be "positive" attributes of this second form of hospitality, calling this unconditional hospitality "pure," "infinite," and "absolute"—terms that are quasi-synonymous but not quite the same, each trying to capture a different aspect of this second kind of hospitality: for example, a hospitality uncontaminated by economic motive or calculation, and so "pure"; a hospitality that is unlimited and not finite, and so "infinite"; and a hospitality that is detached or absolved of relations to duty and to law, and so "absolute." But this second kind of hospitality, which might initially look like the ideal kind, also "risks turning into its opposite," says Derrida, "creating a situation in which no one receives anyone or gives anything, especially not a determinable place, to an identifiable person." While the danger with conditional hospitality is that, by determining and limiting hospitality, it risks always turning hospitality into hostility, the guest into an enemy, the danger with "absolute hospitality" is, says Derrida, that it can open "a savage space of pure violence," *un espace sauvage de violence pure*, that is, a wild, untamed, uncivilized space of pure or unchecked violence that would cause hospitality to lose all meaning, all appearance and so all phenomenality, anything that would look and appear in a public or private space *as* hospitality. The danger of such an "absolute" or "infinite" hospitality would be that one would no longer know who is giving what to whom, since there are no laws or norms or third parties, no contracts to regulate an exchange, no customs or regulations to distinguish, in French, the *hôte* from the *hôte*, that is, the *host* from the *guest*. And so, says Derrida, there is nothing to prevent the guest from becoming the worst enemy, not just the enemy you might escort to your border and say, perhaps, "sorry, nothing personal, it's just the law," but much worse still, much worse and very much more personal.

One would not be wrong, surely, to hear Carl Schmitt in the background here. Insofar as unconditional hospitality opens a beyond of law and politics, the political enemy can ultimately become the private or even the absolute enemy. This is, as Derrida says in reference to Schmitt in *Politics of Friendship*, "the distinction between *polemios* and *ekhthros*," that is, "the enemy of war, the political enemy, and the hated enemy, the object of hatred in general" (*PF* 100). Later in the *Hospitality* seminar, Derrida will say, following, it seems, the same line of argument:

> It is necessary to have absolute hospitality without losing sight of the fact that if one does not provide a body of actual laws, a juridical and political body for this absolute hospitality, it risks being nothing but a utopia, a dream, or worse, a place of savage and barbarous relations where love turns into hatred. (*H* 1 133/183)

This is, it seems, a real objection against this pure, unconditional, absolute hospitality, the kind of hospitality we *might* have thought Derrida, via a certain reading of Levinas—one that ignores, for example, the importance of the third—establishes as the ideal, even if we always, unfortunately, maybe even tragically, fall short of it. Too bad we cannot simply tear down all the walls, we might have thought, open all the doors, and invite the anonymous, infinite other to walk across the threshold. But Derrida is suggesting here that we "must not disregard this risk"; indeed, we must take seriously those who—and Ellen Burt translates this beautifully—"want to set the backfires or establish the safeguards (*garde-fous*) of right against this madness of absolute hospitality." Absolute hospitality is indeed a kind of "mad" hospitality, an aneconomic hospitality that exceeds the reasoned and reasonable, economic hospitality that is called conditional hospitality. Later again in the seminar, Derrida speaks of the madness—or of the "hyperbolically mad hypothesis"—of unconditional hospitality:

> Nothing appears madder [*plus fou*] and more uncanny than this familiarity of the *at-home* as at-home of a family. And perhaps then— this can seem madder still and I put it forward only as a hyperbolically mad hypothesis, but also perhaps as the chance for a thought of hospitality, for thought as well as for hospitality—perhaps then *The* law of unconditional and just hospitality commands us to open hospitality beyond every familial schema, every *at-home* determined as family, and hence (following Hegel's philosophy of right), on the basis of the family, civil society and the state (civil society or state, where the language is paternal rather than maternal): to think then, and to attempt hospitality, beyond any juridico-political determination attached to the family, civil (or bourgeois) society or to the state, these three entities being dialectically indissociable. (*H* 1 164/223–24)

Derrida is here arguing that it is not just the state and civil society but the family that must be rethought or reinvented with regard to absolute hospitality, the only hospitality truly worthy of the name. But he will go on in this same passage to argue that while new "transactions" must be found for the family, the family must not be completely abandoned, for that would just be as irresponsible—and just as dangerous—as getting rid of all those "safeguards" offered by conditional hospitality.

> As there could be no question (it would be irresponsible precisely) of making a clean break, purely and simply, with the family, with every familial, civil or state-national at-home, so as to uphold the claim of and do justice to absolute, just hospitality (a rupture with the father-mother that would have the effect merely of giving free rein to absolute madness and to the all-powerful perversion of the family or of the father-mother), well, there is room only for transaction, for a transaction reinvented at every moment. This transaction is not necessarily an empirical and shameful compromise, it is the place of the gravest, most concrete, most difficult of political, ethical and juridical responsibilities, the place where one must precisely, through reform, revolution, transformation, and mutation, change the family and the state, change the laws, legislation, mores, discourse as much as language, etc. Render the impossible as possible as is possible. (*H* 1 164/224)

There are thus problems or dangers on both sides of this polarity of hospitality, dangers that can never be excluded or ignored insofar as they are constitutive of these two kinds of hospitality. Derrida continues in the passage from the third session that we are still reading:

> In both cases, in a different fashion, hospitality risks contradicting itself or getting carried away from itself. In the first case, because it limits itself and poses its conditions, confirming the power of ipseity; in the second, because, without criteria, without anyone or anything identifiable as guest received or host receiving, it no longer even justifies its name and, in the end, can no longer appear, or can only appear with the least identifiable features. (*H* 1 57–58/88)

Derrida thus ultimately argues, it seems, that both hospitalities are necessary, that we must have both in an impossible "at once" in order to counteract or temper the inevitable possibility of inversion or perversion on both sides, an inversion or perversion that must nonetheless "remain open in both cases in order that a hospitality might be possible." This is yet another iteration, it seems, of the Derridean logic by which any "positive" phenomenon must always run the risk of its negative perversion, the promise being inextricably bound, for example, to the possibility of perjury (of *parjure*), or forgiveness being inextricably bound to foreswearing, to the breach of faith that structurally conditions the possibility of forgiveness or of any other speech act, or the gift being always haunted by the ineradicable possibility of poisonous perversion, and so on.[3] So essential is this possibility of perversion that Derrida seems to have been tempted to call his seminar not "Hospitality" but "Hosti-pitality"—a neologism that seems to have become just a bit too unwieldy to pursue and develop straight through to the end of the seminar. But here, too, the possibility of perversion is not simply a possibility that haunts the positive version with the specter of some future negativity but a possibility that makes that positive possibility possible in the first place. No positive phenomenon without the possibility of the negative, that is, no conditional hospitality to the guest without the possibility of the guest becoming an enemy, and no possibility of a love without limit or condition without the possibility of a limitless hatred. As Derrida will argue much later in the seminar, the possibil-ity of radical evil must remain open—in order, it seems, better to combat it. "Without the open possibility of a possible perversion," says Derrida, "there is neither good nor love nor unconditional hospitality" (see H 1 142/196). It is thus because "unconditional hospitality, left to itself, can become perverted, shift into its contrary," that it is "necessary to have rules, laws, politics, the law" (H 1 162n24/222n1). It is necessary to have laws because what might appear to be the good hospitality, the just one, can always be perverted—according to a certain "logic of the unconscious"—into its contrary. Derrida writes:

> A logic of the unconscious must never be excluded, to be sure, both in thinking *The* law and in thinking the *laws*; . . . [it] must not be excluded either in thinking what I called the possible perversion, the irreducible pervertibility of *The* law of absolute hospitality (apparently the most giving and most just) into its contrary, the self-negation that can win out if no limits in the Kantian style are assigned to it, for instance; and then, above all, and this is what today remains the most difficult politically, juridically, in thinking together this logic of the unconscious and the axiomatics that at present governs the ethico-juridico-political discourse prevailing everywhere, namely a discourse or an axiomatics of intentional consciousness and the egological subject. (H 1 162–63/222)

The risks must thus remain on both sides, ineradicable, though those risks are different from each side. The risk of conditional hospitality, as Derrida argued, is that it "limits itself and poses its conditions, confirming the power of ipseity," that is, the sovereign power of the host. They are the risks associated with the identification of hospitality with identity and power, that is, in a word, with *ipseity*. The risk of unconditional hospitality is, it seems, the risk or the danger of pure difference or difference without distinction, a hospitality that is "without criteria, without anyone or anything identifiable as guest received or host receiving." It is a hospitality, Derrida then adds, that "no longer even justifies its name and, in the end, can no longer appear, or can only appear with the least identifiable features." There is thus a hospitality of identity and a hospitality of difference, if we can put it this way, both of which can lead to the end of hospitality, the one to conflict or war and the other to an all-out, unregulated hatred or xenophobia.

There are, therefore, two hospitalities or two poles of hospitality, neither of which is able, it seems, to justify its name of "hospitality" without reference to the other. The two kinds or types of hospitality are in a relationship that Derrida will later characterize as a paradox, an aporia, or an irresolvable antinomy—philosophical terms that Derrida will multiply in order to try to characterize the relationship between these two hospitalities. But even before those terms, there is the name "law," which marks both sides of the divide. Derrida continues:

> It is basically against this last madness of hospitality (but a madness inscribed in the law of hospitality, a madness dictated by an uncompromising law of hospitality, which commands uncompromisingly that right be renounced; what is at issue here is a law against laws), it is basically against this latter madness of hospitality, against this law without law of hospitality, that Kant's wisdom, his critical, juridical and political prudence, his sense of moderation, warns us, calls us back to the limit. (*H 1* 58/88)

As Derrida here argues, even this second form of hospitality, this pure, absolute, infinite, perhaps even impossible, "hyperbolic" hospitality, this hospitality that goes beyond the law, can nonetheless be identified with a "law." It is, however, a "law" that would be above or beyond all determinate laws, a law above all laws, a law without law (not unlike Oedipus, perhaps, who is described in *Oedipus at Colonus* as being a sort of *anomos nomos*). This law above or without law is, of course, as we just saw, a kind of madness, a law outside the economy of law, a sort of hyperbolic hospitality that, paradoxically, justifies the very name "hospitality" in any conditional law. Much later in the seminar, Derrida will compare this law above the law to what Thoreau called *civil disobedience*, that is, a kind of adherence to a law beyond all determinate law, a law that exceeds all laws of civil society or of the nation-state, a law that would resemble a sort of natural law, exercising a critique of all existing laws (all nation-state laws, for example) in the name of a higher law or a law above the law (see *H 1* 69, 230/102, 306).[4] In another text from around the same time (December 1996), Derrida speaks of "what is called in the United States the 'civil disobedience' by which a citizen declares in the name of a higher law that he will not obey some legislative measure, which he judges to be wrong and unjust, thereby choosing delinquency over shame, and the so-called crime over injustice" ("Q" 90). And so while "everything possible must indeed be done to get the laws of hospitality written into actual laws," when that proves impossible acts of "civil disobedience" seem to be the next best option ("NU" 132).

The example of civil disobedience is helpful but also, of course, imperfect, because one would still be criticizing nation-state law in the name of another law (natural law, as the foundation, say, for human rights), a so-called natural law or a notion of human rights that would itself need to be criticized in the name of, say, Justice, which inspires or motivates all these notions of law but cannot be reduced to them. This is yet another example of what Derrida calls — and we will look at this phrase in much greater detail later — "mediating schema" for thinking the relationship between a singular law, which would be "closer" to the notion of Justice, and plural, nation-state laws, a law above the laws in the tradition of civil disobedience and all determinate, nation-state laws. As Derrida will argue much later in the seminar, it is a question of knowing how to transform the law so as to make it progress.

Derrida is thus clearly *for* unconditional hospitality; he is *in favor* of civil disobedience in certain circumstances. The one, like the other, it seems, is necessary. There could be no ethics without them. And yet, to go back to the other side of the threshold distinguishing the two hospitalities, it is to protect hospitality from the madness of absolute hospitality, from its nonphenomenality, that Kant in *Perpetual Peace* establishes conditions for hospitality. For example, hospitality is to be limited, first, and this goes without saying in Kant, to human beings. There is no consideration whatsoever of offering it to any other living being besides a human being. It is going to be granted, second, only to those coming from nation-states. Third, it will guarantee those coming from nation-states only the right to sojourn in a foreign land for a time, not the right to become permanent citizens. And fourth, it will grant the citizen of another nation-state a sojourn that may be curtailed, the guest expulsed, whenever the invited guest is deemed to be no longer behaving "peaceably" within the host country. Given all this, it is easy to think that Kant's anthropocentric, nation-state-oriented hospitality goes *against* the very idea of hospitality as openness to the other, that it is simply *opposed* to the pure, unconditional hospitality that, as Derrida will later suggest, is the only hospitality worthy of the name. And yet Derrida here suggests that such hospitality, such a prudent, cautious hospitality, is perfectly understandable and, in many respects, wise. Prudent, wise, and so seemingly desirable. For without an effective law of hospitality, the unconditional law of hospitality will remain, says Derrida, a *désir pieux*, that is, a "pious" or "empty" wish, not only ineffective but "irresponsible" (*H 1* 259/343).[5]

But before drawing *that* conclusion, Derrida jumps back over the threshold yet again in order to remind us yet once more of the dangers of conditional hospitality. Returning to the argument with which he began, he recalls that conditional hospitality "confirms itself in its actuality only by denying itself, by placing denial at the heart of the invitation: act as if you were at home, but only *as if* at home, don't forget that you are not at home" (*H 1* 58/89). In other words, *faites comme chez vous, mais ne restez pas trop longtemps.*

That is Derrida's first attempt in the seminar to formalize this relationship between conditional and unconditional hospitality. Later, he will identify the second of these two hospitalities, this absolute hospitality that breaks with the hospitality of right or of law, with a justice that is heterogeneous to all law (*H 1* 83–84/120–21). This should make more sense in light of the passage we just looked at. Absolute hospitality would be on the side of a justice that goes beyond or is heterogeneous to all law, that is, to all determinate laws. And that, as we just saw, is both its promise and its danger, both that which allows it to act as a sort of critical or deconstructive lever to criticize all existing laws and that which, without any guardrails, backfires, or limitations—without any attention to the threshold, precisely—can lead to the very worst forms of violence and injustice.

9

Unconditional and Conditional Hospitality

> Hospitality can take place only beyond hospitality, only by deciding, while letting come, to cross over that hospitality that lets itself get paralyzed on the threshold that it is. It is necessary to let come beyond hospitality, if that is possible. (*H* 1 24/46)

Derrida will continue throughout the seminar to redefine and reinflect this relationship between conditional and unconditional hospitality, going back and forth across the threshold, as it were, between the two hospitalities, or, rather, remarking the threshold continuously *within* the two, as if unconditional hospitality were an enclave within conditional hospitality, within yet somehow heterogeneous to it, at once "bigger" than conditional hospitality yet somehow "contained" within it, and conditional hospitality were what surrounded and limited the unconditional, at once "smaller" than unconditional hospitality yet somehow "containing" it. Derrida will thus continue throughout the seminar to multiply the terms on both sides of the threshold between the conditional and the unconditional, in addition to attempting to rethink the threshold itself, that is, the place of articulation between the two, arguing, for example, as we will see in a moment, that unconditional hospitality "inspires," "motivates," or "orients" conditional hospitality, thereby justifying its very name of "hospitality."[1]

The distinction between the two kinds of hospitality is even reflected in Derrida's language regarding the recipients of that hospitality. While conditional hospitality is offered to the "foreigner," unconditional hospitality, that is, pure, infinite, absolute hospitality, is what is offered to the stranger or, better, to the "absolute other." We thus see Derrida throughout the seminar and in *Of Hospitality* distinguishing or even opposing the *étranger*, the foreigner, to the absolute other. What makes unconditional hospitality "impossible" is thus not only the way it exceeds the power, capacity, or possibilities of the one who would offer it but the impossibility of identifying the one to whom it is offered, the fact that such hospitality is offered *not* on the basis of any lineage or name, any birthright or citizenship, indeed any distinguishing characteristic whatsoever. Again, that which limits hospitality is also that which makes it possible. Derrida writes early on in *Of Hospitality*, in a passage that does not appear as such in the seminar:

> If we wanted to pause for a moment on this significant fact, we would have to note once again a paradox or a contradiction: this right to hospitality offered to a foreigner "as a family," represented and protected by his or her family name, is at once what makes hospitality possible, or the hospitable relationship to the foreigner possible, but by the same token what limits and prohibits it. Because hospitality, in this situation, is not offered to an anonymous new arrival and someone who has neither name, nor patronym, nor family, nor social status. . . . We have alluded to this: the difference, one of the subtle and sometimes ungraspable differences between the foreigner and the absolute other is that the latter cannot have a name or a family name; the absolute or unconditional hospitality I would like to offer him or her presupposes a break with hospitality in the ordinary sense, with conditional hospitality, with the right to or pact of hospitality. In saying this, once more, we are taking account of an irreducible pervertibility. (*OH* 23–25/27–29)

The relationship between conditional and unconditional hospitality is here called a paradox or a contradiction, another way of speaking of that essential pervertibility on both sides, so to speak, of hospitality. The restriction or limitation of hospitality to, for example, the family is at once what makes hospitality possible *and* forbids it by limiting it, restricting it to those whom the host recognizes and knows, those who are like the host, who reflect the host. Such hospitality must thus be opposed to the hospitality offered to an anonymous *arrivant*, to the "newcomer," as it is sometimes translated, without name, patronym, family, or social status (see *OH* 25/29, *H* 1 84/120–21). As Derrida suggests in *Aporias*, a text that predates the *Hospitality* seminar by a couple of years:

> I am talking about the absolute *arrivant*, who is not even a guest. He surprises the host—who is not yet a host or an inviting power—enough

to call into question, to the point of annihilating or rendering indeter-
minate, all the distinctive signs of a prior identity, beginning with the
very border that delineated a legitimate home and assured lineage,
names and language, nations, families and genealogies. The absolute
arrivant does not yet have a name or an identity. (AP 34)

The unconditional or absolute hospitality that one would like to offer to the
other thus entails a rupture with the conditional hospitality of right and duty,
of laws and pacts. For the anonymous other, without name, lineage, or country, is not even recognizable as "someone" with whom a pact might be con-
tracted. Derrida continues in *Of Hospitality*:

> The law of hospitality, the express law that governs the general concept
> of hospitality, appears as a paradoxical law, pervertible or perverting. It
> seems to dictate that absolute hospitality should break with the law of
> hospitality as right or duty, with the "pact" of hospitality. To put it in
> different terms, absolute hospitality requires that I open up my home
> and that I give not only to the foreigner (provided with a family name,
> with the social status of being a foreigner, etc.), but to the absolute, un-
> known, anonymous other, and that I *give place* to them, that I let them
> come, that I let them arrive, and take place in the place I offer them,
> without asking of them either reciprocity (entering into a pact) or even
> their names. The law of absolute hospitality commands a break with
> hospitality by right, with law or justice as rights. Just hospitality breaks
> with hospitality by right; not that it condemns or is opposed to it, and
> it can on the contrary set and maintain it in a perpetual progressive
> movement; but it is as strangely heterogeneous to it as justice is hetero-
> geneous to the law to which it is yet so close, from which in truth it is
> indissociable. (*OH* 25–27/29; see *H* 1 84/120–21)

Absolute hospitality entails opening my home not just to the *étranger*, to the
foreigner, but to the absolute, unknown, anonymous other. It requires, says
Derrida, that I "give place [*donne lieu*]" to the other, that I offer hospitality
without asking for reciprocity, without asking what this other can offer me in
return (based, for example, on their family, wealth, training, job qualifica-
tions, etc.), indeed without even asking for a name (see *H* 1 129/178–79). This
language of "giving place," *donner lieu*, which is so prominent in Derrida's
reading of the *khōra* in Plato's *Timaeus*, would seem to suggest that the "giver"
of absolute hospitality would be something like a *khōra*, offering nourishment
and shelter but also, and perhaps before anything else, simply *space* or *place*,
receiving before anything is even identifiable, just as the protoelements are

received by *khōra* before they are identifiable objects in the cosmos and even before the elements themselves are recognizable as fire, air, water, and earth.

Absolute or just hospitality thus "breaks with the hospitality of law." Though this hospitality might in fact motivate or inspire conditional hospitality, as we will see, it is as heterogeneous to it as justice is to law. Though it might be what inspires Kant's notion of hospitality in *Perpetual Peace*, it is nonetheless heterogeneous to it. For the stranger in the cosmopolitical tradition of Kant is not someone who is welcomed unconditionally but someone with whom one begins by asking his name. The first, minimal demand is: "What is your name? [*Comment t'appelles-tu?*]" (*OH* 27/31; see H 1 84/121). We now begin to see better why Derrida began that fourth session with a question and why the question of hospitality is, in the end, the question of the question. Should we pose a question to the other or not? Does hospitality consist in questioning the newcomer—whether harshly or gently—or does it begin with the welcoming without question, before it is even a question of the question or the name? Is hospitality to be given *before* the other has been identified as a subject, as a subject of law or a nameable subject?

Having looked in some detail at Derrida's first attempt to sketch out a relationship between conditional and unconditional hospitality, let me turn now to what is no doubt the most powerful and condensed form of the argument regarding the two forms of hospitality, that is, to three or four pages of the second seminar session in *Of Hospitality*, the fifth session of the seminar, where Derrida tries to formulate as rigorously as possible the relationship between the two forms of hospitality. As with that first passage, we would do well to read it closely, not quite word by word but at least step by step, *pas* by *pas* (see *OH* 75–83/71–77). Here is the first step, which comes not long after the *pas d'hospitalité* with which the session begins:

> It is as though hospitality were the impossible: as though the law of
> hospitality defined this very impossibility, as if it were only possible to
> transgress it, as though *the* law of absolute, unconditional, hyperbolical
> hospitality, as though the categorical imperative of hospitality com-
> manded that we transgress all the laws (in the plural) of hospitality,
> namely, the conditions, the norms, the rights and the duties that are
> imposed on hosts and hostesses, on the men or women who give a wel-
> come as well as the men or women who receive it. And vice versa, it
> is as though the laws (plural) of hospitality, in marking limits, powers,
> rights, and duties, consisted in challenging and transgressing *the* law
> of hospitality, the one that would command that the "new arrival" be
> offered an unconditional welcome. (*OH* 75–77/71; see H 1 103/146)

We hear even more clearly in this passage the relationship between conditional and unconditional hospitality as the relationship between plural laws
and a singular law. Beginning with an "as if," Derrida says it is "as if" the
singular law of absolute, unconditional, hyperbolic hospitality required us,
as a sort of categorical imperative, to transgress or overstep all determinate,
limited, conditional laws of hospitality. A reference to civil disobedience may
again be helpful: It is as if the unconditional law of hospitality required us,
through a kind of civil disobedience, to overstep all determinate nation-state
laws, customs, and pacts in order to respond to the infinite demand of the
other. As for the term "hyperbolic," it is impossible not to be reminded of
Descartes's "hyperbolic" doubt (which Derrida analyzes in his 1963 "Cogito
and the History of Madness"), his continuous raising of the stakes or upping
of the ante of doubt—moving from common optical illusions that make us
distrust our perceptions, to the phenomenon of dreams, which often seem
just as indubitable as waking life, to, finally, the hypothesis of an Evil Genius
who is causing us to feel and to think everything that we do. But we would
also not be wrong to recall the Platonic origins of hyperbole, Glaucon, for
example, in the *Republic* reacting to Socrates's suggestion that the Good exceeds all Being as *epekeina tes ousias*, "what demonic hyperbole (*daimonias
hyperboles*)," that is, "what demonic exceeding or excess" (see "CHM" 56–57).
Hyperbolic hospitality, as exceeding all determinate laws of hospitality, would
recall or echo all of this—as if the absolute other, without name or identity,
without identifiable characteristics, were a sort of Good beyond Being, a Good
beyond all phenomena, to be sure, but also beyond all essences. It is in this
sense that absolute hospitality cannot be "given," indeed cannot be the object
of an invitation, but is always unforeseen, unpredictable, a visitation rather
than an invitation.[2] Derrida continues his description of absolute, infinite, or
hyperbolic hospitality:

> Let us say yes *to who or what turns up* [*à l'arrivant*], before any deter-
> mination, before any anticipation, before any *identification*, whether
> or not it has to do with a foreigner, an immigrant, an invited guest,
> or an unexpected visitor, whether or not the new arrival is the citizen
> of another country, a human, animal, or divine creature, a living or
> dead thing, male or female. (*OH* 77/73; see *H* 1 103/146; passage added
> to *OH*)

Again, we here see unconditional hospitality going even beyond anthropo-
centrism, beyond all species determination. Moreover, the "yes" at the beginning of this line should make us think that unconditional hospitality is to be
thought in relation to what Derrida speaks of elsewhere as the "yes" before the

"yes," the "yes yes" that would open up hospitality even before any criteria of selection would allow one to say either "yes" or "no." (I recall in passing that the most recent text of Derrida's to be published besides the *Hospitality* seminar is *Penser, c'est dire non*, a course from 1960–1961, where Derrida takes up this title phrase from Alain in order to begin to develop a thinking of the "yes" before any negation.)[3] It is *as if* the law of absolute, unconditional hospitality required us to transgress all the norms and conditions of hospitality, required us to say "yes" to the other, to welcome, to offer hospitality without condition to whoever comes—be it an invited guest or an unknown migrant, a human, an animal, or a god.

Derrida then goes on to try to think the *relationship* between the two kinds of hospitality, using a whole series of terms—some Kantian and some not—to characterize that relationship:

> In other words, there would be an antinomy, an insoluble antinomy, a non-dialectizable antinomy between, on the one hand, *The* law of unlimited hospitality (to give the new arrival all of one's home and oneself, to give him or her one's own, our own, without asking a name, or compensation, or the fulfilment of even the smallest condition), and on the other hand, the laws (in the plural), those rights and duties that are always conditioned and conditional, as they are defined by the Greco-Roman tradition and even the Judeo-Christian one, by all of law and all philosophy of law up to Kant and Hegel in particular, across the family, civil society, and the State. (*OH* 77/73; see *H* 1 103/146)

Derrida here characterizes the relationship between limited and unlimited hospitality, conditional and unconditional hospitality, as an "insoluble," "non-dialectizable antinomy" (somewhat like that between God and Freedom or the antinomies of space and time). Between *the law* of (unconditional) hospitality and the *laws* of (conditional) hospitality, there is a nondialectizable antinomy, a conflict, an "aporia." Derrida continues:

> That is definitely where this aporia is, an antinomy. It is in fact about the law (*nomos*). This conflict does not oppose a law to a nature or an empirical fact. It marks the collision between two laws, at the frontier between two regimes of law, both of them non-empirical. The antinomy of hospitality irreconcilably opposes *The* law, in its universal singularity, to a plurality that is not only a dispersal (laws in the plural), but a structured multiplicity, determined by a process of division and differentiation: by a number of laws that distribute their history and

their anthropological geography differently. (*OH* 77–79/73; see *H* 1 103/146)

Derrida here reinscribes the notion of *aporia* into his thinking of hospitality, along with that threshold that we have been talking about throughout, suggesting, it seems, that there is no hospitality without aporia and a perpetual return to the threshold. In addition to antinomy or aporia, it is the double bind (in English) that gets reinscribed. Here is Derrida in the first session of the seminar, speaking of

> an aporetic crossroads, that is to say, a crossroads or a sort of double postulate, double contradictory movement, double constraint or double bind (I prefer "double bind" because this English expression preserves the link [*lien*] to linking and thus to obligation, to ligament, to being bound [*liance*]). It can seem paradoxical that the experience of hospitality encounters aporia, where people mainly think that the host offers the guest passage over the threshold or border so as to welcome him at home. Is aporia not, as its name indicates, the non-road, barred way, non-passage? Well, my hypothesis or thesis in this seminar would be that this necessary aporia is not negative, and that, without repeatedly undergoing this paralysis within contradiction, the responsibility of a hospitality, hospitality *tout court*—where we do not yet know and will never know what it is—would have no chance of coming about, coming, making or letting well-come [*d'advenir, de venir, de faire ou de laisser bienvenir*]. But this will later become more thinkable for us, if not clearer and more familiar. (*H* 1 21/43)

The antinomy, an irresolvable antinomy, is thus also a double bind, an aporia, giving us no way or passage out. The antinomy concerns a conflict between two laws, or two regimes of law, Derrida here suggests, a singular, absolute law—a law above or without the law, as we saw earlier—and the plural, multiple, historically determined laws. This, in conjunction with the reference to Hegel, sets up, it would seem, the reference to tragedy that soon follows. As Hegel argues in the *Aesthetics* in his reading of *Antigone*, tragedy is the result of a conflict between the law of the city that prohibits Antigone from burying her brother Polyneices and the law of the family that requires her to bury him. For Derrida, the conflict is between the multiple laws of conditional hospitality that require limits, distinctions, filtering, selection, and so on and the singular law of hospitality that demands a welcoming of the other before any such distinctions. That is the tragedy, the conflict not between two

regimes of determinate law but between a regime of determinate law and the
law of laws that seems to rise above those laws. Derrida continues:

> The tragedy, for it is a tragedy of destiny, is that the two antagonistic
> terms of this antinomy are not symmetrical. There is a strange hierar-
> chy in this. *The* law is above the laws. It is thus illegal, transgressive,
> outside the law, like a lawless law, *nomos anomos*, law above the laws
> and law outside the law (*anomos*, we remember, that's for instance
> how Oedipus, the father-son, the son as father, father and brother of
> his daughters, is characterized). But even while keeping itself above
> the laws of hospitality, *the* unconditional law of hospitality needs the
> laws, it *requires* them. This demand is constitutive. It wouldn't be
> effectively unconditional, the law, if it didn't *have to become* effective,
> concrete, determined, if that were not its being as having-to-be. It
> would risk being abstract, utopian, illusory, and so turning over into its
> opposite. In order to be what it is, *the* law thus needs the laws, which,
> however, deny it, or at any rate threaten it, sometimes corrupt or
> pervert it. And must always be able to do this. (*OH* 79/73–75; see *H* 1
> 103–4/147)

The tragedy that is to be found in the conflict between law and laws, the
irresolvable antinomy or aporia between them, also seems to suggest a mutual
albeit irreciprocal relation between them. The laws of hospitality need the
law of hospitality so as not to negate themselves, ruin themselves, and the
law of hospitality needs the laws of hospitality in order to become *effective*.
"It wouldn't be effectively unconditional, the law, if it didn't *have to become*
[devait pas devenir] effective, concrete, determined, if that were not its being
as having-to-be" (*OH* 79/75; see *H* 1 103–4/147). In order not to be simply
"abstract, utopian, illusory" and in order not to "turn over into its opposite,"
which, as we saw earlier, would be a savage, untamed, uncivilized rejection
and maybe even hatred of the other, the law *has to* become effective.

It might thus seem that the problem with the law of hospitality is that it
might always remain empty, merely formal, that one will never attain it, that
it will remain a sort of utopian ideal we can only ever approximate and will
always fall short of. But Derrida wants to argue something more or something
different. Though heterogeneous to laws, the law of unconditional hospitality
requires or calls for laws, exerts a certain pressure on them. Derrida writes in
that critical albeit not altogether transparent phrase: "It would not be effectively unconditional if it *didn't have to become* effective, concrete, determined,
if that were not its being as having-to-be" (*OH* 79/75; see *H* 1 103–4/147). It
is as if the singular law of hospitality requires, calls for, its own transgression

in order to become effective, in order to be, says Derrida somewhat enigmatically, "what it is"—namely, a *law of hospitality*. "In order to be what it is, *the* law thus needs the laws, which, however, deny it, or at any rate threaten it, sometimes corrupt or pervert it. And must always be able to do this" (*OH* 79/75; see *H* 1 103–4/147).

The unconditional requires the conditional, Law requires laws, in order to be effective. And yet, Derrida goes on to suggest, the possibility of perversion, a fundamental pervertibility, continues to haunt the two sides, which is why this antinomy can never be resolved, despite these attempts to connect the two hospitalities, despite the becoming-*effective* of hospitality, or, as we will see, the becoming-law of justice. Unconditional hospitality may put conditional hospitality on the road to an incessant progress, hence that notion of perfectibility, but conditional hospitality is also, perpetually, a perversion of absolute hospitality, which means, it seems, that that incessant perfectibility is always haunted by the possibility of perversion, the possibility of the determinate, conditional laws of hospitality becoming more restrictive, less open and less just. Derrida continues, trying yet again to provide some link, some relation, between the two sides of this antinomical relation:

> For this pervertibility is essential, irreducible, necessary too. The perfectibility of laws is at this cost. And therefore their historicity. And vice versa, conditional laws would cease to be laws of hospitality if they were not guided, given inspiration, given aspiration, required, even, by the law of unconditional hospitality. These two regimes of law, of *the* law and the laws, are thus both contradictory, antinomic, *and* inseparable [emphasis added in *OH*]. They both imply and exclude each other, simultaneously. They incorporate one another at the moment of excluding one another, they are dissociated at the moment of enveloping one another, *at the moment* (simultaneity without simultaneity, instant of impossible synchrony, moment without moment) when, exhibiting themselves to each other, one to the others, the others to the other, they show they are both more and less hospitable, hospitable and inhospitable, hospitable *inasmuch as* inhospitable. (*OH* 79–81/75; see *H* 1 104/147)

It is in this passage that Derrida seems to make his most strident attempt to think the two kinds of hospitality "together," "at the same moment," or "simultaneously." Instead of speaking simply of the pervertibility of both kinds of hospitality, the pervertibility of the unconditional law of hospitality both by the conditional laws of hospitality and, it seems, by its own tendency to turn into its opposite, namely, an unconditional hatred or rejection, and then the pervertibility of conditional laws of hospitality through the limitation and determination of the unconditional, Derrida speaks of a "perfectibility" that would always accompany the "pervertibility." It is this "perfectibility" that would seem to explain, in Derrida's account, the very existence of conditional laws of hospitality in the first place, laws that will have been guided, "inspired," given aspiration—given breath, as it were—by the unconditional law of hospitality. The unconditional would not be what it is, namely, an unconditional *law*, without the conditional, but also, reciprocally, the conditional laws of hospitality would cease to be what they are, namely, laws of *hospitality*, were they not guided, inspired, drawn, given inspiration, given aspiration, by the law of unconditional hospitality.

Elsewhere in the seminar, Derrida uses the language not of "inspiring" or "giving inspiration" but of "orienting" and "orientation." Guided, perhaps, by the Kantian notion of orientation, he says:

> Thus, just as justice, which is not the law, calls for a history of right, a history of laws, a transformation, an interminable reform of the laws, of legislation, which put into effect the conditions for the application of justice—so justice is not the law, but it demands the law and in the same way the law, which is not justice, lets itself be called, *oriented* by the idea of justice. There would be no law either if there were no call for justice. And likewise, conditional hospitality, which is not absolute or hyperbolic hospitality, deserves the name of hospitality only to the extent that it lets itself be *oriented*, guided by an idea of absolute hospitality. So, one has here this strange polarity between these two hospitalities which, in a certain way, come down to a single one. (*H* 1 132/182–83; my emphasis)

Hence, the idea of justice—a certain unconditional hospitality—orients the conditional, historical laws of hospitality. It is this "orientation" of conditional by unconditional hospitality that makes it possible to call these conditional laws laws of *hospitality*.

A bit later in the seminar, Derrida returns to this language of "orientation," suggesting that absolute hospitality "orients" the desire and experience of hospitality. The question then becomes

> how to inscribe this injunction of absolute hospitality, which continues to *orient* the desire for hospitality, the experience of hospitality, into new political, juridical projects, a new political, juridical discourse, new ethical, juridical and political apparatuses. What must be done, what must one think, what must one do in order to comply

with this injunction of absolute hospitality, under the conditions that
are those of the evolution of the state, the nation, of national borders,
international law? (*H* 1 140/193; my emphasis)

What are we to make of this *inspiration* or this *orientation*? A few possibilities. First, it seems that we would not have any concept of hospitality at all, no
concept of a hospitality beyond, say, commercial exchange or what is called
"customer service" in the hospitality industry, no hospitality beyond that of
the innkeeper and the restaurant owner, or beyond the targeted recruitment
of foreigners by a nation-state for economic needs, *without* this unconditional
drive toward the other or this welcoming of the absolute other. There would
be no concept, and there would be no evidence of this concept's universaliza-
tion in history (Kant, for example), if the unconditional were not exercising
this force, a force, it could be said, of deconstruction, the deconstruction of
conditional hospitality in the name of the unconditional, or the deconstruction of law in the name of justice. There would be no concept of hospitality
and, indeed, no name "hospitality," no name for this concept in the law, were
it not for unconditional hospitality. In this sense, it is the law of hospitality that
gives *meaning* to the plural laws; only because they are animated or aspirated
by the law of hospitality do the laws of hospitality "deserve" to be *called* or
named laws of "hospitality." In a brief text titled "The Principle of Hospitality,"
Derrida writes:

> The two meanings of hospitality remain irreducible to one another,
> but it is the pure and hyperbolical hospitality in whose name we
> should always invent the best dispositions, the least bad conditions,
> the most just legislation, so as to make it as effective as possible. ("PH"
> 67/274)

The repetition of "in the name" or "in whose name" would seem to suggest,
again, that there would be no name for "hospitality," or no hospitality worthy
of the name, without that unconditional hospitality that guides, inspires, or
orients conditional hospitality. Derrida goes on in this same text to define the
relationship between the conditional and the unconditional in terms of what
can and cannot be calculated. He writes:

> Calculate the risks, yes, but don't shut the door on what cannot be
> calculated, meaning the future and the foreigner—that's the double
> law of hospitality. It defines the unstable place of strategy and decision.
> Of perfectibility and progress. It is a place that is being sought today, in
> the debates about immigration for instance. We often forget that it is in
> the name of unconditional hospitality, the kind that makes meaningful

any reception of foreigners, that we should try to determine the *best* conditions, namely particular legal limits, and especially any particular implementation of the laws. ("PH" 67/274)

Second, Derrida's invocation of "historicity," which elsewhere in his work is related to the becoming-history of a hyperbolic moment that "exceeds" history, suggests that the relationship between unconditional and conditional hospitality is not that between an ahistorical concept and its historical instantiation but, rather, a becoming-historical of the absolute, thereby making "historicity" the place of a perpetual, ineradicable, and irreconcilable perfectibility/pervertibility between the law of hospitality and the laws of hospitality, a perfectibility/pervertibility that can be summarized by that *pas d'hospitalité* with which Derrida begins the fifth session. Derrida can thus write that "these two regimes of law, of *the* law and the laws, are both contradictory, antinomic, *and* inseparable" (*OH* 79–81/75; see *H 1* 104/147). As for the nature of this inseparability, we might try to think it in relationship to what Derrida will later call in the seminar the structure of the "enclave," that is, the structure of an outside, of an exclusion, within. It is that kind of structure, that kind of relation between inside and outside, inclusion and exclusion, that Derrida seems to be trying to indicate in the following passage:

> Because exclusion and inclusion are inseparable in the same moment, whenever you would like to say "at this very moment," there is antinomy. The law, in the absolute singular, contradicts laws in the plural, but on each occasion it is the law *within* the law, and on each occasion *outside the law* within the law. That's it, that so very singular thing that is called the *laws* of hospitality. (*OH* 81/75; see *H 1* 104/147)

The two regimes of hospitality imply and exclude each other simultaneously; they are at once hospitable and inhospitable with regard to each other.

It is just after this attempt to think the excluded law of hospitality within the laws of hospitality that Derrida makes an attempt to distinguish two kinds of plurality in these plural laws, the first, the plural conditional laws of hospitality all by themselves, as it were, and the second the relationship between those plural laws and the singular unconditional law of hospitality.

> Strange plural, plural grammar of *two plurals that are different at the same time.* One of these two plurals says the laws of hospitality, conditional laws, etc. The other plural says the antinomic addition, the one that adds conditional laws to the unique and singular and absolutely only [*seule*] great Law of hospitality, to *the* law of hospitality, to the categorical imperative of hospitality. In this second case, the plural is

made up of One + a multiplicity, whereas in the first case, it was only multiplicity, distribution, differentiation. In one case, you have One + n; in the other, n + n + n, etc. (*OH* 81/75–77; see *H* 1 104/147)

Derrida is suggesting two different kinds of multiplicity or plurality for hospitality's two regimes of law, one multiplicity or plurality for the series of conditional laws, n + n + n, and another that consists of this same series, n + n + n, plus or preceded by—preceded and, as we just saw, inspired, guided, oriented, given aspiration by—the singular law of hospitality, the One law that comes before and guides or inspires the multiplicity, the One that seems to require its own supplementation by this open set of determinate laws, One + n.[4] The first plurality is that of conditional hospitality, a series of laws that con- dition hospitality, while the second is that of the unconditional One law *plus* the open series of conditional laws. The term "law" would thus itself be one of those mediating schemata between conditional and unconditional hospitality. It allows Derrida to try to think the relationship between the singular Law and multiple laws, a Law beyond the law, an *anomos nomos*, as he says, a Law that guides or orients laws and those laws themselves.

Finally, after characterizing in this long passage that singular law of hospi- tality, that unconditional law of hospitality, as a sort of categorical imperative of the Kantian type, Derrida warns us against seeing too close a proximity between the two. This latter is but a "quasi-synonym" for the unconditional demand of unconditional hospitality. For the unconditional demand of un- conditional hospitality would be, as it were, a demand without "imperative." Derrida writes:

(Let us note parenthetically that as a quasi-synonym for "uncondi- tional," the Kantian expression of "categorical imperative" is not un- problematic; we will keep it with some reservations, under erasure, if you like, or under *epoche*. For to be what it "must" be, hospitality must not pay a debt, or be governed by a duty: it is gracious, and "must" not open itself to the guest [invited or visitor], either "conforming to duty" or even, to use the Kantian distinction again, "out of duty." This unconditional law of hospitality, if such a thing is thinkable, would then be a law without imperative, without order and without duty. A law without law, in short. For if I practice hospitality *"out of* duty" [and not only *"in conforming with* duty"], this hospitality of paying up is no longer an absolute hospitality, it is no longer graciously offered beyond debt and economy, offered to the other, a hospitality invented for the singularity of the new arrival, of the unexpected visitor.) (*OH* 81–83/77; see *H* 1 104/147–48; *gracieuse* added to *OH*)

Notice, once again, Derrida's emphasis on an aneconomic aspect to hospitality, a hospitality before the economy of debt and repayment, a hospitality that is—and we will return to this term in greater detail in the next chapter—"gracious [*gracieuse*]," meaning not only offered with grace, with style, but freely, without any expectation of payment or return.

Notice also Derrida's emphasis on a hospitality that must be "invented." Neither a hospitality that simply follows predetermined laws or norms, that is, a hospitality that begins to cancel itself or to ruin itself just as it begins, nor a hospitality that offers itself absolutely, purely, as well as impossibly insofar as host and guest cannot even be distinguished, but a hospitality that must be "invented," and each time uniquely, as it tries to bring together or cross these two irreconcilable yet inseparable laws of hospitality. Derrida writes in "*Une hospitalité à l'infini*"—a title that might be translated either as "An Infinite Hospitality" or as "A Hospitality to the Infinite"—"hospitality must be so inventive, adjusted to the other, and to the welcoming of the other, that each experience of hospitality must invent a new language" ("HI"101).

But it is here that we begin to see how a deconstructive thinking of hospitality begins to reflect and be reflected in something like a thinking of deconstruction as hospitality.[5] For later in both *Of Hospitality* and the *Hospitality* seminar Derrida refers not only to an invention of hospitality, one that would be each time unique, within hospitable *practices*, if we can speak this way, but also to an invention at the level of *theory*, at the level of thinking the relationship between unconditional and conditional hospitality, an inventive *thinking* of hospitality as what must be at each moment a kind of invention.[6] One sign or expression of this inventive thinking at the "theoretical" level would be the very "mediating schemas" that we have been following here, the use of terms such as "aspiration" or "orientation," the "becoming-effective" of the unconditional law of hospitality, or, soon, the "becoming-law of justice." The very notion of "schemas" would itself then be just such an invention, an inventive reinscription of a term with a long philosophical heritage. Speaking of the distinction between unconditional hospitality and the rights and duties that condition hospitality, Derrida argues in *Of Hospitality*, "Far from paralyzing this desire or destroying the requirements of hospitality, this distinction requires us to determine what could be called, in Kantian language (in an approximate and analogical way . . .), intermediate *schemas*" (*OH* 147/129–131; see *H 1* 124/171). Here is the seminar version of this passage:

> The antinomic distinction between unconditional hospitality and the right to hospitality, far from paralyzing us or from paralyzing the demand or desire for hospitality, requires us to determine what I would

call, using Kantian language, the intermediary *schemata* between
an unconditional law or an absolute desire for hospitality on the one
hand, and on the other, a conditional law, politics, ethics. (*H* 1 124/171)

Derrida thus speaks in the seminar of an "absolute desire" for unconditional
or infinite or impossible or absolute hospitality, a desire that, we might think,
is what animates or aspirates or gives aspiration or inspiration to all conditional laws of hospitality. Between an unconditional law or an absolute *desire*
of hospitality, on the one hand, and conditional laws, politics, and ethics, on
the other, there is "radical heterogeneity" but also "indissociability." The "one
calls forth, involves, or prescribes the other" (*OH* 147/131; see *H* 1 124/171; these
lines seem to have been added to *OH*).[7]

So, aspiration, desire, calling forth: All these are schemas or schemata, it
would seem, ways or attempts to think both the difference and the inseparability between the two forms or two regimes of hospitality. Derrida follows up this
claim with a series of questions: "In giving a right, if I can put it like that, to an
unconditional hospitality, how can one give *place* to a determined, limitable,
and delimitable—in a word, to a calculable—right or law? How can one give
place [or make place, or give rise] to a concrete politics and ethics, including
a history, evolutions, actual revolutions, advances—in short, a perfectibility?"
(*OH* 147–49/131; see *H* 1 124/171). Derrida is asking about a politics, a law, and
an ethics that would be able to meet today's changing demands by inscribing
democracy, international law, and citizenship otherwise. He speaks, for example, of intervening "in the name [*au nom de*]" of this unconditional, "even
if this pure unconditional appears inaccessible," not simply because it is infinitely removed like a Kantian idea but, he says, for "structural reasons," that
is, because of the "internal contradictions" that he will have been analyzing
(*OH* 149/131; see *H* 1 125/171).

There are thus two kinds of hospitality, unconditional and conditional,
heterogeneous yet indissociable, related by means of all these mediating schemata, as different from one another—though also as related—as justice and
law.[8] Derrida writes in *Of Hospitality* in a passage that is based on but that also
significantly modifies a passage from the fourth session of the seminar: "What
is a foreigner? . . . It is not the other, the completely other who is relegated to
an absolute outside. . . . The relationship to the foreigner is regulated by law,
by the becoming-law of justice [*le devenir-droit de la justice*]" (*OH* 73/67–69;
see *H* 1 99/139). Everything is contained in that final phrase, which Derrida
added to the *Of Hospitality* version of the seminar. Hospitality granted to
the foreigner in a given context would be the "becoming-law of justice," the
place or the site where justice, that Law above the law, becomes determinate

law. Though there would be no formula, it seems, for this becoming-law of justice, no law that prescribes it and, obviously, *no guarantee of it*, the very phrase "becoming-law of justice" seems to promise it. In a brief text in *Paper Machine* titled "Not Utopia, the Im-possible," Derrida makes it clear that if this becoming-law of justice happens, and perhaps happens all the time, there can be no project or no program for inscribing or embodying this justice in the law. He there argues:

> Unconditional hospitality is inseparable from a thinking of justice itself, but as such it remains impracticable. It cannot be written into the rules or in a piece of legislation. If one wanted to translate it imme-diately into a policy, it would always carry the risk of having perverse effects. But even as we watch out for these risks, we cannot and must not abandon the reference to hospitality without reservations [*sans réserve*]. It is an absolute pole, outside which desire, the concept, and experience, the very thought of hospitality, would be meaningless. (*PM* 131/361)

Here is yet another formulation, this time from the seminar, of the rela-tionship—the nonoppositional relationship—between the singular, uncondi-tional Law of hospitality and the plural conditional laws of hospitality, that is, between justice and law. Derrida speaks of

> the polarity without opposition, without oppositional distinction, between *The* law of unconditional, absolute, hyperbolic, *just* hospi-tality, and the *laws* of hospitality that are conditional, hypothetical, limitative, violent and, as it were, more juridical than just, in accor-dance with this gap between justice and law that guides me here. (*H* 1 162/222)

Desire, effectivity, the One + n, inspiration or aspiration, the becoming-law of justice: These are just some of the intermediate schemata—just some of the many thresholds, if you will—by which Derrida tries to think the relation-ship between the unconditional law and the conditional laws of hospitality, the intermediate schemata in Derrida's theoretical apparatus that reflect or exemplify the kinds of intermediate schemata that happen or take effect all the time in law and politics.

To summarize: Derrida characterizes and tries to rethink the relationship between conditional hospitality and unconditional hospitality in the following ways: (1) in terms of the *term* for hospitality, that is, in terms of *language*, the very concept and name of "hospitality" entailing a welcoming or a reception beyond mere "exchange," "contract," or "pact," and so entailing something like unconditional hospitality; (2) in terms of "law," singular and plural, the singular law of unconditional hospitality and the multiple laws of conditional hospitality; (3) in terms of *experience*, the *experience* of hospitality, which appeals to unconditional hospitality; (4) in terms of desire, what Derrida characterized as an "absolute desire" for the absolute; (5) in terms of possibility, for without hyperbolic, unconditional, pure, absolute, *impossible* hospitality, no hospitality would be possible, the only possible hospitality being thus the impossible one; (6) in terms of effectivity, that is, the becoming-effective of the unconditional or, relatedly, the becoming-law of justice; (7) in terms of progress toward universality, that is, in terms of *perfectibility* (and its related pervertibility), since we must explain what at least appears to be the drive to criticize or deconstruct conditional laws of hospitality by means of an appeal to unconditional hospitality, that is, by means of the call of unconditional hospitality within conditional laws or the appeal to justice within the law.

These are just some of the ways Derrida tries to think or to characterize the relationship between conditional and unconditional hospitality, this crucial distinction in *Of Hospitality* and the first year of the *Hospitality* seminar that, curiously, recedes into the background during the second year.[9] It is thus necessary to recall both this distinction between the two hospitalities and the indissociability of them, so as to avoid thinking that unconditional hospitality is simply the *good* hospitality, the ideal of hospitality, the favored kind of hospitality, while conditional hospitality is an insufficient hospitality, a betrayal of that best or absolute, unconditional hospitality. A full reading of the first year of the seminar makes it quite apparent that the two hospitalities cannot be opposed in this way, that is, for example, as a good, Levinasian, unconditional hospitality and a bad, Kantian, conditional one. Derrida argues that *both* kinds of hospitality are necessary and that each by itself is insufficient and *dangerous*. While the danger of conditional hospitality seems to be fairly straightforward, namely, the setting of limits or conditions to hospitality, hospitality granted, for example, as we see in Derrida's reading of Kant, only to humans, to citizens in nation-states, hospitality involving only a right to sojourn and not to reside, restrictions or conditions that bring hospitality to an end before it even begins, the dangers of unconditional hospitality are perhaps less obvious but no less ominous, namely, the unconditional, unlimited welcoming—indeed love—of the other that can, without the safeguards or restrictions of conditional hospitality, turn into an unlimited or unconditional hatred for the other outside or beyond all law and all nation-states, an unlimited xenophobia where the very worst can happen. As Derrida very simply puts it in an interview in *For What Tomorrow*, "unconditional hospitality can have perverse effects" (*FWT* 59/102). It is a point that Derrida underscores in several places during the first year of the seminar, particularly when he is emphasizing, somewhat surprisingly, it may seem, the positive side of Kant's *Perpetual Peace*, whose ambitions, on the one hand, have never been lived up to among nation-states and whose conditions, on the other, would prevent the worst kinds of violence from being unleashed. This is, arguably, a particularly important lesson for us today as so much of the world tends toward the rejection of international law and projects of this Kantian variety.[10]

Rather than simply choose one hospitality over another, therefore, we must, Derrida insists, invent intermediary schemata between the two, that is, "negotiate"—negotiate the threshold, as it were—between them. "We will have to negotiate constantly," writes Derrida, "between these two extensions of the concept of hospitality as well as of language" (*OH* 135/119; see *H 1* 120/165). We must thus "invent," "negotiate," find the right "transaction." As Derrida says in an improvised remark in the spring of 1996, as France, as part of a relatively new European Union, defined in part by the Schengen agreement, was imposing new restrictions on immigration through the Pasqua Laws and was considering even stricter measures through the proposed Toubon Law, "the right transaction must be found" between opening up the borders completely (since no one will take that seriously, as Derrida says) and shutting them down (see *H 1* 164–65/224–25). The right transaction must be found, that is, invented, on the threshold, on the border, of the two hospitalities, since it is from that threshold that we are constantly reminded that both kinds of hospitality are necessary. In another text from around the same time, Derrida speaks of the need for "another politics, a politics that is truly other, at once intelligent and generous, that lifts the shame and infamy of current laws, a politics of the foreigner, a right of foreigners that is not an abrogation of justice" ("Q" 91). It is a politics that, clearly, still remains today to be invented.

10

The Art or Poetics of Hospitality

> . . . to penetrate while remaining on the surface or on the threshold,
> etc. Again, a question of hospitality. (*H* 1 38/62)

But now we come to a gesture on Derrida's part that frequently accompanies his thinking of the relationship between conditional and unconditional hospitality but that each time appears as something of a detour, sidestep, or supplement to that thinking. It arrives almost always parenthetically, at the end of a long development of the two hospitalities we have been analyzing, and it represents, at least to my ears, something of a change in register in Derrida's discourse there where what is at issue in hospitality is precisely a question of register, tone, or inflection. I am referring to all those passages where, instead of thinking these two regimes of hospitality in an antinomic or aporetic relation to each other, Derrida speaks of hospitality in terms of *grace* or *graciousness*, as we saw earlier, or as a sort of *art* or *poetics*, a kind of *politesse*. Such an art or poetics clearly cannot be unrelated to that antinomy or aporia between conditional and unconditional hospitality that is so prominent in the first year of the seminar, and it cannot be unrelated to finding or inventing moderating or intermediate schemata between the two laws of hospitality, but it does introduce a somewhat different philosophical register, one that can be heard as approximating a sort of Aristotelian hitting of the mean: to offer hospitality in the right way, at the right time, and in the right amount, that is, not too little and not too much.

To illustrate this, let us return to a passage cited earlier in abbreviated form, this time in order to underscore the rather singular register introduced by the

words *gracieuse* or *gracieusement* at the end of a passage distinguishing unconditional hospitality from an unconditional imperative of the Kantian type:

> To be what it "must" be, [unconditional] hospitality must not pay a
> debt, or be governed by a duty: it is gracious [*gracieuse*], and "must"
> not open itself to the guest . . . to use the Kantian distinction again,
> "out of duty." This unconditional law of hospitality, if such a thing is
> thinkable, would then be a law without imperative, without order and
> without duty. A law without law, in short. For if I practice hospitality
> *"out of* duty" [and not only *"in conforming with* duty"], this hospitality
> of paying up is no longer an absolute hospitality, it is no longer gra-
> ciously [*gracieusement*] offered beyond debt and economy, offered to
> the other, a hospitality invented for the singularity of the new arrival,
> of the unexpected visitor. (*OH* 83/77; see *H* 1 104/147–48)

Derrida here emphasizes, perfectly in accord with the way he has characterized unconditional hospitality, the *aneconomic* aspect of this hospitality, a
hospitality that must remain foreign to the economy of debt and repayment.
But he then adds—and these words were added to the *Of Hospitality* version
of the seminar session—that this hospitality must be "*gracieuse*, offered *graciously* [*gracieusement*]," a gracious hospitality that must be invented each
time in a singular way for the "singularity of the new arrival."

Grâce, gracieuse, gracieusement: The range of these words makes them
almost impossible to translate, and "gracious" or "graciously" are probably
the best one can do with a single family of words. But Derrida is suggesting
here that hospitality must be offered *gracieusement* in the sense of freely, for
free, beyond the circle of debt and economy, though also in an unmerited
way, without desert, just as grace is traditionally understood as something that
is granted (by God) beyond expectation and desert. It also seems to suggest
an act of hospitality that is done, precisely, with grace, gracefully, rather than
following some predetermined, rigid law. While this entire matrix of terms
seems to take us away from the language of the two regimes of hospitality and
of the antinomic, aporetic relation between them, it does seem to bring us
back to a thinking of the threshold, to a certain *practice* or *art* of the threshold, a gracious or graceful negotiation of the threshold that does not follow
some path or *method* but instead unfolds according to a certain *démarche*, an
approach or way of proceeding that must be invented each time anew within
each new, singular context.

This notion of *grace*, of hospitality as a kind of grace or gracefulness, might
be associated with what Derrida elsewhere calls *poiesis*, as when Derrida says

in the seminar, "Hospitality is poetic or is not at all" (H 1 157n9/215n1),[1] or else, as I just suggested, with a certain *"politesse,"* that is, a certain *tact* or *discretion* or *good judgment*, a thinking of hospitality that might initially appear to be, again, a sort of Aristotelian hitting of the mean, somewhere between, say, the extremes of narcissism (an excess of selfhood) and selflessness (a deficiency of selfhood). But it is perhaps even better understood as a *practice* or a *poetics* of the *threshold*, as a way of knowing both how to respect the laws of hospitality *and* how to break them. Each time or each time uniquely, it might be said, one must know how to respect the laws and how to transgress them. It is as if that notion of "civil disobedience" we mentioned earlier was here inscribed within the very antinomy between conditional and unconditional hospitality. Derrida writes:

> That is why *politesse*, like hospitality, is a thing so rare and almost impossible, hard to find, at any rate impossible to prove and determine by a determining judgment. To be polite, it is necessary each time, each unique time, to know, know the rules and know how to pass beyond the rules, know how to do without the rules without contravening the rules. (H 1 156/214)

In an oral aside during the seminar, Derrida himself relates this *politesse*, this politeness or tact, this *délicatesse*, to a sort of "grace," adding that such *politesse*—and by implication such hospitality—is "impossible to prove and determine by a determining judgment": "If there is such a judgment, one can be sure of being mistaken. There is no judgment, no theorem of politeness. It is the grace that consists in inventing each time the right transgression" (H 1 156n8/214n2).

I suggested earlier that this language of grace, poetics, and politesse seems to belong to a somewhat different register than the analysis of the two regimes or poles of hospitality that we looked at in the previous two chapters. It seems, in short, to introduce a different *inflection* to Derrida's discourse. Derrida ends his brief text "The Principle of Hospitality" by suggesting that between the question asked as an invitation (an invitation that would be closer to an unconditional hospitality than a conditional one) and the question as a police interrogation (an interrogation that would obviously be much closer to conditional hospitality) there is "a difference both subtle and fundamental, a question that arises on the threshold of 'home,' and on the threshold between two inflections. An art and a poetics, but an entire politics depends on it, an entire ethics is decided by it" ("PH" 67/275). Derrida is speaking here of a question, a perhaps very simple question such as, "So, who are you?"—a question that can be asked aggressively, violently, but that can also be asked with a kind of modesty or reserve, not in order to gain information but in order, precisely, to welcome.

These terms and this thinking, this change in tone, can be found in the second year of the seminar as well. Here is Derrida in the ninth session, contrasting the kinds of discourse and language one should and should not have with a guest, that is, the form and length of a discourse that would belong to a genuine art of conversation, within an art of hospitality, and those that would not:

> One ought not to inflict on the guest a theoretical treatise, a presentation, a discussion. You don't invite someone in order to discuss, you invite someone to make conversation. The mode of hospitable discourse is conversation, not a sermon, or discussion, or a theoretical treatise, or the law: moderate conversation in its time, conversation [*l'entretien*], and not infinite [*Laughter*], finite conversation. That's what hospitality is. If there is an art of hospitality, it is an art of conversation, to know how to speak just as much as necessary and with the necessary tone, not too serious. You don't invite someone in order to work. You invite someone for leisure, not to work. (H 2 231/317)[2]

Derrida speaks here of moderate conversation, a form of speaking that is not determined by the economy of work. He speaks of a "just" or "right" speaking, which, again, sounds more like an attempt to find a mean than negotiate an aporia. Indeed, Derrida seems to be invoking a series of terms often associated with Aristotelian ethics or, indeed, with the second kind of measurement highlighted in Plato's late dialogue *Statesman*, not the relative measures of the big and the small, the heavy and the light, where one can say only that something is bigger or smaller, heavier or lighter, than something else, but the kind of measure that allows for ethical, practical, and aesthetic judgments, namely, the appropriate, the fitting, the suitable, the proper, the opportune — categories that all take into account a particular situation and that allow for judgments of praise or blame.[3]

Again, terms or categories such as grace, graciousness, gratuity, art, poetics, *poiesis*, cannot be inconsistent with, or opposed to, an aporetic crossing or, indeed, negotiation between the two regimes of hospitality or the invention of a "rule" that would somehow mediate between the conditional and the unconditional. But they do seem to give a different inflection to Derrida's discourse. He continues:

> That is why the question we are always asking here about immigration, immigrant workers, the politics of immigration, finally, despite the

proximity, is not a question of hospitality once it is a question of workers. Hospitality is not offered to people who come to work. Work does
not belong to the world of hospitality. That is why the talk between a
host and a guest ought not to be anything other than a conversation
and should not talk about work, a finite conversation on subjects that
are not-serious in the sense of work. Without work, without program,
without constraint, without commerce, as leisure, gratuitous, grace.
Gratuitous hospitality is graceful and that is why it is an art; and what
is offered to the guest is something like a music salon. One doesn't
offer a lecture to a guest. One gracefully offers them art, as an artist, as
a poet. (H 2 231/317–18)

These words all seem to point toward what Derrida calls in Kantian terms
a moderating schema. But the whole semantics of grace, of something that is
unmerited, that is outside economy, beyond the marketplace (a bit like Aristotelian *scholē*), or that is free, *gratuit* or *gracieux*, that cannot be determined
by any kind of law, and that is also graceful or artful, seems to introduce a
different language or register to Derrida's analysis of hospitality.[4]

The question of hospitality requires a rethinking, as we have seen, of the
singular and the multiple, the one and the many, the extreme of the absolute
or unconditional and the extreme of the conditional, but then also, between
extremes, as it were, between the unconditional and the conditional, a sort of
"mean," one that could never be attained and maintained once and for all but
must be constantly, perpetually, renegotiated, since it can, at any instant, veer
off into deficiency or excess. At any point in time, a host may go from being
hospitable to inhospitable by saying or giving or asking too little or too much,
that is, in short, by failing to negotiate the threshold artfully or gracefully. For
the threshold between the hospitable and the inhospitable is obviously not
located simply between the inside and the outside of the house, there at the
door, on the threshold. It is redrawn or marked out everywhere throughout
the house—at the table, in the living room, etc. It is redrawn and so must be
renegotiated at every point in time. At the level of the state, too, the threshold
between the hospitable and the inhospitable may have an exemplary place
at the border or in the immigration office, but it is traced out everywhere
throughout the state or the city, anywhere that hospitality might be extended
to another. It is another way of saying that the threshold is everywhere and that
it must be perpetually negotiated.

Allow me, then, to reproduce here a rather hilarious example of this constantly renegotiated threshold between the hospitable and the inhospitable
from the second year of the hospitality seminar, a somewhat extended example

that Derrida offers his class more or less extemporaneously, an example that demonstrates one more tool in Derrida's kit for approaching the question of hospitality: humor. Here is Derrida in the spring of 1997, breaking away from his written text in order to give an example of hospitality turning into something else, something that is not exactly its opposite but that is no longer simply hospitality because the one offering it is being just a bit too hospitable, a bit too enthusiastic in his giving. Here is the setup for the example:

> Another example of this im-possible I was thinking about—which obviously covers everything we are talking about here—is the example, very simply, stupidly, massively, of presence or absence to the other. When one receives someone, when one offers hospitality to someone, must one be present to them or must one not be present to them? Must one absent oneself, let be, or must one be there, attending? Where is there more hospitality when one receives someone? The art of receiving is to be there, but also not to be there. If, when you receive someone, you are there all the time, behind, beside—come sleep at my house and then I stay in your bedroom to see if you are sleeping well [*Laughter*]. One must know how to efface oneself, but not too much either, because if I am not in the house, if I am totally absent, that is not okay either. Must one be *da* or *fort*? Must one be present or absent? Both. The same question arises about knowing whether one must speak or not speak to the one being received. You receive someone, you offer them hospitality, so naturally you have to speak; you can't receive someone without saying anything to them. But one must speak *a little* [*Laughter*].[5] (H 2 226/311)

Then comes the example:

> I was on an airplane the other day, I was returning from Italy, on an Alitalia flight, and then as soon as the plane takes off, the pilot begins to talk and says, at the beginning it was the usual information, "and then we are going to turn right, and we will take . . ." I say to myself at least the pilot is hospitable, he doesn't behave like a mechanic, like a technician. He is receiving us in his airplane—the question being whether one can receive in an airplane, we talk about "air hostesses"— but, in any case, he is behaving as if in a house; he tells us where we are going, welcome, we will ascend to such and such an altitude, we are going to turn right, we are going to fly over, etc. And I thought it was very good: here is someone at least who knows how to live and who receives us like guests in his home. And then he went on [*Laugh-*

ter] and he went on and he went on! The flight lasted an hour and a
quarter. [*Laughter.*] At which point, I said to myself, well there, hospitality, no, one has to know when to stop. He flew over Paris and he said
"Paris is the most beautiful city," etc. [*Laughter.*] He thought we had
never been to Paris. "Rome is not bad" —he was saying this in French
and Italian—"Rome is nice, but it is antiquity, I much prefer Paris,"
etc. He drowned us in words for an hour and a quarter. [*Laughter.*] So,
hospitality, what is the right measure? If he had been silent, that would
not have been good; talking too much is not good either. The question
is whether or not there is a measure for good hospitality. There is no
measure. If there were a measure, if one said: "Okay, the pilot has the
right to speak for ten minutes, after that he shuts up" [*Laughter*], that
is not hospitality either. It's necessary [*il faut*] that at every instant—
this is the event—it's necessary that in every singular experience one
invent without a rule the time of speech. It must not be a set rule. If
there is a regulated procedure, if there are norms and criteria, it is not
hospitality. It is necessary for the host, in agreement and in harmony
with the guest, to decide at every moment if he or she must be silent or
speak, without a rule. They must invent and invention is impossible.
Likewise, they must decide at every moment to be present or absent,
to show themselves or hide. And for that, there is no rule either. This
is the invention of the impossible possible, at every moment. (*H* 2
226–27/311–12)

It is perhaps noteworthy that these moments or examples in a somewhat different register are often to be found at the end of an analysis, frequently in an oral
aside, like a sort of supplement to the more formal analysis. And it is perhaps
no coincidence that they are often very funny.[6] It is as if Derrida realizes that
there is another aspect to hospitality that his more formal analysis of the two
regimes is simply unable to capture or do justice to.[7] Something, perhaps,
like an art of hospitality or indeed, if hospitality and deconstruction must be
thought together, an art or a poetics of deconstruction.

11
But Why So Much Kant?

Today a reflection on hospitality presupposes, among other things, the possibility of a rigorous delimitation of thresholds or borders: between the familial and the non-familial, the foreign and the non-foreign national, the citizen and the noncitizen, but first of all between private and public, private right and public right, etc. (*H* 1 92/130; see 204/272)

As we have seen, Derrida at once criticizes Kant and, somewhat more surprisingly, defends him, and he does so not once but repeatedly throughout the first year of the seminar on hospitality. Before continuing, it will be worth our while to try to explain precisely why it is that Kant is such a crucial reference for Derrida in his thinking of hospitality. Indeed, Derrida actually begins the entire seminar simply by reading, with minimal commentary, that *Third Definitive Article of a Perpetual Peace* (*Dritter Definitivartikel zum ewigen Frieden*), which states that "*Cosmopolitan right* shall be limited to conditions of universal *hospitality*."[1] Derrida makes a point of saying that this text is being cited at the beginning of the seminar as a sort of extended epigraph that would precede or stand above it, even watch over it, a bit like — and this is a somewhat perverse analogy that Derrida himself invites — the "laws of hospitality" that are put under glass, framed, and then put up on the wall above the bed of the guest bedroom in Klossowski's *Roberte ce soir* (see *H* 1 2–7/20–26).

So why the centrality of Kant? A first answer would be that Kant gives us the *best example* of what Derrida will go on to call somewhat critically a "conditional hospitality." While Kant's hospitality will aim for a certain universality, it will nonetheless be limited, conditioned, and, as such, it will begin to "ruin" the kind of hospitality that Derrida will call unconditional, the only hospital-

ity truly worthy of the name. We have already mentioned some of these limitations or conditions in abbreviated form. Here they are in a bit more detail.

First, the kind of hospitality outlined in *Perpetual Peace* will be the result
of a treaty or pact among nation-states. As such, it would seem to be restricted
to citizens of nation-states (see *H* 1 2–7/20–26, 58/88–89), and it depends upon
the sovereignty of nation-states (see *H* 1 257–58/340–42). Kant would thus have
little to say about the kind of hospitality that might be granted to those without a state, to stateless migrants and refugees, which in the twentieth and
twenty-first centuries have come to make up a greater and greater proportion
of those asking for asylum or refugee status and who most need the kind of
hospitality that Kant would seem to want to promote. Moreover, in order to
determine whether the one asking for hospitality or asylum is coming from
such a nation-state, he or she would need, as we have repeatedly said, to
answer a series of questions, beginning, no doubt, with the question of their
name (see *H* 1 84/121).

Second, and relatedly, the kind of hospitality of which Kant speaks is offered
always by those with the power and authority to offer it (see *H* 1 2–7/20–26).
Such hospitality thus remains related, as Derrida shows with the help of
Benveniste and others, to a certain law of the *oikos* (see *H* 1 58/88–89) and
thus to the long history, at once political and philosophical, linking selfhood
(*Selbstheit*) to power and authority, to that conjunction of power, authority,
and self-identity that Derrida calls *ipseity* (see *H* 1 43–44/69–70). In the case
of both Kant and Hegel, there would be three primary instances or three
circles of ipseity, the family, civil society, and the nation-state (see *H* 1 63/95),
and while there is in Kant a sort of homology between these three, hospitality
as understood in *Perpetual Peace* would be the province or the prerogative of
the nation-state.

Third—and this is rather obvious, though what is obvious often needs to
be pointed out—hospitality in Kant is limited to the human. It is an "anthropological" hospitality, or maybe better a *humanist* hospitality, which excludes
from the outset—from the threshold, indeed even before the threshold because it will never even come into question—hospitality to animals, plants, or
gods (see *H* 1 3/22, 133–34/184–85). It is a purely human hospitality that does
not ever entertain the possibility of a hospitality to the nonhuman. We will
look at this aspect of hospitality in more detail in Chapter 18.

Fourth, Kantian hospitality assures the right to visit but not the right to reside. That is, it assures the right to a temporary sojourn or stay but not the right
to reside permanently or to become a citizen. The reason for this, it seems, is
that when one grants someone permanent residency it is no longer hospitality
that is being offered but something else. But one could then counter that if all

sojourns must come to an end, might not the guest upon his return face the same kind of dangers or threats that hospitality was meant to protect him from in the first place (see *H* 1 5/24, 54–55/83–85, 174–76/237–38, 257–58/341–42)?

Fifth, the one who receives hospitality must agree to remain "peaceable" during his or her stay, a reasonable condition, it might be thought, though one that could easily be used as an excuse or an alibi for expelling or extraditing foreigners accused of no longer visiting "peaceably" because of the critical or uncomfortable questions they are posing to the host country or the critical discourses they are producing or promoting (see *H* 1 55/85). Now it is true that there is a reciprocal condition imposed on the nation-state that is offering hospitality, namely, not to turn the foreigner away or to return them to their home country if this will lead to their *Untergang*, that is, as the French translation has it, their *perte* (*H* 1 54–55/83–84, 145/199). But this condition too, as Derrida suggests, is sufficiently vague as to be used as an alibi by any host country, which could claim, for example, that if someone were returned to their homeland they might indeed suffer some *perte*, some loss, some fall or downfall, some punishment or harm, but not necessarily their *Untergang* understood more narrowly as their *death*.

These are some of the conditions that Derrida sees operating in Kant and some of the reasons why Derrida can say that the kind of hospitality we find in Kant is not hospitable to the other *as other* (see *H* 1 57/87). It is hospitable to the other as human, as peaceable citizen of another nation-state, and so on, but it is not hospitable to the other as other and so is not, it seems, a "hospitality" truly worthy of the name. There is an inevitable perversion or pervertibility to Kant's conditional hospitality that seems to limit it, even ruin it, right there on the threshold (see *H* 1 57–60/88–91, 97–99/136–39). As Derrida puts it, such conditions limit or, indeed, condition hospitality to such an extent that the concept of hospitality itself implodes or deconstructs (see *H* 1 5/24).

And yet, *et pourtant* — and it is here that we jump onto the other side of the threshold — it is not simply *in spite of* these conditions but *because* of them, *thanks* to them, that hospitality can become real or effective, offered to a determinate someone rather than an anonymous anyone. It is only by *restricting* hospitality as Kant has done that hospitality can become effective or concrete. If Kant thus gives us the "best example" of conditional hospitality, that is, the exemplary or paradigmatic example, he also seems to provide the "best example" of how to prevent unconditional hospitality from remaining ineffective or merely utopic. So let us now count some of the ways in which Kant is, for Derrida, such a *good example*.

First, Derrida recalls that Kant in *Perpetual Peace* speaks of hospitality as a "right," an "international right," and not a moral obligation. One offers hospitality not out of philanthropy, out of sentiment, out of love for other human beings, but as a matter of right or law (see *H 1* 3–4/22, 12/32–33). While this may seem to be a disadvantage, it means that hospitality is not dependent on the good feelings or sentiments of those being asked to offer it.[2] It is a matter of right, and this right or obligation to hospitality is based upon something that all humans share and should be able to recognize, the common possession of the surface of a finite earth and the natural right of all humans to inhabit that earth (see *H 1* 5–6/24–25, 61–63/92–95, 175–76/237–38). Because the world is finite—finite and round—people cannot disperse infinitely across it. Were they able to do so, Kant seems to suggest, there would be no need for a right to hospitality, since someone rejected or expelled by one state could simply keep moving until he or she has found some uninhabited place in which to settle down. If the earth were infinitely large, one could inhabit and even own parts of the earth without that ownership impinging upon the rights of others. But because the earth is finite, finite and round, one will eventually come back to one's point of departure by continuing to move in the same direction. The right to hospitality is thus based on a natural right to share the surface of the earth. It is on the basis, then, of this natural right, this shared or common possession of the surface of the earth, that Kant is able to establish the goal of a cosmopolitan constitution. This goal, this telos, remains on the horizon, a *teleology* or "infinite idea of Cosmopolitical right" that promises to lead to a cosmopolitical, universal hospitality (see *H 1* 17/38, 122/168). Though the state of nature is, for Kant, a state of war, this natural right remains a sort of horizon, a natural right that guides and inspires cosmopolitical, universal hospitality. The idea is thus infinite not because it extends across an earth that is infinite but because it aims at approximating that natural right to the possession of the earth by means of a more and more comprehensive and just pact or treaty among nation-states.

This is clearly one of the aspects of Kant's project that Derrida admires most—despite its conditions. Though it is, to be sure, a product of its times, Kant's cosmopolitanism elicits Derrida's deep admiration for its ambition and its progressivist vision. The very forces that, at the end of the eighteenth century, led to colonialism (the kind that Kant condemns in *Perpetual Peace*, with its vision of the world unified only by expansionist and exploitative projects), also led to Kant's cosmopolitical project, a project that would bring together in peace distant parts of the world. If that shared surface of the earth had become like a single body, where something felt in one part of the earth is felt everywhere, Kant sought to establish a cosmopolitical treaty that would reflect and take advantage of that global communication.

The cosmopolitical in Kant is thus, for Derrida, conditional and restrictive.

And yet there is also a certain generality if not generosity to this Kantian/
Enlightenment hospitality that Derrida seems to suggest we still have not
realized, indeed that we are in some ways getting further and further away
from (see *H* 1 225–26/301). Kant seems to suggest that the human race can
be unified or brought together under a cosmopolitical constitution, a sort of
League of Nations or United Nations before the fact, a form of international
law among sovereign nation-states that would lead to the great though incomplete and flawed achievements of the twentieth century (see *H* 1 61–63/93–95,
184–85/249). As Derrida put it in an oral aside, "If Kant, from a certain aspect,
is behind the times concerning a certain technological modernity"—an aspect of Kant's work we will turn to in a moment—"he is also truly the thinker
of our epoch, of international law, of the problems of international law today"
(*H* 1 63n21/95n2).

The right to hospitality in Kant would be, in the end, the precondition for
perpetual peace, the absolute condition for perpetual peace, an exceptionally
worthy ambition that Derrida seems to admire and, it seems, wishes himself
to approximate or take as a model, at least up to a point. For what Derrida
will call unconditional or absolute hospitality, the kind that guides, orients,
or inspires conditional hospitality, or that leads to the deconstruction of conditional laws of hospitality in the name of justice, looks very much like the
perfectible hospitality of which Kant speaks, the kind he puts on the horizon
for humankind (see *H* 1 220/293–94). Indeed, when Derrida speaks of laws or
rights being subject to a more natural right, with one right being guided by
another (see *H* 1 58/89, 61–63/93–95), then one would not be wrong to think
of Kant's *Perpetual Peace* (see *H* 1 131–34/181–85). Indeed, such a Kantian notion of the infinite idea will look so much like the unconditional hospitality
that animates or motivates conditional hospitality that Derrida will attempt
repeatedly, and in various ways, to distinguish his thinking from Kant's on
that score. For example, Derrida will argue that his understanding of unconditional hospitality is not teleological or progressivist in the way Kant's is. We
saw Derrida speak of both the perfectibility and pervertibility of both conditional and unconditional hospitality. Because of this, Derrida's unconditional
hospitality cannot be set on the horizon as a goal or telos in the way Kant's
notion of a cosmopolitical hospitality that would lead to a perpetual universal
peace can. Also, Derrida's unconditional hospitality is not grounded, as Kant's
cosmopolitical hospitality is, in any kind of human or natural right. For the
appeal to a natural right is always, for Derrida, an appeal to a sort of surrepti-
tious or concealed divine or theological right, the idea, precisely, that all finite
beings have a common possession, a fraternal share, of the world of their cre-
ator. As Paul says in his Letter to the Ephesians: "You are no longer foreigners

and strangers, but fellow citizens with God's people and also members of his household" (2:19). This will help explain in part why Derrida claims that the cosmopolitical tradition of Kant is in many ways a secularized version of a Christian cosmopolitanism, a cosmopolitanism that combines Greek stoicism with Pauline Christianity (see *H* 1 256–57/339–41).

In addition to these differences between Kant's cosmopolitical project and Derrida's thinking of hospitality, Kant's emphasis on a shared earth does not take into account nonterrestrial spaces. This is, of course, perfectly understandable for someone writing at the end of the eighteenth century. But to be effective in the twenty-first century, cosmopolitanism would need to account for other cosmic bodies besides the earth, as well as space itself, which can now be inhabited and where a certain hospitality can take place (on the International Space Station, for example). We thus need, it seems, another kind of cosmopolitanism that would go beyond the limits of the earth (see *H* 1 58–59/89–90).

Perhaps even more important, Kant's cosmopolitanism also cannot account for the kinds of virtual hospitality afforded by teletechnologies such as cell phones and the internet, innovations that, again, Kant can hardly be criticized for neglecting, but that anyone who would like to renew or refine the Kantian project would need to take into account. Derrida writes:

> At the time, of course, Kant could not take into account the telephone, the fax, email, the internet, television, panoptic satellites, multimedia, CD-ROMs and information highways, access to nonterrestrial spaces, so many radical de-localizations that call for another experience of the relation to the other and so another experience of hospitality, or even already another right to hospitality, another duty of hospitality. (*H* 1 60/91)

How, then, does hospitality change, how does it need to be rethought, in a world where delocalizing teletechnologies have made space less and less relevant (see *H* 1 58–61/88–93)? How can hospitality be rethought in order to account for changes in our conception of the world or the world-wide, in order to account for a twenty-first-century conception of globalization (see *H* 1 63–64/95–96)? Derrida asks:

> One may wonder whether it is possible to translate the essential reference that Kant makes in this text to the earth's surface, to translate this earthliness, this terrestriality of Kantian right into a modern *cosmos* that opens onto a political and techno-political appropriation of non-terrestrial spaces and places: . . . not only an appropriation of

the moon then, where one can now "land," as it were, moonland, not only of space as ground (lunar or terrestrial or planetary in general), but also of space as non-ground, the appropriation of a space and time no longer having ground or surface. . . . Appropriation by means of teletechnologies . . . (*H*1 59/89–90)

Though this virtualizing, delocalizing dimension of hospitality in the form of writing, publication, letters, and so on was not completely unknown to Kant, his cosmopolitanism did not take it into account theoretically, making it less useful to us than it might have been (see *H* 1 58–61/89–93). (In Chapter 14, we will look in much greater detail at this relationship between hospitality and teletechnology.)

Finally, the fact that Kant speaks only of public hospitality and not private hospitality seems to reveal, indeed seems to be perfectly aligned with, his emphasis on transparency and publicity, the imperative to veracity both in the public square and in the private sphere, even across the threshold of one's home (see *H* 1 97–99/136–39, 228/304). This imperative to veracity extends, famously, all the way to telling the truth to assassins when they come asking about the person seeking refuge in one's home.[3] At the end of the fifth session of the seminar (and at the end of *Of Hospitality*), Derrida contrasts the good Kantian, who gives up his guest in the name of veracity or truth, with Lot, who subordinates everything, including his daughters, to an ethics of hospitality (see *H* 1 125–27/172–76; see also 151–52/207–9).

In this biblical story, to recall it briefly, Lot takes into his home in Sodom two strangers—two angels—and he refuses to hand them over to the men of Sodom when they come to his home with the intention of "knowing" them. Lot gives the men of Sodom his own virgin daughters instead of the guests in his house. For Lot, a breach in the laws of hospitality, that is, betraying his guests, seems to be more serious than offering up his own virgin daughters to the Sodomites, who intend to "know," that is, to "penetrate" them (*OH* 151/133; see *H*1 125–26/172).[4] Derrida concludes his discussion of this scene by asking whether and to what extent we would be the inheritors of *this* tradition of the laws of hospitality (see *OH* 155/137; see *H* 1 127/176).[5] It is a story that raises not only the question of the prioritization of truth and/or hospitality but, obviously, the whole question of the relationship between hospitality and sexual difference, as well as hospitality and violence, which Derrida will return to throughout the seminar.[6]

Whereas Lot is willing to subordinate all kinds of other ethical or moral obligations—including those toward his daughters, perhaps in conformity with the sexual ethics of his time—to the laws of hospitality, Kant would seem to subordinate the call to offer hospitality to the imperative to tell the truth. Derrida's turn to the question of veracity in Kant appears to be motivated by the worry that a certain zone of privacy, and thus a certain space of hospitality, can easily yield to an imperative to *tell the truth* (OH 67–69/63–65; see H 1 97–99/137–39). He is worried that when truth becomes the overriding value, when the unveiling of one's thoughts in a public space becomes more important than privacy or hospitality, when "the imperative to veracity [becomes] absolutely unconditional," then there is no distinction—no threshold, as it were—between public and private, outside and inside (OH 67/63; see H 1 97–98/137). By founding the freedom of the subject upon a social bond that is rooted in this imperative to tell the truth, Kant, according to Derrida, takes away the individual's interiority, that is, anything that would *not* be open to the public. In the name of "pure morality," Kant, therefore, in Derrida's words, "introduces the police everywhere" (OH 69/65; see H 1 98/138), not just in the public square or in the home but in our own relation to ourselves, that is, inside our very heads. The truth detectors are then operating everywhere, the police listening in to our every conversation, even those we hold on our "internal telephones" (OH 69/65; see H 1 99/138). In this saturation of private space by the public by means of the imperative to tell the truth, there is no place for secrecy, no genuine interiority, no place outside the realm of public hospitality from which to offer hospitality to another (see H 1 201–2/269–70).

As Derrida reads it, Kant's discourse ends up destroying the very possibility of the hospitality it tries to preserve and universalize. It destroys it because one now admits the guest only under the condition of telling the truth about them no matter what, indeed even if it leads to their loss or their death. Derrida sees no coincidence in Kant's example of giving up one's "guest" whom one is hiding rather than lying about their whereabouts (OH 71/67; see H 1 99/138–39). For Kant, it is better to break the law of hospitality than not obey the imperative to tell the truth. Hospitality is here conditioned by the unconditionality of truth that founds the law. Derrida will, in a sense, reverse these: What will be unconditional will be hospitality, though this will entail not, of course, an unconditional adherence or obedience to some particular code or pact of hospitality but, rather, an unconditional offering of hospitality to the absolute other, an offering that then immediately becomes inscribed in law or must immediately negotiate with the law. It is for all these reasons—in addition to all those conditions that limit hospitality—that Derrida's thinking is not simply Kantian on the question of hospitality, despite the universal ambitions of Kant's text.

And yet—once again "and yet"—Derrida will speak of Kant's *sagesse*, his "wisdom," his "sense of moderation," and his "critical, juridical, and political prudence [*prudence*]," that is, his caution and his carefulness, against the "madness of (unconditional) hospitality" (*H* 1 58/88). There is a wisdom to Kant's conditional hospitality, a wisdom or prudence in recognizing the dangers of unconditional hospitality without limits, without *ipse* (see *H* 1 131–33/181–83). While Derrida is far from endorsing such a *wisdom* or *prudence* in his own name, he clearly sees the merits of Kant's discourse and approach. And, as we have seen, he will not refrain from using without completely appropriating or endorsing other kinds of Kantian vocabulary, speaking, for example, of the *antinomy* between conditional and unconditional hospitality or of the need for intermediary *schemata* between the conditional and the unconditional, or indeed of a certain *regulative idea* (see *H* 1 124/171).

It is this Kant or this part of Kant that Derrida will continue to admire, this Kant and the tradition that he will have initiated.[7] It is what allows or motivates Derrida to speak of "the right to hospitality in the cosmopolitan tradition which will find its most powerful form in Kant and the text [*Perpetual Peace*] we have read and reread" (*OH* 27/29–31; *H* 1 84/121). "Read and reread" is a perfectly apt description of the way Kant's text—unlike any other, one is tempted to say—is treated throughout the *Hospitality* seminar. In a text in *Paper Machine* titled "Not Utopia, the Im-possible," Derrida repeats both his admiration for a Kantian "cosmopolitan law" governing "universal hospitality," which would be, he says, "a great advance," and his belief that one must, for all the reasons we have seen, go beyond it ("NU" 133).

12

Xenos Paradox: Hospitality and Autoimmunity

> It can seem paradoxical that the experience of hospitality encounters aporia, where people mainly think that the host offers the guest passage over the threshold or border so as to welcome him at home. Is aporia not, as its name indicates, the non-road, the barred way, the non-passage? (*H* 1 11/43)

A seminar on hospitality would have to be, it seems, a seminar that tries to understand, define, explain, and give examples of the "concept" of hospitality. But Derrida begins the first session by admitting that he does not know what hospitality is and that, as a result, he is unable to explain, define, and give straightforward examples of a pure and rigorous concept of hospitality. And yet that does not prevent him from deploying the language of hospitality, at once mentioning it as the topic or the subject of the seminar and using it in order to welcome his students into the seminar in accordance with what are recognized to be the codes of hospitality (*H* 1 7/26).

But in what way does this "concept" of hospitality remain unknown at the beginning of the seminar? There are several possibilities, various ways for something to remain unknown. It may be that we do not *yet* know what hospitality is, even though it is knowable, and that the aim of the seminar will be to discover exactly what it is. It may be that it is unknown and will or must forever remain unknown, unknowable, a mystery or an enigma, a sort of noumenal X that the seminar will, perhaps, try to indicate but will never be able to attain or define. But it may also be that we do not know what hospitality is or means because hospitality is a "concept" that is not one with itself or the same as itself, present to itself in the way a good concept should be. It may be that there is something within the concept of hospitality that cannot be fully received or thought, something "within" it that cannot be made fully present. It may be that it is from the start divided, divided against itself—those two regimes of hospitality, the conditional and the unconditional, being just one of the most visible signs of that internal division. In such a case, the aim would not be, indeed could not be, to arrive one day at a single, univocal, clearly definable concept of hospitality by crossing over the threshold from the unknown to the known. Indeed it may be that the concept of hospitality is inherently self-contradictory, paradoxical, self-deconstructive, or, as Derrida was able to say in 1995–1996, *autoimmune*, this last adjective becoming available to Derrida because of newly emerging discourses, both scientific and more popular, re-garding HIV and AIDS. It is a term that Derrida developed and deployed a year earlier in his important text "Faith and Knowledge," as he himself recalls in the seminar (*H* 1 183n11/247n12). He writes in the opening pages of the first session, that is, the session of November 15, 1995:

> Hospitality is in itself a contradictory concept and experience, one that cannot but self-destruct or protect itself from itself, auto-immunize itself in a way, that is, deconstruct itself on its own—precisely [*juste-ment*]—rightly [*justement*], by exercising itself. (*H* 1 5/24)

While this might easily seem to be Derridean hyperbole, an overinterpre-tation of the concept of hospitality, which, it might be thought, is complex, difficult, complicated, but hardly self-deconstructive or autoimmune, pretty much everything *in the tradition* already points in this direction. Derrida's claim is thus hardly radical, certainly not an imposition or hyperbolic in-flation, but simply a recognition and explicit elucidation of everything that suggests just such an autoimmunity in the concept of hospitality, beginning with the etymologies of Benveniste, which, as we have already seen, suggest a troubling affinity between *hospes* and *hostis*, this latter meaning at once stranger and enemy in Latin, suggesting some kind of proximity or relation be-tween hospitality and hostility (*H* 1 26/48). Derrida himself speaks elsewhere of the "troubling kinship between the words *hostis* (*hôte*, stranger or enemy) and *hospes* (hôte, *guest*) and the troubling logic that will have associated *and* dissociated, contaminated *and* distinguished between them . . . *hostility* and *hospitality*, the stranger as *enemy* and the stranger as *friend*" ("D" 122–23). It is because of these etymological peculiarities that Derrida can say that the *word* "hospitality" harbors within itself, like a Trojan horse, as we will hear, or like an enclave, or an unconscious—its opposite, namely, hostility.

Even in Kant, in the opening lines of that "Third Definitive Article of a Perpetual Peace," the very *concept* of hospitality is related to its opposite, that is, to hostility, as if the shadow or ghost of hostility were always right there on the border or the threshold to threaten it. Kant writes: "Here, as in the preceding articles, it is not a question of philanthropy but of *right*, so that *hospitality* means the right of a foreigner *not to be treated with hostility* because he has arrived on the land of another" (cited by Derrida at *H* 1 4/22–23; my emphasis of this last phrase).

Then there is Levinas's insight, at once linguistic and analytic, that the subject is not only a "host" (see *Totality and Infinity*, 27) but a "hostage" (*Otherwise Than Being*, 112) (*OH* 109/99; see *H* 1 112/156; see also 15/36). It is a point that Levinas is able to make through a reinterpretation of subjectivity based on a relationship to the other, that is, to a certain infinity that would come before the totalizing movement of the subject or the ego. It is a point that is then expressed, consolidated, even clarified through the linguistic resources of the French language (*hôte/otage*). And, finally, it is a point for which Derrida will find confirmation in so many of the texts he reads. For example, among the many themes Derrida will draw from *Oedipus at Colonus* will be the idea that hospitality can always be a danger for the host, who can always become the hostage of his guest, Oedipus's final prayer to remember him looking very much like a threat: If you do not remember me, Theseus, your city will be destroyed. A guest can also always become the hostage of his host, to be sure, and that is no doubt what Oedipus would have become had he returned to Thebes at the behest of Creon. But in *Oedipus at Colonus*, it is Theseus, the *host*, who becomes a sort of *hostage* of Oedipus, his guest, the hostage of a dead man to whom he has sworn an oath and whose secret, if preserved, will save the city, but, if divulged, will destroy it.

In Klossowski's novel *Roberte ce soir*, we find the very same danger and chance, the very same threat and opportunity, as the host awaits his guest as his liberator or his emancipator, that is, in a sense, as his host. It is as if the guest, and not the host, were the one who held the keys, as if the stranger were the one to "save the master and liberate the power of his host," "as if the master, *qua* master, were prisoner of his place and his power, of his ipseity, of his subjectivity (his subjectivity is hostage)" (*OH* 123/111; see *H* 1 116/161). Hence the host ends up being invited into his own home, becoming thereby the *hôte*, that is, the guest, as well as the hostage, of his own guest (*H* 1 14/34–35). He becomes, as it were, *chez lui chez l'autre*, at home in the home of the other, the logic of substitution ultimately making "everyone into everyone else's hostage" (*OH* 125/111; see *H* 1 116/161).

There is also, as we have already mentioned in several places, the question of the "enclave" in relation to hospitality, that is, the question of an outside within, of a pocket or a zone of radical exteriority within, which Derrida frequently relates to a logic of the unconscious (see *H* 1 183–90/248–56). It is the enclave that can exercise a certain deconstructive force against that in which it is lodged; it is a force that confronts the inside not head-on, from the outside, but, more perniciously, more penetratingly, from within. In a rather suggestive passage from the second year of the seminar, Derrida speaks of the concept of hospitality in terms of a Trojan horse, and he then relates that concept or conception to conception itself, a conception that counters conception in the form of a contraconception or contraception (whether Ramses or Durex or, more likely here, Trojan). He writes:

> We have no idea, of course, but we know enough to tell ourselves that hospitality, what belabors hospitality in its bosom, what belabors it like a labor, like a pregnancy, like a promise as much as a threat, what installs in it, in its inside, like a Trojan horse, the enemy (*hostis*) as well as the future, intestine hostility, is indeed a contradictory conception, a countered conception, or a *contraception* of expectation, a contradiction in the welcome itself. (*H* 2 97–98/145)

We have also already seen in some detail how the two forms of hospitality need yet also interrupt, "deconstruct," one another. This would be, it seems, an autodeconstruction or autoimmunity against which there can be no reliable prophylaxis. But one will recall that Derrida in his discussion of those two poles or regimes of hospitality seemed to suggest that the very name "hospitality" could be justified only through a nondialectizable movement between the two. What he meant by that, it seems, is that there would be no historically determined, conditional and conditioned "hospitality" without the absolute hospitality that inspired or motivated it and, on the contrary, no absolute, unconditional "hospitality"—no name and no concept for such a "hospitality"—without that limited, historical "hospitality."

We saw Derrida earlier speak of hospitality as "a contradictory concept and experience" that cannot but "auto-immunize itself in a way, that is, deconstruct itself on its own—precisely [*justement*]—rightly [*justement*], by exercising itself" (*H* 1 5/24). The translator left the French in brackets here not only to indicate to the reader that the same French word has been translated, rightly, by two different English words, but because Derrida no doubt wants us to hear something of that "justice" that inspires or motivates or guides or, indeed, *deconstructs* the "law." In an interview in *Sur Parole*, we see Derrida putting together the two regimes of hospitality, justice and law, by means of this same *justement*:

> I tried indeed to show that justice is irreducible to law, that there is an excess of justice with respect to law, but that justice, in order to be

concrete and effective, nonetheless demands to be embodied [*s'in-carner*] in law, in legislation. Naturally, no law could be adequate to justice, and that is why there is a history of law, it is why human rights evolve, it is why there is an interminable determination and an endless perfectibility of the juridical, because the call for justice is precisely [*justement*] infinite. Again, justice and law are heterogeneous and indissociable. They call out for [*s'appellent*] for one another. (S 72)[1]

This is yet another way to think the necessarily autoimmune or self-deconstructive movement of hospitality. The one hospitality calls out for the other; it at once justifies the name of the other and interrupts it, shows both its promise and its insufficiency. There are two movements or two laws that require each other but cannot be reconciled in a single, dialectizable "moment." There is both a formal or formalizing movement, in this case, a general or generalizable structure of "hospitality," "hospitality" as a sort of quasi-transcendental (absolute or unconditional hospitality), and a historical or historicizing movement of "hospitality" (conditional hospitality). Derrida speaks of the "impossible chronology of this hospitality," or the "incalculable *timing* [in English] of hospitality" (OH 127/113; see H 1 116–17/162), not, again, because hospitality is some timeless, unknowable thing or concept but because it must be thought in two times or in two movements that can never be reconciled. From this perspective, the autoimmunity of the concept of hospitality is attributable at once to its inscription in language, in speech, in what Derrida calls archē-writing, that is, in a temporalizing movement that determines it as an historical possibility, and to its relation to a general structure of "hospitality" that always exceeds that temporalization without becoming some kind of atemporal or ahistorical essence. What Derrida says about these two moments or movements in *Hospitality* is thus not unlike what is called, in "Faith and Knowledge" and elsewhere, a general messianicity and a historically determined messianism, or else a general or generalizable revealability (*Offenbarkeit*) and a historically determined revelation (*Offenbarung*).

It is this relation or alternation between a generalized hospitality, that is, a generalized welcome or receptivity, an opening to the future, on the one hand, and a determined historical hospitality, on the other, that accounts in large part for Derrida's many comments throughout the seminar on the importance of the "date" (and datability, *Datierbarkeit*) (see H 1 235/312–13).[2] It is a theme that had been important to Derrida from at least the time of "Shibboleth," the relationship between, say, a general datability and a historically determined date. On the one hand, one must date things, Derrida suggests, not out of some kind of historicism but in order to acknowledge their singularity (see H 1 206/276). The date is a sort of signature of the here and now. On the other hand, the date is related to a fundamental *historicity*, a historicity that—without being in any way ahistorical—is more fundamental than any particular historical inscription of hospitality, any particular crisis or pact of hospitality, any particular religion or historical movement (see *H* 1 232/309).[3]

It is just after these references to the date and datability that Derrida sketches out a plan to treat three crucial texts related to hospitality, the homely, the homey, and so on, three central texts of the twentieth century, Joyce's *Ulysses*, Heidegger's "Building Dwelling Thinking," and Freud's "The Uncanny." All three of these texts push the boundaries of their genre, that is, of literature, philosophy, and psychoanalysis respectively; all three are about a crisis; and all three raise serious questions about spectrality and the uncanny, not to mention questions about hospitality (*H* 1 236–37/314–15). Moreover, all three texts were written during or in the wake of wars that led to huge numbers of immigrants, exiles, and displaced persons—hence the importance of the date.[4]

Derrida does not really carry out the more detailed analysis and comparison of these three texts that he initially promises, but he does say a few words about *Ulysses*, another great book about exile and return, like Homer's *Odyssey* and Hegel's *Phenomenology*, and a work that, like Freud's "The Uncanny," has many scenes of hospitality, Greek and Jewish (*H* 1 222/296). Derrida speaks of a couple of them, for example, the strange scene of "hospitality" in the house of prostitution in Nighttown (*H* 1 239/317–18). But Derrida does not mention the famous scene of "the Citizen" (Polyphemus), who receives Leopold Bloom (Odysseus) only to reject him or kick him out a bar and thus, symbolically, out of Ireland. It is a scene of perverted hospitality, of a hospitality turned to hostility, a scene of violence, xenophobia, and antisemitism that would have illustrated yet again the fundamental autoimmunity of hospitality that Derrida develops throughout the seminar.

There is one final aspect of this relationship between a general form or historicizing structure of hospitality and the historical inscriptions or determinations of that structure that helps explain the autoimmunity of the concept of hospitality. It has been presupposed in everything said thus far about the autoimmunity or self-deconstruction of hospitality, but it now needs to be said more explicitly. Whether we are talking about etymologies, hosts becoming hostages, or the relationship between historically determined hospitalities and a general historicizing structure or form, all this happens, as it were, of its own accord, without the need of Derrida or anyone else to bring it about. As Derrida once put it, "deconstruction is what happens" ("SST" 85). It is what happens everywhere, though perhaps, as we are soon to see, in an exemplary way in hospitality. It is the case with the concept of hospitality and, as it were, with the "thing" hospitality, as new technologies, for example, change the very meaning and practice of hospitality, or, indeed, deconstruct it. Speaking of the "strangeness" of his approach to the question of hospitality in the seminar, using, on the one hand, philosophical and literary texts to develop a general and abstract formalization of the question and, on the other hand, current political examples that demonstrate the urgent nature of this question, Derrida argues that these current urgencies "seem, as though of themselves, to *deconstruct* these inheritances or the prevailing interpretations of these inheritances" (OH 139/123; see H 1 121/167; my emphasis). As we have already mentioned and will treat in more detail in Chapter 14, new technologies are transforming our experience of space, home, territory, etc., leading to a "deconstruction," as it were, of hospitality through these technological mutations.

What, then, is deconstruction, deconstruction itself, as a result? One of the best definitions—for there is no single one, and for essential reasons—is that deconstruction is the case, or better, that it "is what happens, what is happening today in what they call society, politics, diplomacy, economics, and so on and so forth" ("SST" 85). It is not a philosophy or a method but, simply, *what happens*, what happens to living organisms, to states and societal structures, and, yes, to concepts and texts—to anything, one might be tempted to say, with a threshold. Throughout this work, I have been trying to argue—and to show—that deconstruction is hospitality. It is hospitality to what is other than it, to what is other to the tradition; it invites otherness at the risk of its own destruction, or at the risk of becoming something else. For example, as we will see, if deconstruction is hospitality and hospitality is self-deconstructing or, indeed, beginning in the 1990s, autoimmune, then deconstruction is perhaps itself—and this would be another quasi-definition—autoimmunity. And autoimmunity is itself what happens: It is what happens to organic bodies, to states and nation-states, to texts and concepts.

Because no concept is self-identical, closed in on itself, because each is open to all the others and open even to what would appear to be its opposite, every concept is autoimmune—or, put otherwise, "hospitable" to the others. That is why, as I suggested earlier, the concept of hospitality is exemplary of the autoimmunity of the concept. Derrida more or less says this very thing in a couple of places in the seminar, perhaps most explicitly and overtly during the second year. If the second year of the seminar is, in general, much more focused than the first, with many pages devoted to detailed readings of Levinas and Louis Massignon, it also contains some of the most interesting and powerful methodological remarks about Derrida's approach to the question of hospitality and this approach in relationship to deconstruction itself.[5] Here, for example, is Derrida during the second year speaking about the relationship between hospitality and literature, though the remarks can no doubt be extended beyond literature:

> The concept of hospitality is so hospitable and so evasive or contradictory in its contours that it is a challenge to find a work that is not positioned either to illustrate, which is always less interesting, or to unfold actively, as its own writing, what we can call "hospitality"—and this already says something significant about the structure of this concept and its supposed limits. (H 2 81/124)

A session later, Derrida extends this hospitality of the concept of hospitality beyond a strict relation to literature and then eventually beyond the concept of hospitality to nothing less than the concept of the concept itself. Derrida is here speaking about the messianic, which, as we suggested a moment ago, is always in a deconstructive, autoimmune relationship with messianicity, when he suddenly begins talking about the concept itself. After speaking of "the messianic that introduces deconstructive disturbance or madness into the concept of hospitality, the madness *of* hospitality, or even the madness *of the concept of* hospitality," Derrida turns to the concept more generally:

> I indeed say "or even of the concept of hospitality" since the contradiction (atopic: madness, extravagance, in Greek: *atopos*) we are talking about produces or registers this self-deconstruction in every concept, in the concept of the concept: not only because hospitality undoes, ought to undo, the grasp, the grip (*Begriff, Begreifen*, the capture of *concipere, cum-capio*, of *comprehendere*, the force or the violence of *prendre* [to take] as *comprendre* [to comprehend]: hospitality is, *ought* to be, *owes it to itself* to be inconceivable and incomprehensible), but also because—we have tested this very often—every concept in hospitality opens up to its contrary, reproducing or producing in advance in the relation of one concept to another the contradictory and deconstructing law of hospitality. Every concept becomes hospitable to its other, to an other than itself that is no longer even *its* other. (H 2 100/148–49)

There is thus the concept of hospitality, which is itself autoimmune, like every concept, open, like every concept, to what is outside it. But insofar as "hospitality" describes as well as any other lexicon—for there is no "proper" lexicon for this, no metalanguage for it—the way in which every concept is open, receptive, to the outside, then the concept of hospitality is exemplary of the hospitality of the concept itself, exemplary of the autoimmunity of the concept itself. In short, the concept of hospitality is autoimmune, and hospitality is another way of speaking of the autoimmunity of the concept. That is what eventually leads Derrida to affirm in this extraordinary passage that "hospitality is a name or an example of deconstruction," that is, an example of the work of deconstruction, of what happens in or by deconstruction, and a name—another historical name, like autoimmunity—for deconstruction itself. Derrida goes on to write in a passage that is initially about hospitality—in this case the hospitality of the concept—but that then leads to a claim about what deconstruction itself will have been from the very beginning:

> If every concept shelters or lets itself be haunted by another concept, by another than itself that is no longer even its other, then no concept stays in place any longer. At stake is the concept of concept, and that is why I suggested a moment ago that hospitality, the experience, apprehension, exercise of impossible hospitality, of hospitality as possibility of the impossible (to receive an other guest that I am incapable of welcoming, to become capable of that of which I am incapable) is the exemplary experience of deconstruction itself, when it is what it has to be and undergoes what it has to undergo, that is, the experience of the impossible. Hospitality is a name or an example of deconstruction. Of the deconstruction both of the concept, of the concept of concept, and by the same token, of its construction, its house, its home. Hospitality is the deconstruction of the home [*le chez-soi*], deconstruction is hospitality to the other, the other of self, the other of "its other," an other that is beyond any "its other." (*H* 2 103/151–52)

Since it is hard to imagine any concept or practice of hospitality that does not involve in some way the provision of nourishment, food and drink—with all the perfections and perversions this can entail—let me conclude this look at the autoimmunity of the concept of hospitality by quoting a single line from Derrida about food and cooking that is related, rather remarkably, to this self-deconstruction or "autoimmunity" of the concept. The line is drawn from a text of Derrida's that comes well before the time in which he or anyone else was speaking about "autoimmunity" under this name, though the logic should be perfectly recognizable (demonstrating just how "hospitable" the very notion of "deconstruction" is or will have been). The line is drawn from *Glas*, a great text about, among so many other things, Hegel's family and, of course, hospitality. The line in question speaks of the concept in Hegel, the concept in general and its expression in speech, or rather, its expression in a form of "writing" understood as a coded structure of repeatability, a form of "writing" that therefore includes speech. The line runs in French, with an absolutely sumptuous economy: *"Dès qu'il est saisi par l'écriture, le concept est cuit"* (260), which I translate—though translation will hardly be adequate—"As soon as it is seized by writing, the concept is cooked."[6]

In other words—since other words are necessary to understand this extraordinary phrase—as soon as it is seized by writing, grasped or understood by writing, gotten hold of by writing, which is also to say by time, by history, by the other, the concept is done for, done in, in a word, cooked. "Being seized" by writing would thus seem to be inscribed in the very concept of the concept, for in German—as Derrida often recalls, and even recalls in *Hospitality*, as we just saw (*H* 2 100/148; see also *H* 1 10/30)—the concept, *der Begriff*, is related to *ergreifen*, that is, to seize. Hence the very word for "concept" in German, the very word for that which *should* promise a conceptual grasp that would go beyond speech and writing, beyond language, if you will, is related to or is associated with words in German having to do with grasping or seizing. So, as soon as it is seized by writing, the concept as it is understood by the tradition is seized by understanding, and seized by a particular language, in this case German, and so is, as a result, done for, done in.

As soon as it is seized by writing, therefore, the concept is done, that is, it is no longer raw, no longer purely natural but already civilized, cooked. As soon as it is seized, *saisi*, by writing, it is cooked, no longer untouched by the materiality of language but, now, drawn into language, and so cooked, done in, and thus burned by it.

That is already a rather powerful and complex economy, but there is yet another meaning of *saisi* to be taken into account, *saisi* not as seized but as *seared*, as in cooking, as when one heats up a pan to be so hot that *as soon as* a piece of food (meat, fish, or vegetable) is dropped onto it, which is to say, almost immediately, it is done, "seared," *saisi*. This would seem to suggest that there is in effect no time, no extended time, before the concept is seized or comprehended, seared or singed, by writing, and thus done or done in. As soon as it is *saisi* by writing, and that happens right away, in an instant, as soon as it is seized by a series of repeatable signs, and that is immediate, the concept is seared, singed, cooked, done for, though also perhaps, for a certain Hegel, ready to be served up in history.

As soon as it is seized, seared by writing, the concept—the concept of hospitality or of anything else—is done in, no longer some putatively ideal meaning transcendent to all particular languages but a concept already marked by a language, seared or grilled by a particular language and its unique economy— an economy, for example, where *saisi* means at once "seized" and "seared" and *cuit* at once "cooked" and "done for." As soon as it is seized by writing, and that is right away, it can no longer be said that the signified comes before the signifier, that the signifier is simply the secondary or accidental inscription of that signified. For as soon as it is seized by writing, and this happens immediately, the concept is no longer raw, disembodied, or transcendental. And perhaps most significantly, it, the concept—like the phrase itself—cannot be grasped all at once, in a single go, and that alone is enough to do in a concept. It cannot simply be grasped, understood, but must now be *read*—and more than once, in more than one time. It is another way of saying that there is no metalanguage and that anyone who has tried to say the contrary has inevitably gotten burned by the language in which they tried to say it. As soon as they will have tried to speak of or in that metalanguage, they will have been done for.

As soon as it is seized by writing, the concept—and perhaps in an exemplary fashion the concept of hospitality—is cooked. As soon as it is seized by language, and this happens already on the threshold, it is done for as a concept, at least in the traditional sense. As soon as it crosses over the threshold, it becomes just another threshold phenomenon, which is to say, no longer a concept worthy of the name. Unless, of course, it is thereby served up, freed up—there on the threshold—to become something even more open and hospitable than a concept in the traditional sense, a concept, a phrase, that is now offered up to reading.

PART III

*The Wall, the Door, the Threshold,
the Hotspot*

13

Dirty Foreigners: The Question of Purity

> The borders are no longer places of passage but places of prohibition,
> thresholds that one regrets having opened, limits toward which one
> hastens to escort people, threatening figures of ostracism, expulsion,
> banishment, and persecution. ("Q" 74)

Derrida speaks during the first year of the seminar of two maelstroms that were
threatening Europe at the time, two maelstroms that have changed in configuration but have done nothing but grow in magnitude and intensity in the intervening years. The first is the problem of citizenship, of immigration, which
was the object of controversy in Europe at the time from two directions, that
is, from the relatively recent unification of Europe under the Schengen agreement, a unification of countries once foreign to one another, sometimes even
enemies to one another, and from immigration problems related to conflicts
in the former Yugoslavia (H 1 65/97–98). And the two were not unrelated, for
the French government was saying publicly at the time that it would apply all
the provisions of the Schengen agreement only when it was assured that other
member states would reinforce the borders surrounding or protecting Europe
from migrants coming from a host of places, including Eastern Europe. This
first maelstrom related to problems of immigration and citizenship loomed
over the entire seminar, and it was augmented or amplified by the contemporaneous discovery in the former Yugoslavia of mass graves and horrific stories
of "ethnic cleansing" (H 1 181/245, 184/248).

Derrida thus recalls throughout the seminar that Europe was just beginning to find its footing in the wake of the Schengen agreement of 1990, which
had the effect of loosening restrictions between European countries while

tightening them and reinforcing borders between Europe and its outside (see *H* 1 65–66/98, 227/303). A loosening within and a tightening without—such seemed to be at the time the effects of Schengen, and there were discourses aplenty, as there are today, about the need to protect and even "purify" a particular state or people from the effects of immigration, and discourses from the other side about the extreme nationalism or "xenophobia" of this rhetoric.

Though it is beyond the scope of this work to reconstitute the historical premises for these discourses, it is important to follow the marks they have left in the two years of Derrida's seminar, which ran, let me recall again, from November 1995 to May 1997. During the first session of the seminar Derrida recalls the newly instituted Pasqua Laws restricting immigration to France, and he calls them, not without sarcasm, "anything but Kantian" (*H* 1 54/84). Much later in the seminar, after citing at length a document related to a 1938 law on hospitality (*H* 1 206–7/277–78), Derrida takes up the proposed Toubon Law—named after Jacques Toubon, then minister of justice—which would have extended the already very restrictive Pasqua Laws (*H* 1 228–30/304–7). The proposed law would have in essence treated any act of hospitality given or offered to someone in an "irregular" situation as nothing less than an act of "terrorism" (*H* 1 228/304–5). It was in reference to this law that one began speaking of a "crime of hospitality," that is, a *délit d'hospitalité* (*H* 1 12n27/32n13), a phrase that Derrida cannot quite believe and to which he returns throughout the seminar. How can something that is almost universally considered to be a good, a virtue, be designated a "crime"? Derrida writes, for example, in the third session, "while in general everyone agrees with the positive evaluation of the idea of hospitality as a good and also as the idea of a cosmopolitical right and perpetual peace, that doesn't prevent French law from speaking of a 'crime of hospitality'" (*H* 1 69/102).[1] One can understand Derrida's shock and outrage, but it turns out that the expression "délit d'hospitalité" or "délit de solidarité" had never been part of the French penal code and was not actually part of the proposed law itself but was used, starting in 1995, by various associations, including the Groupe d'information et de soutien des immigrés (GISTI), to *characterize* the law, which would sanction and propose penalties, including fines and imprisonment, for anyone "facilitating or trying to facilitate the irregular entry, movement, or stay of a stranger in France."[2]

Bracketing the question or the provenance of that frightful phrase, the Toubon Law, like the Pasqua Laws before it, would have nonetheless been motivated, according to Derrida, by some of the worst xenophobic tendencies in France at the time. Derrida speaks in a text from around the same time of a "politics of racist allergy, of protectionist xenophobia," of a "convulsion" that is at once "national-protectionist, identitarian and xenophobic, an ancient and renewed figure of racism" ("Q" 84). His remarks there, as in the seminar, are addressed primarily to French politics, but Derrida also recalls in the very same passage that in the United States there are actually, as a consequence of this same logic, "organized efforts to hunt down 'illegal immigrants'" ("Q" 85). It is as if, says Derrida, "one no longer realized that the at-home [*chez-soi*] of a house, of a culture, or of a society also presupposed an hospitable opening" ("Q" 75).

After recalling that this proposed law seemed to be in contradiction with the Schengen agreement, which makes allowances for "disinterested" hospitality, that is, hospitality offered without any financial motive (*H* 1 229/305), Derrida reads at some length a document protesting this proposed law (*H* 1 229–30/306–7). Earlier in the seminar, he had evoked the not-so-hypothetical case of someone offering hospitality to, for example, Basque separatists (*H* 1 200/268). Must those offering support to such people ask for authorization from the police in order to put them up or offer them hospitality? Such cases pose serious questions regarding the relationship between private hospitality and public hospitality (*H* 1 201–2/269–70). It was in response to such an intolerable situation, Derrida recalls, that he and a few others had recently engaged in acts of "Civil Disobedience" by helping Algerians come to France without visas, as was required by the Pasqua Laws (see *H* 1 69/102; see also *DE* 100).

These recent laws in France were at once a response to the Schengen agreement on the part of a government opposed to it either in part or in whole and a reflection of a growing xenophobia in France, the beginning of a rise of the far right that continues to this day. This leads to numerous remarks throughout the seminar regarding the political enemy, whom one fights but does not hate, and the personal enemy, whom one comes to hate outside or beyond all politics. Derrida comes to this distinction, made famous by Carl Schmitt, by comparing Arendt's discourse to Schmitt's on the political enemy (*H* 1 138/189–90). In the course of addressing during a discussion session a question about Hannah Arendt and the appropriation of man by man in the Declaration of Human Rights (*H* 1 141/194), Derrida treats Schmitt's objection to the notion of a crime against humanity. For Schmitt, this notion spells the end of the political, which is born of the distinction between friend and enemy, the friend and the enemy who fight each other, and even risk their lives doing so, but who do not hate each other (see *H* 1 146–49/201–4).[3] We have already heard traces of this Schmittian discourse — traces, at least, of his analysis or diagnosis, though not his remedy — in Derrida's remarks, which we treated in Chapters 8 and 9, regarding an absolute or unconditional hospitality that makes it impossible to recognize who is inviting whom, who is host and who is guest, a situation that, Derrida says, can quickly turn to hatred.

Arendt argues somewhat similarly in *The Origins of Totalitarianism* that after the breakdown of politics following World War I there was no longer hostility but, precisely, hatred (*H* 1 138–39/190–91). What motivated that hatred was not nationalism as such but the breakdown of nationalism, the loss of a political culture. Hatred arose between two world wars not because enemies were able to recognize, identify, and hate one another but because the enemy could *not* be identified. Instead of identifying a foreign enemy, hatred was directed toward those who were closest (*H* 1 161/220).

Elsewhere in the seminar, Derrida's analysis of the *chez* leads him to talk about this closeness and proximity from a different, though related, perspective. What distinguishes what is close, the neighbor, for example, from what is different or distant, that is, from the foreigner, is related to the difference between what is one's own (*propre*, in French) and what is the other's, which is itself related to the difference between what is clean (*propre* once again in French) and what is dirty (*sale*) (see *H* 1 180–84/244–48). And this would be the case not only from an analytic, if not psychoanalytic, point of view but also linguistically. Derrida speaks of "the troubling semantic neighborhood between *proper-improper* and *clean-dirty* [*propre-sale*] or *repugnant*" and the fact that this language can be "quickly converted into a lexicon of hospitality if one considers that the xenophobic drive naturally inclines, as it were, toward a phobic repulsion with respect to what is presumed to be not only im-proper, not-proper, foreign, but also dirty, contagious, contaminating, impure" (*H* 1 181/245). Having spent so much time developing these questions and themes in previous texts, Derrida says he will simply mention or situate them during the seminar. He thus relates "ethnic cleansing" to this "xenophobic drive," this *pulsion xénophobique*, and thus to the opposition between the proper and the improper, that is, the foreign, dirty, repugnant, and impure. Hence the "immunological dimension" mentioned by Derrida, since the phobic drive must be motivated by the fear that the impurity, that the dirty and repugnant, is not only objectionable or damnable but *contagious* (see *H* 1 182/245–46).[4] Whence the desire to cut oneself off—from everyone, including and especially those closest to us:

> Contact must be cut off and the border shut or the nearest one exterminated, the orifices, eyes, ears must be blocked and sutured, the skin must be hardened all the way to the heart so that nothing can pass in [*passe*], I would say even so that nothing takes place [*se passe*], and especially not the nearest one. (*H* 1 183/248)

What is "closest," "nearest," is thus that from which I must cut myself off or that of which I must be purified. This is the beginning of an explanation for xenophobic hatred. While "the foreigner is the one against whom the proper [*le propre*: also, the clean or pure] is affirmed, is posed, is called for" (*H* 1 72n41/106n2), xenophobia is not, paradoxically, a hatred of what is completely other. One does not exterminate foreigners, Derrida suggests, but always those who are too much like us in some way. As he puts it in an aside—and even goes on to illustrate on the blackboard (in what must have resembled a sort of deconstructive version of the so-called uncanny valley phenomenon):

> In the place of these two oppositions, we have this chiasmus: it is the proper that is dirty, the proper in the sense of the near, in the sense of my dear ones too, that is dirty, that inspires repulsion, immuno-logical xenophobia. One does not exterminate foreigners pure and simple; one exterminates near ones, near in a certain manner. (*H* 1 182n8/246n2)

This suggests, among many other things, that the stranger or foreigner is perhaps also always, potentially, a little uncanny, *unheimlich*, the stranger being an uncanny and frightening double. Insofar as the uncanny bears an "undecidable force of resistance" between the familiar and the foreign, it be-comes a crucial notion for hospitality (*H* 1 218/291; see 239–41/318–21), which explains Derrida's turn to Freud's "Das Unheimliche" essay later in the sem-inar. Here is Derrida explaining the necessity of thinking the uncanny in re-lation to hospitality but also, toward the end of this passage, the way in which the theme of the uncanny runs through several of his most recent seminars, making it necessary to return to this essay again and again from a different perspective—yet another aspect of Derrida's perpetual return to the threshold, this time not within a single seminar but *between* seminars:

> With the apparent and shifting, unstable, contradiction of "at-home-at-the-other's- house," the theme of the "*Unheimliche*," yet another word so difficult to translate, a theme that will have been for many years the obsession of this seminar, along with all those obsessions that I recalled last week (the proper and the near, expropriation, exappropriation, the oppositions between proper or proximate (*prope*) versus far off or foreign, clean [*propre*] *versus* dirty or contaminating or contagious, and then the immunological, auto-immunological paradox that inscribes a chiasmus between these two oppositions, with the result that the proxi-mate or the proper becomes also the dangerous or hateful contaminat-ing thing), the theme of the *Unheimliche* then, such as it resonates in Freud's work as well as in Heidegger's—after having travelled through seminars on nationality, friendship, cannibalism, the secret or testi-mony—again becomes decisive here in speaking about hospitality. (*H* 1 218/291)[5]

This xenophobic hatred of those *close* to us, those with an uncanny sim-ilarity to us, might also help explain Derrida's rather strident response to a question during a discussion session about whether there might be a sort of solidarity between peoples based on our common "foreignness to ourselves," a foreignness that might become the basis for welcoming or appreciating the foreignness of others. In his reply to this question, Derrida is very clear that one must never say that the other, the foreigner, makes us realize how foreign we are to ourselves or that foreigners are great to have in France because they enrich the culture. The welcome of the foreigner must be beyond all such calculation or comparison, Derrida suggests. One cannot "cultivate" one's own strangeness or foreignness to oneself in order to appropriate it in that way. Indeed, one's foreignness must remain, precisely, foreign to the self (*H1* 129–30/179–80).

These themes of purification and immunization also raise the whole question of immunity, another major theme in the seminar: the immunity of embassies, for example, of hospitals, sometimes even of universities, but perhaps especially of churches (*H* 1 202–3/271). During an improvised session late in the year, in May 1996, Derrida addresses an event that was taking place at the same time as the seminar: the expulsion of undocumented migrants who were seeking refuge, as well as immunity from arrest and expulsion, from the Church of Saint-Ambroise in Paris, an expulsion that eventually took place not only with the consent of church officials but perhaps even at their initiative. All the while acknowledging that he does not know all the details of the case, Derrida questions certain arguments and statements by church officials and asks about the implications of this case for the long tradition of immunity or sanctuary in religious places, in this case, in Catholic churches (see *H* 1 260–64/345–49). This event is part of what motivates Derrida to take up the question and history of the right to sanctuary in churches—a right that, Derrida notes, is becoming more and more restrictive and more and more rare—and, later, the project of renewing a biblical and medieval tradition of "cities of asylum" or "cities of refuge" that would make the city something of an enclave within the nation-state, a place immune from persecution or prosecution, exile or extradition. (We will look at this notion of a renewed tradition of "cities of asylum" in Chapter 17.)

What is clear is that a new politics or political response to these questions and problems must be invented. The "political task" must be, as Derrida argues in yet another text from around the same time, to find the best "legislative" transaction or "juridical" conditions in order to change "laws, habits, phantasms—a whole 'culture,'" including, it seems, all the phantasms of self, the nation-state, and God that so often lead to xenophobia and nationalism ("NU" 131).

14

Homing Devices: Teletechnology and the Question of Private Space

In the typescript, several words have been added by hand: "No step/ step of negation [*pas de pas*]: private/public. No more threshold [+ *de seuil*]." (*H* 1 102n3/145n3; editors' note)

Derrida speaks in the third session of the first year of the seminar of *two* maelstroms. The first of these, which we looked at in the previous chapter, was immigration, related, as we saw, to questions of purity and purification, propriety and cleanliness. The second, says Derrida, is teletechnology, that is, the way teletechnology has completely transformed the way we think about a foreign body, a *corps étranger*, and, therefore, about hospitality. As Derrida says, "the foreigner is never present or presentable as such" (*H* 1 66/99) — that has always been the case — but certain teletechnologies will have completely altered our relation to the foreign body, causing us to rethink all our "concepts and norms of the propriety of the body proper, of its relation to the foreign body (grafts, artificial insemination, viral contagion, analysis and possible transformation of the human genome, etc.)" (*H* 1 67/100).

This theme or question of technology, or, as Derrida more frequently calls it, teletechnology, runs throughout the *Hospitality* seminar. That should not be so surprising, for if hospitality always involves a relationship between an inside and an outside, an inside that does or does not receive or welcome something from the outside — a living being, for example, be it their living body or perhaps just their voice, their writing, or their image — then the question of technology becomes inevitable. Again, technology or teletechnology will have *always* been central to hospitality, even if, as we saw, it was one of the aspects of hospitality that Kant seemed to ignore. But more recent kinds of technology—television, email, the internet, cyberspace, the telephone, and especially, as we will see in Derrida, the mobile phone—will have made this structural law linking hospitality to technology all the more palpable, pressing, and, indeed, unavoidable for any contemporary thinking of hospitality.

To introduce Derrida's approach to technology in the seminar, let me simply quote Derrida at some length from an improvised session during the first year in which he is reading aloud and commenting on a newspaper story in *Le Monde* from the previous day about a technology called the "xenograft" and the controversy surrounding it. The story concerns the experimental treatment by which cells from a baboon are transplanted into a human in order to achieve immunity from HIV.[1] Derrida's comments are telling both for the way they show him interpreting the xenograft for the purposes of the seminar on hospitality and for the way they illustrate his way of reading and operating more generally, particularly with regard to technology and the animal. Here, for example, would be one rule of thumb: Find a concept that is defined by the tradition in a relatively narrow sense (here the "xenograft," elsewhere "writing") and then show that, according to the very definition or understanding of that concept in the tradition, the concept should have a much wider application (here covering all grafts, elsewhere all language) in order to argue that what was thought to be a narrow or marginal case is in fact the rule. Derrida breaks away from his written text to say during this session of December 20, 1995:

> And since I am speaking of the foreign [*l'étranger*] and the graft, I will refer to something I read in *Le Monde* yesterday that had a very interesting word, which is "xenograft." What is a xenograft? First, it is the foreign. So, it is the graft, all grafts are xenografts, but these xenos are more xeno than others. And so what are they? You may have read this article, "Man, the Baboon, and AIDS." I will read it to you, basically it is clearer than what I could tell you. (*H* 1 67n28/100n1)

After thus prefacing his reading with that very quick but decisive claim that will guide his entire reading, namely, that "all grafts are xenografts," Derrida begins reading the article, with his accompanying comments placed in brackets by the editors:

> Although no one can explain it, the fact is not contested: baboon cells are naturally immunized against the HIV-1 virus, which is responsible for the great majority of cases of AIDS. On Thursday, then, Jeff Getty underwent a high-risk transplant whose potential beneficial effects could be considerable. If everything unfolds as expected, millions of

baboon cells are going to mix with those of the patient [you see here, the question of the foreign body beyond the human, the animal, what is called the animal], millions of baboon cells [which are going to be welcomed, to which one ought to offer the hospitality of man's body proper] are going to mix with those of the patient, to proliferate and help to reconstruct a new immunizing potential [the question of immunity or auto-immunity will later be at the center of this seminar] resistant to the effects of the AIDS virus. Hence, it is not a matter of acting on HIV but of reinforcing the defenses of the body against its manifestations [further on, this operation is named "xenotransplant-ing," *xeno* because it comes from somewhere other than humankind: it is then to the foreigner as an animal that the hospitality of transplant into human tissue is offered]. But xenotransplants, these grafts of ani-mal tissue onto man, provoke lively controversy [further on, under the title "Russian roulette," the word "xenograft" appears.] The detractors of xenografts that constitute [. . .]

Derrida then breaks off his reading of the article to comment:

Immediately the debate is no longer scientific, there are controver-sies in a place where there is no purely scientific discourse, there are detractors, how can one be a detractor of xenografts? Either it works or it doesn't, it's true or it isn't, one cannot be a detractor of xenografts. Thus, so those who are xenograft detractors are already xenophobes, people who worry; there ought not be any non-scientific polemic about these things. We will return to the question of *xenos* later. . . . I close this parenthetical remark here. (*H* 1 67n28/100–1n1)

This is, as we said, a rather simple and straightforward example of Derri-da's way of proceeding. As generally understood, a xenograft is a tissue graft or organ transplant from a donor of a *different* species from the recipient. But Derrida argues that every graft, insofar as it comes from another, from a foreigner or a stranger, from a *xenos*, or from somewhere else, some foreign part, is a xenograft. Of course, we might — indeed we should — within this gen-eralizable structure of xenografting distinguish the grafting of a piece of tissue taken from one part of a single individual onto another part of the same indi-vidual, a graft that generally has, of course, fewer risks (though not none) of rejection, from the graft of tissue or of an organ from another individual of the same species, from — and this is the controversy in question in the article — the grafting of a tissue or an organ from a member of *another* species. We ought to distinguish between these various kinds of xenograft, especially in relation to what works and what does not. But in all these cases we are talking about a xenograft, according to Derrida. Though the "foreignness" of the last example, the graft from one species onto another, seems greater than the first two, and so may be more prone to rejection, that is something that would need to be determined by science. But the controversy emerges not from some debate over whether the xenograft from another species works less well than the xenograft from the same species and so should not be used. It emerges because of the fear, a sort of fantasmatic fear (and we will return to this notion of the fantasmatic in Chapter 18), that something will happen to the human when another species mixes with it, invades it, contaminates it. What Derrida is suggesting here is that the *binary logic* that feeds the fantasmatic fear of those who oppose such xenografts, the binary logic that simply and massively opposes the human to all other species, needs to be replaced by a more complex, refined, *differential logic* that shows a compatibility between humans and other species in some ways and not others. (As genetic sequencing has proven in the time between Derrida's seminar and today, we share no less than 94 percent of our DNA with baboons, 99 percent with chimps and bonobos.)

The question here, says Derrida, is not whether this is acceptable but whether it works. It is only when there is an assumed opposition between one's own species and another, what is mine and what is other, what is human and what is not, that one begins to worry or to claim that something is unacceptable. What we should be talking about here, then, are various levels or degrees of xenografting—a differential logic of the xenograft, as it were—and not an oppositional or binary logic that would draw a clear line between the xenograft and what might be called the "autograft." Indeed, it is as if the very term *xenograft* had been coined with that binary logic in view, a logic that would oppose the graft from a foreign species, from a *xenos*, to the graft from one's own species. But the fact that rejection of tissues and organs happens not only between species but also within them suggests that every graft is in essence a *xenograft*, and thus the opposition between interspecies grafts and intraspecies grafts breaks down. As long as what is being grafted is not "the same"—and no graft would or could ever be the grafting of the same onto the same—then it is xenograft.

To be clear, there may be other reasons, ethical or otherwise, to object to the grafting of tissues or organs from another species or even another individual of the same species (questions of consent, for example, of animals or even humans being used as a mere means toward an end), but objecting to the xenograft solely on the basis of it coming from another species, as if this would create, with no medical basis for such a belief, a medical monster, is what Derrida finds objectionable and in need of critique.

To recall the more general point about Derrida's argumentative, decon-structive strategy, it is, notice, the extreme case, the graft of tissue or of an organ from *another* species, that allows one to begin to think, retrospectively, as it were, every graft as a xenograft. We see this elsewhere in Derrida with regard to speech and writing. In works such as *Of Grammatology*, Derrida would come to criticize or deconstruct in a similar way or on similar grounds the relationship between speech and writing in the Western philosophical tra-dition, a tradition beginning with Plato and Aristotle and running up through Hegel and Heidegger that consistently prioritized speech over writing insofar as the former was considered to be more natural, closer to life, to presence, to intention, to what is one's own, and so on, while the latter was artificial, related to death, absence, lack of intention, the foreign, and so on. (Recall that, in Plato's *Phaedrus*, Theuth, the inventor of writing, was himself a for-eigner, Egyptian and not Greek.) But when one looks at justifications for this distinction in, for example, the myth of writing in the *Phaedrus*, one sees that speech is in the same relationship to thought, to what Plato calls "writing in the soul," as writing is to speech, so that the *opposition* between speech and writing is no longer tenable, and *both* can then be thought under the aegis of archē-writing, that is, a differential series of signs, written or spoken, that come to signify through their relations among themselves rather than through some immediate connection to intention or to some signified.

That's one similarity between the way Derrida treated speech and writing in early works and the way he treats the xenograft here. But there are ad-ditional correspondences—for example, their relation to technology. What made the analytical point about the similarities between speech and writing even clearer and more difficult to ignore was, undoubtedly, the development of certain technologies for reproducing the written word and, perhaps espe-cially, beginning in the nineteenth century, the spoken word (phonographs, tape recorders), that allowed us to see that speech is indeed a "kind" of writing. As soon as speech leaves my mouth, it, like writing, is potentially reproducible in my absence, without my intention, even beyond my life, and so on—all those attributes once thought to apply uniquely to writing. It was, therefore, the technical advances of print and voice reproduction that made it even more possible to see or to understand what *will have always* been the case, namely, that there is no rigorous way to oppose speech to writing. Similarly, it was ad-vances in the medical technology of grafting organs or tissue from one species onto another, the xenograft in the narrow sense of the term, that made it even more evident that every graft is a xenograft and that grafting from one spe-cies to another cannot simply be opposed to intraspecies grafting. And, as we mentioned earlier, DNA sequencing would make all this even more evident.

Once again, therefore, a technical advance—a technological "mutation," as Derrida often calls it—will have led to the deconstruction of an opposition that had hitherto gone unquestioned or had been considered axiomatic. (And notice Derrida's grafting of the term "mutation" from evolutionary biology onto philosophy in order to suggest something that happens of its own accord, without any particular intention or conscious actor behind it.) In the case of hospitality, therefore—to return to the subject at hand—it will be a series of mutations in the modalities, the growth, and, especially, the efficacy of tele-technologies that will have been transforming, as if of their own accord, our categories of time and space, distance and proximity, and causing us to rethink our understanding of hospitality.

Derrida gives numerous examples over the course of the seminar of the ways in which teletechnologies are changing, for example, the relationship between public and private space and, thus, the very terms of hospitality. He speaks of telephone call intercepts, phone tapping and recording, in short, various forms of "bugging" or "spying" on the part of the state, teletechnological innovations that threaten or redefine the "interiority of the home," the "interiority of our chez soi" (*OH* 53/51; see *H* 1 93/131). And he speaks not only of governments intercepting phone calls but also of readily available technologies that allow private people to do so, to listen in to the phones of others and even to clone them (see *OH* 59/57; see *H* 1 95–96/134). It is thus becoming more and more difficult to distinguish between the surveillance possibilities of the police and those of private citizens, not to mention, we would want to add today, the possibilities available to communications networks and social media platforms. Derrida evokes the case of an internet provider (CompuServe) giving up the identity of its clients to the police, comparing it to hotels giving over their list of guests to the police or to the post office allowing the police to open private mail (*OH* 63/59–61; see *H* 1 96–97/135–36). We recall the way in which Kant, in the name of ethics, said that we must not lie, not even to assassins, prompting Derrida to say that Kant "introduces the police everywhere" (*OH* 69/65; see *H* 1 98/138; see also 227/303), indeed even into our own relation to ourselves. As Arendt saw, in such a situation the police begin no longer simply to enforce the law but to *make* it (*H* 1 253/335),[2] posing enormous problems for the relationship between public and private.

While individuals will thus often appropriate certain technologies of the nation-state, the nation-state is itself trying to catch up with and appropriate the teletechnologies of corporations and industry that often exceed it and go beyond it (*OH* 57/55; see *H* 1 94–95/133). Hence the struggle between nation-states and entities that are larger, richer, and more powerful than many nation-states—Facebook, for example, with about as many users as the entire populations of China and India combined (a contemporary fact that would have surely interested Derrida). As Derrida goes on to say, "the democratization of information" seems to be coextensive with its policing (*OH* 57/55; see *H* 1 94/133). It is a law of teletechnology that seems to confirm many of the things that Derrida argued back in "Signature Event Context" and elsewhere: "The more one encodes, the more one decodes, the more one encrypts the more one decrypts." That is because every time one encodes in order to keep something secret one is yielding yet another codified thing to the structures of iterability and readability. As Derrida says with an incontestable clarity and simplicity: "I can hide a letter only by separating myself from it and thus by yielding it to the outside, by exposing it to another, by archiving it, a document thereafter accessible in the space where it is deposited" (*OH* 65/61; see *H* 1 97/136; added to *OH*). In other words, once I separate myself from my letter, and that happens as soon as it is written, it becomes readable for a third beyond me. And, of course, as we recalled earlier, what holds for the letter holds also for speech. As soon as I speak, into a microphone, into a telephone, on Zoom, to another who may record me or simply remember what I say, I make my words accessible to them and to others in my absence. It is thus perhaps even easier to understand today Derrida's seemingly cryptic phrase from *Ulysses Gramophone* of some four decades ago: "In the beginning was the telephone" (*UG* 270/80). If the delocalizing power of the telephone is already there in speech, in the word, in logos, then the virtualizing, delocalizing power of a voice that becomes separated from its origin from the origin, conveyed through air or over wires through various kinds of technologies, will have been there from the beginning as well.

It is these same delocalizations brought about through teletechnology that are behind all the "reaction and resentment aimed at purity" (*OH* 53/51; see *H* 1 93/131) that we looked at in the previous chapter. We can imagine a scenario in which one wants to keep one's home, the place where one typically offers hospitality, so pure of these outside interferences, so free of these teletechnological parasitical intrusions, that one ends up closing the doors and windows so tightly that one can no longer offer any hospitality at all. This then leads to a sort of perversion of the very law of hospitality. As Derrida writes: "The perversion, the pervertibility of this law (which is also a law of hospitality) is that one can become virtually xenophobic in order to protect or claim to protect one's own hospitality, one's own at-home which makes possible one's own hospitality" (*OH* 53/51–53; see *H* 1 93/132). One becomes xenophobic out of a desire to keep one's home safe and sound and open for hospitality, that is, in order to protect one's home for future hospitality. It's a strange paradox, or, as Derrida would call it, an autoimmune reaction. One becomes xenophobic by wanting to protect one's own hospitality, the proper of one's own home that makes hospitality possible.

Telephone surveillance, wiretapping, telephonic "parasiting," cloning: Hospitality cannot be thought today without all these things, which are in and of themselves neither good nor bad but always and from the beginning potentially both, essentially pervertible. As Derrida nicely couches the paradox: "The blessing [*bénédiction*] of vision and daylight is also what the police and politics want" (*OH* 57/55; see *H* 1 94/133). While there would be no violations of our private space if there were no points of access to the outside, no points of vulnerability, as it were, there would also be no hospitality. For a home to offer hospitality, it must have openings to the outside, windows, doors, and thresholds, various means of accessibility (*OH* 61/57–59; see *H* 1 96/134–35). Were one able to master one's home to the point of controlling absolutely all its points of entry and exit, thereby protecting one's sovereign ipseity and preserving it from all intrusion, there might well be no intrusions, but there would also be no hospitality. Indeed, were someone to master his home to this degree, he would no longer really be living in a home at all, which seems to require not only a certain interiority but access to that interiority from the outside.

But while this has always the case, this law of accessibility or opening has today taken on some very new and different forms. As a result of all these teletechnological delocalizations

> hospitality can be granted or refused under conditions that no longer have anything to do with what is ordinarily called place or territory. To welcome someone into an internet network or even into a national or international telephone conversation, is already an experience of hospitality no longer commanded by the crossing of a limit or territorial frontier. (*H* 1 59–60/90–91)

The whole question of the relationship between public hospitality and private hospitality must thus be posed anew, along with the relation between public and private law (*H* 1 104/272–73; 208/279). Kant's *Perpetual Peace*, for example, as universalizing and cosmopolitan as its ambition was, concerns only *public* hospitality, progress in view of a perpetual peace among nation-states. A separate agreement would need to be made, it seems, for any kind of private hospitality (see *H* 1 201–2/269–70). In this regard as well, one has to go beyond Kant's cosmopolitanism, however ambitious and laudable it may be. For there is simply too much it cannot account for:

> the telephone, the fax, email, the internet, television, panoptic satellites, multimedia, CD-ROMs and information highways, access

to non-terrestrial spaces, so many radical de-localizations that call for another experience of the relation to the other and so another experience of hospitality, or even already another right to hospitality, another duty of hospitality. (*H 1* 60/91)

Derrida asks throughout the seminar how the internet and email have changed the structure of so-called public space, indeed the very relationship between public and private. Cyberspace is in our home, yet it has windows onto the world and allows the world to look into our home. Derrida gives the example of state censorship of pornographic websites on the grounds that the internet is a public space, an action that, all by itself, raises the question about whether these exchanges on the internet are private or public, where the boundary is between private and public, and, indeed, where the borders between nation-states are to be found on the internet (see *OH* 47–49/47–49; see *H 1* 91–92/129–30). It is a question that has everything to do with hospitality, a question that, twenty-five years later, is obviously far from being resolved. It is surely no coincidence that so many words having to do with what Derrida calls these technological virtualizations or "radical delocalizations" (*H 1* 60/91) have to do with the home and appeal to a certain language of domesticity or hospitality— "hosts" and "servers," "home pages" and "chat rooms," Windows and Zoom "invites," and so on. It is no coincidence that we speak of "cybersecurity" in the same terms as "home security," of "viruses" that enter our computers like "viruses" that enter our bodies, or of our systems and networks being held "hostage" by intruders asking for "ransom" for the data they have stolen or the control over our systems that they have gained. So while hospitality will have always been hospitable to a certain thinking of technology, since, as Derrida reminds us in "The University without Condition," "as soon as there is a trace there is virtualization; that's the abc's of deconstruction" ("UWC" 210/25), there is an acceleration and multiplication of venues for these technologies to enter our systems and our states, whether invited or uninvited, offering new possibilities and problems for thinking hospitality or cosmopolitics today.

Derrida would have thus hardly been surprised by the sort of phenomena we today know all too well, marketing by logarithm and mega data, electronic profiling and pay-per-click advertising, the experience, for example, of using what we had considered to be our private computer in the privacy of our own home to go on to some website in order to research, say, some hotel to stay at, some book on hospitality to read, or some hospitality program at some university to enroll in, only to discover the very next day that that supposedly private computer, in what we thought to be our own private space, is now receiving "personalized messages" from that hotel or about that book or university program. We thought we were looking onto some public venue from the privacy of our own home, and, lo and behold, that publicly accessible venue was looking at us, registering our every keystroke and causing unexpected and often unwanted incursions into what we thought to be our private space.

What is being redrawn is thus the relation between public and private, where the border is in a process of perpetual "destructuration-restructuration" and where "every element of hospitality finds itself disrupted" (OH 51/49; see H 1 92–93/130–31). What is happening is a sort of deconstruction of the line between self and other, public and private, as one invites others into one's ear via the telephone or into one's home via the internet with a rapidity and frequency that far surpass our ability to invite them into our home in a more traditional way.

By transforming our relationship to space, teletechnologies have also completely changed our relations to power. Delocalizing in its very essence, detached from land or territory, that which is small but virtual can today exercise an unprecedented power over what is large but concrete. Derrida reminds us:

> One can have more power, and hence more means of hospitality, by wielding a certain tele-technological power over a ridiculously small territory, far more than those who would dispose of endless territories without telephone, fax, television, surveillance satellites, etc. (H 1 59n13/90n3)

Again, while this power of delocalization or deterritorialization has always played a part in hospitality, making it necessary to think hospitality beyond territory, recent advances in teletechnology have made this thinking or rethinking all the more necessary (see H 1 61/92–93). Derrida thus speaks throughout of the inevitable "pervertibility" that effaces the limit between private and public, the secret and the phenomenal, the "at-home" that makes hospitality possible and the violation of the home inevitable (OH 65/61; see H 1 97/136–37).

Teletechnologies have led to a redrawing or a reconfiguration of the lines between public and private, the state and what is outside the state. That is, they have made apparent what has *always* been the case, namely, that the self—the home, the inside, the state—is what it is only in relation to the outside, even if the self, the inside, the state, society, might claim in a kind of phantasmatic way that it comes before and is independent from that outside. Derrida is always very clear that, for him, it is not a question of something radically new but of a mutation or transformation as a result of new modalities, rhythms, and powers.

It is not a matter of opposing a *before* and an *after*, along a historical line that would see possibilities or mutations, in particular in
techno-scientific powers, coming one after the other. One must, of
course, take into account these events and mutations that transform
in a structural, quantitative, and qualitative way the experience and
juridical conditions of hospitality, the condition and exercise of rights,
beginning with property rights—that is to say, in an extended sense,
the structure of the juridical person and of ipseity in general before
any determination as person or ego. (*H* 1 60/91)

Once again, the technological supplement makes apparent what will have
been the case already from the beginning, namely, the fact that as soon as a
signifier becomes separated from a signified, as soon as I hear myself speak,
it is already the case that I can be tapped or taped, wiretapped or recorded,
intercepted and reproduced. The teletechnological machines of the past few
decades that bring the inside into our home reveal this millennial truth in a
most striking way.

And yet, even if not absolutely new, something rather different seems to
be happening today. As Derrida puts it: "What has always been so structured
today multiplies in absolutely unprecedented proportions and modalities both
the at-home and the at-home's accessibility" (*OH* 61/59; see *H* 1 96/134–35).
Derrida evokes this unprecedented and, it has to be said, somewhat uncanny
relation between the home and teletechnology at the beginning of the fifth
session of the seminar. He begins with this question because, as he says, he did
not quite say what he wanted to when the question arose during the previous
session. Here he is in an oral aside making even more explicit than he had before the relationship between teletechnology and hospitality in relationship to
the threshold and the *pas*, the step, and then linking it to the televised funeral
of François Mitterrand that we spoke of in Chapter 5:

What I failed to remark upon last time in the development on the
internet, fax, email, etc., etc., and especially what these technological,
tele-technological mutations affect when it comes to hospitality, what
I had failed to underscore, was precisely the *pas*. In the traditional
problematic of hospitality, to offer hospitality is to leave passage for a
step [*pas*], a step that crosses a threshold, the threshold, for instance,
between public and private, outside and inside, and what these new
technologies transform—in this century, at least, or since the end of
the last century and in an accelerated way today—is what in hospitality belongs to the step. Today, we enter into the inside, notably

the private space, without a step [*sans pas*]. What the telephone or television make enter into the inside of the space of the at-home, into a private space, for example, or a non-private space but one that is the space of an at-home—the nation, city, national territory, etc., etc.— well, that happens [*se passe*] without a step, without the time of a step, and without walking. Before then, until the end of the nineteenth century, hospitality presupposed that someone walked and crossed a threshold, a border—or even on horseback when an army invaded or when a guest passed over a border or a threshold—it was a walking step, the walk of a living being, that was the condition of hospitality. Today, hospitality no longer passes [*ne passe plus*] by way of the step [*pas*], neither by the time nor the movement of the step; from the moment that something like a telephone or television or fax is to be found in an at-home, what happens is that one welcomes—or does not welcome, one is invaded by an intruder, by the intrusion of what does not pass by way of the step [*ne passe pas par le pas*]. So, all of a sudden, in one's at-home, telephone, answering machine, television, there is a coffin, in your bedroom or your living room, the coffin of the head of state, and naturally that transforms profoundly the relationship of hospitality or non-hospitality between public and private space. (*H* 1 102–3n3/145–46n3)

In a word or a line or a lyric, "where have all the thresholds gone?" And what happens next, what is the next step for hospitality, when there are no more thresholds or—perhaps the same thing—when they are everywhere?

15

Phantasms of Fatherlands and Mother Tongues

These are questions that await us on the threshold. [*Voilà des questions qui nous attendent sur le seuil.*] (H 1 179/243)

In the sixth session of *Hospitality* 1, Derrida brings together a set of rather odd and seemingly incongruous terms and images to characterize language or, more particularly, what is called a "maternal language" or "mother tongue." Here is Derrida speaking in a session dated February 7, 1996:

> . . . this familiarity of the at-home in language, in my language called maternal or familial [*dans ma langue dite maternelle ou familiale*], this language as milieu of auto-affection, about which we have sometimes recalled here, comparing it to a mobile telephone, that it is often apprehended by emigrants, exiled, deported and displaced persons, by the stateless . . . as the soil that they carry with them on the soles of their shoes. (H 1 155/213)

So, the at-home, auto-affection—these might reasonably be understood in relation to a mother tongue—but then Derrida goes on to speak of the mobile phone, the stateless, and the soil on the soles of one's shoes? It is not easy to see how all these things fit together into anything like a coherent whole, much less a whole that might characterize a mother tongue, which Derrida thinks it necessary to explain in relation to hospitality. The aim of both this chapter and the next is to do little more than unfold and explain this compact set of terms and images in order to show how, for Derrida, the maternal language or mother tongue, while never simply pure, natural, or one's own, nevertheless lends itself to the *phantasm* of being one's own, and particularly by displaced persons, by the stateless, a phantasm of property and of life that brings the mother tongue together with the fatherland, the tongue in one's mouth together with the shoes on one's feet, Hannah Arendt together with Georges Danton, nature together with technology, airwaves together with the earth, and life together with death. That, as we will see, is the "twisted" nature of a mother tongue and of the phantasms that always seem to attend it.

Now, Derrida comes to question of a mother tongue in his seminar on hospitality in the course of evoking what he calls the two nostalgias or two longings of all exiled or displaced persons. The first is the longing to return to the place of one's buried ancestors, something we saw in *Oedipus at Colonus* and in Antigone's lament for a site to mourn her father. Derrida writes of all these displaced or exiled peoples:

> *On the one hand*, they would like to return, at least on a pilgrimage, to the places where their buried dead have their last resting place . . . the city or country where relatives, father, mother, grandparents are at rest in a rest that is the place of immobility from which to measure all the journeys and all the distancings. (*OH* 87/81; see *H 1* 105–6/149)

So, nostalgia for the resting place of one's ancestors, a desire to return to a sort of immovable center, an axis mundi, as it were, for all one's travels, a family tomb or sepulcher in the old country or in one's native land.

The second longing is a longing for language, a nostalgia for language, that is, for a particular language known as a "mother tongue." Like the first nostalgia, it is related to a certain inheritance, to some assumed origin or source, but, unlike the first, which can always be thwarted or frustrated by war or politics or any number of personal happenstances (like having Oedipus for a father), this second nostalgia is easily answered or satisfied, or so it seems, insofar as one always carries one's mother tongue around with one, even into exile. Derrida continues:

> *On the other hand*, exiles, the deported, the expelled, the rootless, the stateless, lawless nomads, absolute foreigners, often continue to recognize the language, what is called the mother tongue [*la langue dite maternelle*], as their ultimate homeland [*leur ultime patrie*], and even their last resting place [*leur dernière demeure*]. That was Hannah Arendt's response on one occasion: she no longer felt German except in language, as though the language were a *remains* of belonging. (*OH* 87–89/81–83; see *H 1* 106/149–50)

The second nostalgia shared by all exiled or displaced persons would thus be more easily answered or overcome, the return more easily made, since neither war nor politics typically takes us away from our mother tongue, which accompanies us wherever we go. Or at least that is the *phantasm*, as Derrida is preparing us to see, since, as he says, "things are more twisted" than this.

Derrida will have already put us on notice by speaking not exactly of "the mother tongue" but of "what is called the mother tongue," "the so-called mother language," *la langue dite maternelle*, thereby marking his wariness or skepticism with regard to this term, the distance he wishes to take from it, his unwillingness to take it for granted or to appropriate and use it in his own name. After having thus spoken of the maternal language or the mother tongue as what would seem to be a *"remains* of belonging"—as if the first nostalgia, returning to the place of the *remains* of one's ancestors, were here coming together with the second nostalgia—Derrida goes on to explain the reason for his skepticism:

> In fact . . . things are more twisted. If it seems to be both, and by that very fact, the first and the last condition of belonging, language is also the experience of expropriation, of an irreducible *exappropriation*. What is called the "mother" tongue is already "the other's language." (OH 89/83; see H 1 106/149–50)[1]

The maternal language, the "so-called" maternal language, as Derrida repeats, the seeming condition of all belonging, is in fact, Derrida seems to be suggesting, and despite all appearances, *already* an exappropriation, indeed an irreducible exappropriation. Though it is—or though it *appears* to be—what is *most* one's own, it comes always *from* the other and belongs always *to* the other. What appears to be most our own belongs already from the beginning to the other; what appears to be the condition of all our future relations of property and appropriation is itself *already* an exappropriation. As Derrida puts it elsewhere, *"une langue n'appartient pas,"* that is, a language does not belong, that is, it does not belong to anyone, it cannot be owned, it cannot be anyone's, even though everyone uses a language as if it were his or her own (see SQ 97–107). That is the paradox or the twisted nature of what is called the "mother" tongue.[2]

But things are even more twisted than this first twist would lead us to believe. Derrida will go on to compare the apparent belonging offered by the so-called mother tongue to a fatherland, *une patrie*, bringing that second nostalgia into even greater convergence with the first. The unique power of the so-called mother tongue seems to stem from the fact that those in exile carry it around with them *like a fatherland*, a fatherland right on the tip of their tongue, a fatherland from which one can never be exiled. For if one can be forever exiled from one's native land, from one's fatherland, made to wander to the ends of the earth, that land or fatherland called the mother tongue will nonetheless accompany one on all one's travels. Unlike the family sepulcher, which stays put, fixed, forever unmoving, the mother tongue would be the moving-unmoving condition of all belonging, a portable or mobile home, a *chez soi* that never leaves one no matter how far one wanders or is exiled from one's native land. Derrida continues:

> If we are saying here that language [*la langue*] is the native land [*la patrie*], namely, what exiles, foreigners, all the wandering Jews in the world, carry away on the soles of their shoes [*à la semelle de leurs chaussures*], it is not to evoke a monstrous body, an impossible body, a body whose mouth and tongue would drag the feet along, and even drag about under the feet. It is because this is about the *step*, once again, of progression, aggression, transgression, digression. What in fact does language name, the so-called mother tongue [*la langue dite maternelle*], the language you carry with you, the one that also carries us from birth to death? Doesn't it figure the home [*chez soi*] that never leaves us? (*OH* 89/83; see *H* 1 106/150)

The "mother tongue," the so-called mother tongue, would thus seem to combine, through its identification with that first nostalgia, at once nostalgia and its eclipse, distance and proximity, immobility and mobility, not-belonging and belonging, a fatherland and a maternal *chez soi*.

It is right at this point, right when it seems that things could not get more twisted, that Derrida introduces the even more twisted notion of a *phantasm*. Having already suggested that language *is* an irreducible exappropriation, Derrida will want to explain exactly why it nonetheless *appears* as what it is not, namely, as the condition of all belonging or appropriation:

> The proper or property, at least the *phantasm* [le phantasme] of property that, as close as could be to our bodies, and we always come back there, would give place to the most inalienable place, to a sort of mobile habitat, a garment or a tent? Wouldn't this mother tongue be a sort of second skin you wear on yourself, a mobile home? But also an immobile home since it moves about with us? (*OH* 89/83; see *H* 1 106/150)

The mother tongue would appear to be what is most one's own, closer to one's self than the garments one wears on one's back or the tent one carries around as one's home in the desert. Conflating nature and culture, it appears more like a second skin, absolutely inalienable, a "nature" that is inherited rather than a culture that must be learned, appropriated, adopted.

The phantasm of the mother tongue would seem to be the phantasm of a sort of inalienable, unmovable, even natural language, a language that one takes along with one as if it were a part of one's very body, a tongue on the tip of the tongue. Though the phenomenon of the maternal language is *also*, indeed though it is *primarily*, though it is *in truth*, an experience of exappropriation, we have the impression of it belonging to us insofar as it *seems* to be within us, or seems to *be* us, that which is to be found in our most intimate interiority. Indeed, the phantasm would seem to be first and foremost the phantasm of the proper or of propriety itself, the phantasm of selfhood itself and of all the relationships of belonging that come along with it. This is, therefore, not one phantasm among others but, it would seem, the very condition of every subsequent phantasm of belonging, the phantasm of *Selbstheit* itself, the phantasm of an autonomous, self-identical, powerful self, indeed, the phantasm of *ipseity*, which Derrida argues is even more original than *Selbstheit*.

The so-called mother tongue, the second nostalgia of all exiled or displaced people, would thus be a particularly powerful and tenacious phantasm. As Derrida says in *Of Hospitality*, in what appears to be an addition to the fifth session of the *Hospitality* seminar:

> What we are describing here, which is not the same as endorsing it, is the most unbreakable of phantasms [*le plus increvable des phantasmes*]. For that which doesn't leave me in this way, language, is also, *in reality, in necessity*, beyond the phantasm [*au-delà du phantasme*], that which never ceases to depart from me. Language only works *from* me. It is also what I part from, parry, and separate myself from. What is separated from me in parting from me. (*OH* 91/85; compare to *H* 1 106–7/150–51)

The twisted nature of the so-called mother tongue seems to stem precisely from the fact that it *appears* as what it is not, that is, as a *phantasm* of proximity and naturalness, of belonging, a phantasm that remains, no matter how hard we might try to overcome it, indestructible, undefeatable, indefatigable, undeflatable, an "unbreakable" phantasm that resists all our attempts to puncture or overcome it. Derrida will go on to suggest that even though I am always, in truth, *in* language, always *chez elle*, I nonetheless always have the impression—the unbreakable phantasm—of carrying this maternal language along with me, as if it were me, *chez moi*, the source of all my relations of belonging (see *H* 1 155/213).

But there is, here, one final twist, if not one last irony. This unbreakable phantasm of a mother tongue or a maternal language that I take with me wherever I go is, in some sense, a "natural" or even a "normal" phantasm. It is a phantasm that is as common as having a mother tongue, a phantasm that perpetually denies the undeniable truth that when it comes to having a language, and even a maternal language, we are always at home in the home of the other, always *chez soi chez l'autre* (see H 1 156–57/214–15). It is here that Derrida deploys yet another deconstructive strategy, namely, to show or to reveal by means of a certain pathology that this "normal" phantasm, this unbreakable phantasm, is itself a kind of pathology, in this case, a pathology that conceals the "truth" that we are always at home in the home of the other.

Derrida begins by recalling the pathology of some elderly people who no longer recognize their "chez soi," that is, who have a problem of orientation and are no longer familiar with the things around them. Derrida says he himself has experienced this with someone in his "entourage" (H 1 196–97/262–63). Thinking no doubt all along of this someone, Derrida reads the humorous portrait "The Absent-Minded" ("Le Distrait") by Jean de la Bruyère (1645–1696), the tale of a man who considers himself to be at home in the home of others, with all the humorous consequences that can result from such a situation. It is the inverse of the elderly person who no longer recognizes his or her own home, but it comes down to the same thing. In both cases, one no longer recognizes one's own home, no longer knows who is the host and who the guest (see H 1 190–95/256–61, 218/291).

This is, of course, a pathology, and Derrida does not want to minimize the harmful if not tragic effects of it. But insofar as we are always—whether in our language or our dwelling—at home in the home of others, the pathology demands to be read as a quasi-universal or transcendental condition (H 1 196–97/263). Indeed, Derrida suggests that this pathology, which one treats or tries to treat, is possible only against the backdrop of that transcendental pathology of being always *chez soi chez l'autre*, at home in the home of the other.[3] Derrida thus takes what is assumed to be a pathology, in this case the comic pathology—thinking one is at home when one is in the home of the other, as well as the related, more tragic pathology of not knowing at all where home is—and he asks whether we do not all share this pathology to some degree, whether we are not all, always, in one way or another, to one degree or another, at home in the home of another, despite all phantasms to the contrary. Hence Derrida takes the marginal example, the example in the margins, and he shows how the rule or the general condition must be understood in relation to that marginal example, how the pathological must be thought through a differential logic rather than in opposition to the normal.

What seems to be a mistake or a pathology turns out to be, for Derrida, the condition for all dwelling: Because we are all, in some sense, at home in the other's home, to mistake another's home for our own is simply the realization of this transcendental condition. When one invites someone hospitably into one's *chez soi*, one should thus not be completely surprised when that guest feels so at home that they treat you as their guest (see *H* 1 194–95/260–61). All this proves yet again, as Derrida argues, and in a very different context, that a letter can always *not* arrive at its destination, that "the letter itself can be distracted," that "the distracted thing [*le distrait*] is the missive that is diverted [*est distrait*] from its proper destination" (*H* 1 193/259).

So, notice, while the natural, normal phantasm is that we consider ourselves to be at home when we are at home, at home in our home, even though we are always at home in the home of the other, the pathology of Le Distrait leads him to believe that he is at home not in his own home but in the home of the other. The normal phantasm is thus a sort of imaginary fiction, while the pathological condition reveals an undeniable—and thus perpetually denied—truth: We are always at home, or perhaps better "at home," only in the home of the other. As the subtitle of Barbara Cassin's book *Nostalgia* puts it, and in the form of a question: "When are we ever at home [*chez soi*]?"[4] It is a question that could have been asked from the time of the *Odyssey*, when Odysseus had to prove, through memory, through signs inscribed in the olive tree around which his chamber and palace were built, that he is in fact in his own home. But it is also a question that should resonate with us every time we are sitting at home, in what we believe to be our home, and our cell phone rings or receives a text. For that too is perhaps a contemporary pathology that reveals to us the pathology of thinking we are at home when we are always in the home of another.

16

Phantasms of Mother Tongues and Mobile Phones

... and the *aporetic* crossroads, that is to say, a crossroads that is also like an infinite threshold, the place of a waiting or a *différance* both finite and infinite ... (*H* 1 33/56)

The phantasm of the mother tongue is the most unbreakable, seemingly natural and normal phantasm, a phantasm that requires an entire pathology in order to be exposed. But what is the exact source of this phantasm, the phantasm of a mother tongue as the phantasm of property and of selfhood? From where does the phantasm get its unique, unbreakable power, and why would it be attached especially to language? It is here that Derrida's rethinking of the phantasm of language in the context of hospitality returns to some of the claims he had been making for some three decades regarding speech and the phenomenon of hearing-oneself-speak, a unique form of auto-affection that leads to the phantasm of being the source or origin of one's own speech, the immobile zero-point of one's own speech or language.

Let me work backward, as it were, from a text that is more or less contemporaneous with the seminar on hospitality, *Monolingualism of the Other* (1996), to some of Derrida's earliest works on speech and language, *Of Grammatology* (1967) and *Voice and Phenomenon* (1967). In all these works, it is the unique nature of speech (as opposed, for example, to writing), the unique experience of hearing-oneself-speak, and no doubt first and foremost hearing-oneself-speak a "mother tongue," that lends itself to the impression, illusion, or, indeed, the phantasm of identity, property, and belonging, in a word, to the phantasm of *ipseity*.

In *Monolingualism of the Other*, Derrida speaks, just as we heard him speak in *Hospitality* 1, of language as an irreducible alienation, as coming always from the other, before going on to explain the relationship between this alienation and the phantasm to which it gives rise, the alienation and the phantasm that would seem to be a *reaction* to it:

> This structure of alienation without alienation, this inalienable alien-
> ation, is not only the origin of our responsibility, it also structures the
> peculiarity and property of language. It institutes the *phenomenon* of
> hearing-oneself-speak in order to mean-to-say [*vouloir dire*]. But here,
> we must say the *phenomenon* as *phantasm*. (MO 25/48)

Though it is, as Derrida says, a structure of alienation, of inalienable alien-ation, that leads to the phenomenon, to the phantasm, of hearing-oneself-speak, this phantasm suggests or leads us to believe in a *nonalienation* of the self from itself in language. It leads us to believe in a coincidence between the self that speaks and the self that hears-itself-speak in a *vouloir dire* or a meaning-to-say, the immediate apprehension of a self by itself in a meaning-to-say or an intentionality. Though the phantasm as *phenomenon*, that is, as an appearing to the self, always introduces iterability and, thus, *difference* into every self-relation, the phenomenon of the *phantasm* brings about the expul-sion, repression, or purification of this iterability or this difference, that is, in short, an erasure of the very phenomenality of the phenomenon, a purifica-tion of interiority of everything (distance, space, exteriority in general) that threatens to contaminate it.

Just a few pages later in *Monolingualism of the Other*, Derrida explicitly relates the phantasm to purity and, as a result, to deconstruction. In the midst of some rather compelling autobiographical pages in which Derrida avows that the only purity he ever loved and ever sought was the purity of the French language, he writes: "I have never ceased calling into question the motif of 'purity' in all its forms," and he then opens a parenthesis to add, "the first im-pulse of what is called 'deconstruction' carries it toward this 'critique' of the phantasm or the axiom of purity, or toward the analytical decomposition of a purification that would lead back to the indecomposable simplicity of the origin" (MO 46/78–79). Deconstruction would thus be, first and foremost, a deconstruction of the phantasm but also, and especially, a deconstruction of any *putatively pure origin*, any claim to absolute purity, any seemingly self-evident or axiomatic origin, any seemingly indivisible, inviolable center, and, when it comes to language, any supposedly intact interiority, beginning, per-haps, with any language—any mother tongue—that would present itself as natural or as naturally ours.

Monolingualism of the Other is very clear about why language must be understood as an originary alienation that nonetheless gives rise to a phantasm of property or belonging in a seemingly originary meaning-to-say, in an auto-affection that would seem to come before all exteriority and all alterity.[1] But it is in works such as *Of Grammatology* and *Voice and Phenomenon* that Derrida develops in greatest detail this critique of a supposedly pure auto-affection in a meaning-to-say and lays down all the premises for his later thinking about the phantasm and the mother tongue.

In *Of Grammatology*, the voice is already characterized as a pure auto-affection that is transparent to itself, able to efface—or at least that is the illusion—the exteriority and materiality of the signifier itself. Derrida argues:

> The voice *is heard* (understood)—that undoubtedly is what is called conscience—closest to the self as the absolute effacement of the signifier: pure auto-affection that necessarily has the form of time and which does not borrow from outside of itself, in the world or in "reality," any accessory signifier, any substance of expression foreign to its own spontaneity. (OG 20/33)

The fact that this effacement of the signifier or this experience of effacement is but an illusion or phantasm does little to weaken or dampen its effect. On the contrary, the effect—the affect—seems to come precisely from the fact that it *is* an illusion or phantasm. As Derrida goes on to argue: "This experience of the effacement of the signifier in the voice is not merely one illusion [*illusion*] among many—since it is the condition of the very idea of truth. . . . This illusion [*leurre*] is the history of truth and it cannot be dissipated so quickly" (OG 20/34). In other words, it is the illusion of such an effacement of the signifier, the phantasm of total transparency and spontaneity, that makes possible the very constitution of truth as ideality. "It is the unique experience of the signified producing itself spontaneously, from within the self, and nevertheless, as signified concept, in the element of ideality or universality. The unworldly character of this substance of expression is constitutive of this ideality" (OG 20/33–34). The stakes of the phantasm of auto-affection, and thus of the mother tongue, could obviously not be greater.

In *Voice and Phenomenon* from the very same year (1967), hearing-oneself-speak, pure auto-affection, is again presented by Derrida as nothing less than the temporal process of signification purified of all exteriority or spatiality. Though Derrida will go on to argue that this "pure interiority of speech or of the 'hearing-oneself-speak' is radically contradicted by 'time' itself" (VP 74/96), that repetition, space, exteriority, and the other are also essential to the constitution of time, the lure or *phantasm* of this pure auto-affection nonetheless remains. Moreover, it is the lure or phantasm of such an auto-affection that actually gives rise, through the reduction of all exteriority, to the constitution of universality itself.

> Insofar as it is pure auto-affection, the operation of hearing-oneself-speak seems to reduce even the internal surface of one's own body. . . . This is why hearing-oneself-speak [*s'entendre parler*] is lived as absolutely pure auto-affection, in a proximity to self which would be nothing other than the absolute reduction of space in general. It is this purity that makes it apt for universality. Requiring the intervention of no determinate surface in the world, *producing itself in the world as an auto-affection* that is pure, it is an absolutely available signifying substance. For the voice encounters no obstacle to its emission in the world precisely insofar as it produces itself *as pure auto-affection*. (*VP* 68/88–89)

This pure auto-affection, that is, this *putatively* pure auto-affection, purified of all exteriority and otherness, indeed, of all difference, would seem to be the spontaneous source of an immediate, living presence. As Derrida argues, again in *Voice and Phenomenon*: "This immediate presence is based on the fact that the phenomenological 'body' of the signifier seems to erase itself [*s'effacer*] in the very moment it is produced" (*VP* 66/86). In the end, what the erasure of the signifier seems to give access to is not only a living presence but the spontaneous origin of life itself:

> My words are "alive" because they seem not to leave me, seem not to fall outside of me, outside my breath, into a visible distance . . . in this way, the phenomenon of the voice, the phenomenological voice, is *given* [se *donne*]. (*VP* 65/85)

The voice is thus *given* in this way; it presents itself or gives itself in this way, gives itself as alive inasmuch as it seems not to leave or to fall outside the living speaker. It thus presents itself in a way that seems to efface its signifying body, that is, its dead, mechanical body, giving access to the thing itself, indeed, to *life itself.*[2]

The entire history of metaphysics, Derrida argues, is ultimately bound up with this project or projection of a voice that would seem to be coincident with itself, present to itself, able to speak without exteriority or alterity, without difference or deferral, that is, without *différance*, a voice that would thus be without death—though also, on Derrida's account, in Derrida's terms, without life.

> *The history of metaphysics is the absolute wanting-to-hear-itself*
> *speak. . . . A voice without différance, a voice without writing is at once*
> *absolutely alive and absolutely dead.* (VP 88/115)

The *experience* of the voice lends itself to just such an interpretation, even though, upon scrutiny, upon reflection and analysis, such an interpretation is inconsistent with a general theory of signification. For Derrida, the problem arises both from experience and from the *interpretation* of that experience, as the *seeming* priority of the voice is uncritically opposed to the secondariness and exteriority of writing, of difference, so as then to be adopted as the ideal of signification in general.

The first phantasm would therefore appear to be the phantasm of a self purely present to itself, a self able to hear and coincide with itself in the immediacy of a *vouloir dire*, through signs that are understood immediately and without delay, that is, through signs that go beyond the sign, signs that appear so natural that we treat them as a kind of second skin. If the experience of the voice gives us or presents us with the phantasm of pure self-presence, auto-affection, and auto-appropriation, analysis and scrutiny of the form of speech, the *reality*, so to speak, of the voice and of language in general demonstrates precisely the opposite, namely, a constant distancing of the self from itself and an ex-appropriation of the self by itself. Indeed, it demonstrates that the voice is never simply one's own but is from the outset taken up in structures of signification that lead it away from itself.[3]

But what we *seem* to experience in hearing-oneself-speak, what we *seem* to bear witness to in a voice that is as close as possible to the living breath, is nothing other than the self-production of *life itself*. As Derrida argued in *Voice and Phenomenon*:

> We must consider, *on the one hand*, that the element of signification—
> or the substance of expression—which seems best to preserve at once
> ideality and living presence in all of its forms, is living speech, the
> spirituality of the breath as *phōnē*. On the other hand, we must con-
> sider that phenomenology, the metaphysics of presence in the form of
> ideality, is also a philosophy of *life*. (VP 9/9)

It should already be pretty obvious how these early analyses of hearing-oneself-speak from the mid-to-late 1960s were still informing and animating Derrida's thinking about language some three decades later. All these references to life and to a so-called living presence bring us back to *Of Hospitality* and the seminar on which it is based, where we find once again that at the heart of the phantasm of a mother tongue there is not only the phantasm of selfhood and of self-belonging but, inevitably, a phantasm of life. Later in the seminar, Derrida returns to this theme of the phantasm, suggesting, almost parenthetically, that the phantasm of interiority, auto-affection, hearing-oneself speak in a closed circle of interiority, and so on needs to be thought in relation to the autonomy and automobility of *living beings*. Derrida says:

> The auto-mobile of this "language we carry with us" . . . is not separate from all the technological prostheses whose refinements and complications are in principle unlimited (the mobile phone is only a figure of this), or, on the other side, if we can put it like that, from the aforementioned auto-affection of which the consensus is that it belongs, as its particular possibility, to the auto-mobility of the living thing [*du vivant*] in general. Is there hospitality without at least the phantasm of this auto-nomy? of this auto-mobile auto-affection of which language's hearing-oneself-speak is the privileged figure? (*OH* 137/121; see *H 1* 120n40/166n1)

It thus appears that *life* itself is the phantasm, that self-movement, perhaps the autonomy and self-sufficiency of living beings, and particularly of the living voice, is what lends itself to phantasm. For even though my voice too always comes from outside me like the voice of another, *as* the voice of another, before being interiorized as what I take to be most fully my own, we cannot resist this most unbreakable, undeflatable phantasm of a voice *living* within me.[4]

Derrida's analysis of phenomenology as a philosophy of *life* would have thus been at the origin, it seems, of his rethinking some thirty years later of the mother tongue in relation to hospitality. While this sense of a mother tongue, this sense of a most intimate interiority, this sense of what is most one's own as the condition of all belonging, this sense of *life*, is, in the end, an *illusion* and so is in a certain sense "false," it cannot simply be dispelled by revealing or pointing out this illusion or this falsity. This is why it is the most persistent of phantasms, a phantasm of belonging or of self, of property or the proper, even more, a phantasm of self-production, spontaneity, and life.

But if Derrida's *Hospitality* seminar is perfectly consistent with these earlier works on the phantasms of a so-called living voice, it is not as if nothing had changed since those early works. In the fifth session of the seminar, for example, Derrida adds one further twist to his rethinking of the mother tongue and of life that he could not have included in the 1960s. Having characterized the mother tongue as what is supposedly most natural or inalienable, as what is most one's own, Derrida compares it to what was in the mid-1990s a relatively new but quickly expanding form of teletechnology, namely, the cell phone or, better, the *mobile phone*. The mother tongue would be like a mobile phone, like a second skin more or less permanently glued to one's ear, or, post-Derrida, attached at one's fingertips. It is an image, a comparison, that was obviously not available to Derrida in the 1960s, an image that Derrida could thus graft onto those earlier texts in order to supplement, augment, and inflect them, that is, in order to "animate" them anew. Here is Derrida again reaffirming the phantasm of hearing-oneself-speak and bringing that phantasm into conjunction with the mobile phone:

> We brought up [earlier] those new teletechnologies, the telephone, the television, the fax or e-mail, the Internet as well, all those machines that introduce ubiquitous disruption, and the rootlessness of place, the dis-location of the house, the infraction into the home. Well, speech, the mother tongue, isn't only the home that resists, the ipseity of the self set up as a force of resistance, as a counterforce against these dis-locations. Language resists all mobilities *because* it moves about with me. It is the least immovable thing, the most mobile of personal bodies, which remains the stable but portable condition of all mobilities: in order to use the fax or the "cellular" phone, I have to be carrying on me, with me, in me, as me, the most mobile of telephones, called a language, a mouth, and an ear, which make it possible to hear yourself-speaking. (*OH* 89–91/83–85; see *H* 1 106–7/150–51)

Passages such as these from the *Hospitality* seminar remind us that Derrida lived well into the age of mobile phones, the age of privately owned and operated and very widespread (though not yet absolutely ubiquitous) cell phones or mobile phones. He did not live to see a world full of texts, tweets, memes, and selfies, but he did live long enough to see where things were headed.

It is, however, a rather surprising comparison, this comparison of the mother tongue to a mobile phone, for it seems to bring what is most natural in language—or at least that is the phantasm—with the cutting edge of personal technology circa 1996: the cell phone or mobile phone, what is called in French *un portable*, or even, jumping ahead in time, for Derrida would have surely made much of the name—an "iPhone," a phone that I carry around with me as if it were me, as if it were the condition for me being and saying "me" or "I," the very condition of my *ipseity*. The cell phone or mobile telephone would nonetheless seem to oppose the mother tongue on almost every count, introducing otherness, absence, distance, exteriority, teletechnology, and so on into what would seem to come before and resist all these things as self-same, present, self-present, proximate, natural, and so on. The only remaining point of comparison or convergence would thus seem to be the *mobility* or, rather, the *unmoving mobility* of both, the fact that we are able to take the one and the other along with us wherever we go. It is on the basis of this shared immobile-mobility that Derrida will be able to compare this most seemingly originary and natural thing, a mother tongue, with this most advanced form of personal teletechnology, a mobile phone. Because I bring *my* voice and, with it or in it, my maternal language along with me wherever I go, my mother or maternal tongue would be the most mobile of mobile phones and, it has to be said, the cheapest and most reliable, with no roaming fees or batteries to be recharged, and if you get the family plan your children can share in the same phantasm at no extra charge.

In the fifth session of *Hospitality* 1, from January 1996, Derrida contrasts in a very striking way the deracinating, universalizing force of teletechnology with the (putatively) rooted and resistant yet absolutely mobile power of the voice or of speech, the power of a mother tongue, which is then itself compared to one of these very same teletechnologies, namely, the mobile phone, the mother tongue thereby becoming a sort of cell phone before the fact, a mobile phone *avant la lettre*. Whereas all these teletechnologies introduce distance, uprootedness, and disruption within the home, the speech of the so-called mother tongue resists—or, rather, *seems* to resist—all this disruption and dislocation, even if, in truth, the mother tongue is itself also the place of an inalienable alienation. Derrida writes:

> Hearing-yourself-speaking, this "auto-affection" [*la dite "auto-affection"*] of hearing-yourself-speaking-yourself, hearing-ourselves-speaking to each other, hearing-ourselves-speaking in the language or by word of mouth, that is the most mobile of mobiles, because the most immobile, the zero-point of all mobile telephones, the absolute ground of all displacements; and it is why we think we are carrying it away, as we say, with each step, on the soles of our shoes. But [and here is the reservation, the breaking, as it were, of the phantasm—a line added by Derrida to *Of Hospitality*] always while being separated from oneself like this, while never being quits with that which, leaving oneself, by the same step never stops quitting its place of origin. (*OH* 91–93/85; see *H* 1 106–7/151)

The voice, or the maternal language attached to it, is thus at once absolutely rooted and resistant and absolutely mobile and portable, a center or home that I carry along with me wherever I go. At once rooted and portable, resistant and mobile, the self-presence and auto-affection of the voice bear all the signs of what Derrida called from some of his very earliest texts right up through his last a *phantasm*. The maternal tongue is—or *appears* to be, *seems* to be, gives the *impression* of being, creates the *illusion* of being—the movable zero-point of our identity, a zero-point that we can carry along with us, that we can wear, as it were, like the soil on the soles of our shoes, that we thus transport with us wherever we go, with absolute ease, like the best and most advanced of mobile phones. It is an analogy that at once naturalizes technology (by comparing the mobile phone to a mother tongue) and technologizes what is natural (by comparing the mother tongue to a mobile phone), making the one and the other into something like a natural technology or an artificial nature.

Things could hardly be more twisted. In order to understand the power and novelty of today's teletechnologies, one must first, it seems, contrast them with the so-called mother tongue, so as then to compare, in a second moment, one of those same teletechnologies, the mobile phone, to a mother tongue, which can then be understood as a sort of mobile phone before the fact. One is then able, in a third moment, and precisely by means of this initial contrast and this secondary comparison, to introduce all those things associated with all tele-technologies, including the cell phone—difference, otherness, dislocation, irreducible alienation, and so on—into the living heart of a mother tongue.

As Derrida reads it, the mobile phone both lends itself to the *phantasm* of immediacy in hearing-oneself-speak and begins the undoing or the defla-tion of that ultimately undeflatable phantasm. The technological supplement would thus make apparent the fact that we are always in a relation to ourselves by way of the other, by way of what is outside us, by way of some kind of ex-pression or some *technology* that immediately and from the beginning takes us out of and away from ourselves, leaving, it seems, no prior interiority intact. It is thus the mobile phone that helps us understand or recognize the kinds of things Derrida argued in *Voice and Phenomenon* in his reading of Husserl. It shows us or helps reveal that all *supposed* auto-affection is *in fact* preceded by and is the effect of a hetero-affection, beginning with language, with speech, which is never simply one's own, but then including all the extensions or pros-theses of language or speech in the form of writing, audio recording, email, internet, and so on.

Derrida in *Of Hospitality* and in *Hospitality* 1 will spend a good deal of time thinking through the strange sort of mobility offered by the mobile phone and the sorts of phantasms to which it lends itself. It is on the basis of this distinc-tion between the phantasm of a mother tongue, or at least the nostalgia for the uniqueness of a mother tongue, the possibility of carrying one's mother tongue into exile, and, as it were, the puncturing or at least the questioning of this phantasm, along with the originary multiplicity of languages to which that questioning gives rise, that Derrida will contrast Arendt's views about language—and particularly the mother tongue—with Levinas's:

Whereas Arendt declares that nothing can replace the maternal language, and that one continues to speak it therefore as the familiar at-home, in some sense the soil [*le sol*] that one carries about on the soles of one's shoes [*à la semelle de ses chaussures*], Levinas, in contrast, who wrote and taught philosophy in the French language, spent almost his entire life in it although Russian, Lithuanian, German, Hebrew (sacred and modern) were his other languages (known, used, familiar). Levinas, then, made the gesture of eradicating, uprooting, of even removing the shoes of this adherence to the maternal tongue about which Arendt speaks, and not only of suggesting that everything ought to be able to be said in the language of Greek philosophy, as a foreign language in some sense, but also that for him French had become the "soil" (that's his word): the soil of the French language was for him the French soil, just as Arendt says of German, that it was in some sense the maternal soil that she carried to the United States, every maternal language being a soil. But Levinas speaks of it as a soil that was first foreign for him and that became, as language, the language as soil, the soil on which he chose to reside. (H 1 165–66/226)[5]

Derrida thus opposes Levinas to Arendt on several counts. Whereas the latter remains Heideggerian in her attachment to German and to her mother tongue, there is in the former an injunction to break with the madness of the mother.

The mother tongue, auto-affection, exile, the mobile phone: It should now be clear that all these belong to a single configuration, no matter how twisted it might first appear. But what about that odd phrase, which we have now heard Derrida repeat three times, of carrying language like the soil on the soles of one's shoes? While Derrida never identifies its provenance in the *Hospitality* seminar, it would seem to be a quasi-citation of the great French revolutionary figure Danton (Georges Jacques Danton, 1759–1794), who, when urged by a friend to leave France and go into exile during the Reign of Terror to avoid the guillotine at the hands of Robespierre, is said to have responded: "Est-ce qu'on emporte la patrie à la semelle de ses souliers?"[6] "Does one carry one's fatherland on the soles of one's shoes?" Danton was obviously suggesting that, no, one does not and cannot take one's fatherland away with one; one cannot take it abroad or carry it into exile. As a result, Danton seemed to be saying, it is necessary to stay where one is and fight for one's fatherland. As he went on to say: "It is better to be guillotined than to be one of the guillotiners"—a preference that he would, of course, die by the guillotine defending.

There would thus be no phantasm of carrying one's country, one's father-land, along with one into a foreign land. Exile or flight from the fatherland might leave one nostalgic for that fatherland, but it does not leave one with the sentiment or the impression of still having the fatherland with one in exile. But when it comes to a mother tongue, one *does* have the impression of carrying it along with us, not simply on the soles of our shoes but in our very interiority. We have the impression—thanks to its phantasm—of carrying that origin of property or propriety along with us wherever we go, a mother tongue as a fatherland, perhaps, that will always stay with us—or at least *can* stay with us (for mother tongues can also sometimes be forgotten)—wherever we go. Almost exactly two centuries after Danton, Derrida will suggest that, contrary to this phantasm, we do not carry our maternal language around with us any more than we carry our fatherland on the soles of our shoes, even if it *appears* that we do.

In an oral aside during the fifth session of the *Hospitality* seminar, Derrida repeats, rephrases, paraphrases, but with some interesting differences, many of the terms and images used in the passage with which we began to describe the mother tongue. He speaks of

> the mobile telephone, auto-affection, the tongue [*la langue*: also "language," as Ellen Burt translates it here: MN] that one carries about with one . . . the fact that the exiled, the expelled, the deported con-tinue to keep their tongue as their home, because the tongue, speech, is a system of auto-affection that, in principle, has no need for any *technē*, or so one thinks, no exterior auxiliary, or so one thinks, it is a pure circle of auto-affective hearing-oneself speak [*du s'entendre-parler auto-affectif*], a phantasm of absolute auto-affection. That is the tongue as at-home [*chez-soi*]. (*H* 1 120n40/166n11)

The phantasm of auto-affection, of hearing-oneself-speak, which Derrida in other texts, beginning with *Voice and Phenomenon*, had related to a pure *circle* of auto-affection, is here related, in the context of a seminar on hospitality, to the "at-home," the *chez-soi*, as if the interiority that results from this auto-affection, the phantasm of this putatively pure interiority, were not only that of a self but of home, a dwelling, a *chez soi*, a place of belonging, an interiority of the self that begins to expand beyond that relatively restricted circuit of hearing-oneself-speak. What was in *Voice and Phenomenon* the closed circuit or circle of mouth and ear, or mouth and tongue, in the auto-affective circle of hearing-oneself-speak is thus expanded in *Hospitality* 1 to envelop the en-tire body, a maternal tongue linking head to foot, the tongue to the soles of one's shoes, making one a living-breathing-walking-talking tongue, a mobile tongue whose circle can then be compared to a mobile home, a home and a homeland, a motherland and a fatherland, an ever-expanding circle that would seem to know no limits and would seem to be the source not only of all nostalgia but, for these too are the stakes of a mother tongue, all nationalism. Such is the power, the indefatigable, undefeatable, undeflatable, inflationary power of the phantasm.

17

On Cosmopolitanism and Cities of Refuge

. . . places from which one wishes the other welcome (but what is a "welcome"?) and grants a sort of right of asylum in authorizing the other to cross a threshold . . . (*H* 1 8/27–28)

In this chapter we turn to Derrida's "On Cosmopolitanism," a text that was first presented as one of the final prepared sessions of the first year of the *Hospitality* seminar of 1995–1996. This needs to be kept in mind as we read this text. Indeed, we need to remember throughout that the "original context" for "On Cosmopolitanism" was, in some sense, the *Hospitality* seminar that we have been examining, the seminar actually beginning, we recall, with a reading of Kant's *Perpetual Peace* and the cosmopolitical tradition that arises out of it.

"On Cosmopolitanism" was thus first presented, summarized in large part, talked through, during the session of March 20, 1996, and it was then read just a couple of days later for Derrida at a conference in Strasbourg that he was unable to attend on the question of cities of refuge, organized under the auspices of the International Parliament of Writers from March 21–22, 1996 (see *H* 1 245/325). I propose weaving together here just a few comments on what Derrida wrote for the Strasbourg conference, in other words, what would eventually be published in French as *Cosmopolites de tous les pays, encore un effort!* and in English as the first part of *Cosmopolitanism and Forgiveness*, with Derrida's own presentation and sometimes development of that text during the seminar.

Let us begin with the title, the French title, *Cosmopolites de tous les pays, encore un effort!*, which is a condensation or combination, as Derrida explains, of two texts. The first, of course, is the famous line from Marx's *Communist Manifesto*: "Proletarier aller Länder, vereinigt euch!," usually translated into English as "Workers of the world, unite!" and into French—and one can better hear Derrida's play in the French translation—as "Prolétaires de tous les pays [or de "tous pays"], unissez-vous!"[1] The second text Derrida is playing on is the Marquis de Sade's *Philosophy in the Bedroom*, whose subtitle is "Français, Encore un effort si vous voulez être Républicains": "Yet Another Effort, Frenchmen, If you would become Republicans." By playing on or off the titles of those two well-known manifestos, Derrida seems to be suggesting that his text too should be heard as a manifesto of sorts, as a programmatic or aspirational text, understood in the same spirit, perhaps, as what Derrida in *Specters of Marx* called "The New International."

Derrida is thus playing here, but in the most serious of ways. He wants at once to criticize and renew or radicalize the cosmopolitan tradition that begins in the West with the Stoics and then Paul in the New Testament and extends up through Kant, who, in *Perpetual Peace*, gives us what, as we saw, Derrida considers to be the most radical understanding or extension of cosmopolitanism. Derrida's text is about the origins of the figure of cosmopolitanism that he had been talking about and developing during the seminar. As he phrases his question or series of questions during the session of the seminar:

> Whence does this figure of cosmopolitanism arrive [*arrive*] to us? And what is happening [*arrive*] to it today? What is occurring today with cosmopolitanism, as also with the figure of the citizen of the world, which is what "cosmopolitical" means, as you know, always supposing that cosmopolitanism and this concept of citizen of the world have any future? One wonders whether there is still a legitimate place today for some determining, decisive distinction between these two forms of City (*polis*) that are the City [*Ville*] and the State [*État*]; *polis* is sometimes translated by city, sometimes by state, cosmopolitanism refers to the world city or state. (*H* 1 245–46/325–26; see *OCF* 3/11)

Derrida thus recalls here the origins of the word "cosmopolitanism" in order to link the questions of hospitality and asylum that he had been treating throughout the seminar to the specific question of the *city* that is central to the conference for which Derrida prepared his text. "Cosmo-politan," Derrida recalls, comes from the Greek *cosmos*, meaning "world" or "world order," and *polis*, meaning, of course, "city" or "state" or indeed, as it is often translated, "city-state." A *cosmopolite*, or cosmopolitan, is thus a world-citizen, someone who would treat the world as his or her city or consider him- or herself a citizen of every city in the world.

But the city is central to this text not just because of the etymological origins of the word "cosmopolitan." It is central because the text was written to
address a meeting or congress in Strasbourg on the subject of cities of refuge
or cities of asylum. It is thus a text written *about* cities that was to be presented
in a very particular and, for Derrida, a very *special* city, Strasbourg, a border
city, a French city right near the German border, a city that has had a complex and contested status because of its location between these two nation-
states and that had recently taken a leading role in rethinking the relationship
between the city, the nation-state, and the world by becoming the seat of the
International Parliament of Writers, the group that had organized the meeting and had solicited Derrida's participation. Derrida thus prepared this text
about hospitality and thus cosmopolitanism in the context of a conference
organized in Strasbourg, not one city among others, around a new project to
establish a series of "cities of refuge," "cities of asylum," or "sanctuary cities"
throughout the world.[2] It is a project that would have interested Derrida from
the start for a number of reasons.

First, Derrida would have been interested in the fact that the very designation "cities of refuge" or "sanctuary cities" was a reference to or a reinscription of older notions and traditions, beginning with the biblical tradition, as
Derrida would have been reminded by Levinas, and including an important medieval tradition. As such, this new project to found "cities of refuge"
would have looked like a sort of putting into practice of that notion of "paleon-
omy"—taking an old word and reinscribing it in a new context—that Derrida
speaks of in an interview in *Positions* (see *P* 71).

Second, Derrida had just a few months before followed rather closely in
his seminar someone seeking refuge in what was more or less explicitly called
a city of refuge, namely, Sophocles's Oedipus seeking refuge in Athens. As
we will see in a moment, there would even be certain affinities between the
tradition we see evoked in Sophocles and that analyzed by Levinas when he
looks at the biblical tradition of cities of refuge.

Third, the strategy here was not to reform international law as such, and
not even the nation-state as such, but the status of the city within the nation-
state within the international community, making the part different from, and
in some sense greater than, the whole. Derrida was always interested in this
logic, whether it was to be found in the logic of the enclave that he develops
during the *Hospitality* seminar or in the old Jewish joke he liked to tell of the
four Jewish tailors whose shops were next to one another in the same street of
a large city. The four shops had coexisted in a state of more or less perpetual
peace for generations, without any competition between them, until one day
everyone came to work to see that one of the four shops had put out a new sign

advertising itself as "The Best Tailor Shop in the City." The next day, a sign appeared outside the second of the four shops advertising itself as "The Best Tailor Shop in the Country." On the third day, everyone came to work to see that the third shop had put up a new sign that read "The Best Tailor Shop in the Whole World." On the fourth day, it was not just the other tailors but everyone from the neighborhood who came to see how the last tailor shop would respond to the escalating challenges posed by its competitors. When they arrived, they were greeted by a sign outside the fourth shop that read, simply, "The Best Tailor Shop on the Street." It is in this way that the smaller can be larger than the largest, a city, for example, larger or more important when it comes to asylum than the country or nation-state in which it is located.

It is for all these reasons, no doubt among others, that Derrida would have been especially predisposed to such a project to rethink the city and to reinscribe the old notion of "cities of refuge" within a new discourse and politics. Cities and *not* states, notice, even though it is not, as Derrida emphasizes in an interview at the time, a matter of outright rejecting the state. But it might be at the subnational level, beginning with the city, that such initiatives have the greatest chance of success, that is, of having an effect. Instead, then, of being simply "for" or "against" the state, one must invent new rules, new transactions, "accept complex and differential practices" ("NU" 127), invent authorities that go beyond the nation-state without, however, advocating for some "world-state" ("NU" 133). It is this notion of *invention* that makes the project to establish "cities of refuge" not only a political project but a philosophical one. As Derrida affirms in this same interview, "all political experimentation has a philosophical dimension"—yet another very good reason why Derrida would have been interested in such a project ("NU" 127).

But Derrida would have been particularly predisposed to this project, it might be thought, because it was associated with Strasbourg, a city in which Derrida had good friends, including Philippe Lacoue-Labarthe and Jean-Luc Nancy, and a city that Derrida came to love, as he bears witness to in the collection *For Strasbourg* and especially in its opening text, "Der Ort sagt . . . Strasbourg." And, of course, as I recalled earlier, Strasbourg was the site of the International Parliament of Writers, a group that would organize or lend assistance to the project concerning cities of refuge insofar as some of the leading and most celebrated figures in the parliament were themselves refugees or asylum seekers. The idea for a project to rethink cities of refuge was thus motivated, as Derrida reminds us, because of the violence against so many intellectuals, scholars, journalists, and writers in many countries, violence against so many who dared to speak out in public in their home countries, including, for Derrida, Algeria, which was then in the midst of a civil war (see *H* 1

248/328–29).[3] Derrida mentions Salman Rushdie, the most famous writer in the world living under a perpetual threat of assassination, at the same time as he recalls that most of the victims of such violence or threats are anonymous, living outside the public eye, and that this new project of cities of refuge must also aim to protect them (see *H* 1 248/328–29). Derrida will later recall in this regard Arendt's reminder of the eternal complaint of refuges, namely, being anonymous, anonymity being the essence of the refugee, "the authorities do not know who I am," and so on (*OCF* 15/39; see *H* 1 253/336).[4]

During the seminar, Derrida briefly explains the International Parliament of Writers in Strasbourg and why it was appropriate for the project to found "cities of refuge" to be carried out under its auspices. It is thus perhaps worth recalling here Derrida's narrative in *For Strasbourg* of the founding or the initial gathering of this International Parliament of Writers in Strasbourg and of the ingenious lengths the city went to protect the parliament's first president.

> After having participated in various *Carrefours des littératures*, overseen by Christian Salmon, Philippe, and Jean-Luc, always with the kind support of Catherine Trautmann, whom we will never thank enough for her help and advice, for the hospitality she so generously offered, first as Mayor and then as Minister of Culture, I experienced, along with others, these great moments when, in the spirit of these *Carrefours*, we all took part in founding the International Parliament of Writers, alongside "personalities," as they are called, who are well-known in the media, Pierre Bourdieu, Susan Sontag, Toni Morrison, Salman Rushdie, and so many others. This Parliament is today still very active, though under a new name, INCA, the *International Network of Cities of Asylum*. It continues to develop through publications and the designation of cities of asylum. I still take part in it in a more or less active way. But so as not to have to recount this long history, already more than a decade long, a complex, international history, let me take refuge once again in a local anecdote. It was on the occasion of the arrival in Strasbourg for the International Parliament of Writers of the person who was to be its first president, Salman Rushdie, that I witnessed one of the funniest and most astonishing things in the life of a large city. The fact is that, in Strasbourg, the city's security services are able to change the name of a street for a single night, so as to throw off, for example, potential assassins who might have tried to execute the *fatwa* pronounced by the Ayatollah Khomeni, the night when Salman Rushdie, surrounded by bodyguards, came to have dinner with us at a private residence in the city. I've forgotten the original

and permanent name of the street, I've forgotten its substitute name or its name for a night, but I recall the surprise of my Strasbourgeois friends before the simulacrum of a brand-new street sign whose name they did not recognize. The feared assassins could have thus known in what city, Strasbourg, in what bourg, they were pursuing their victim, but they had lost the trace of the evil and the *Strasse* of the crime they had premeditated. Strasbourg, I concluded, is a city that can change countries, Strasbourg is a city that can change the name of its streets for a night, but the place name(d) [*le lieu dit*] Strasbourg remains and dictates Strasbourg: "*Der Ort sagt . . .*" (FS 14)

Derrida begins "On Cosmopolitanism" by speaking about the possibility, the dream, of a "novel status for the city, and thus for the 'cities of refuge'" (*OCF* 3/12; see *H* 1 246/326). He suggests that we must dream of another politics of the city, even if this appears utopic (see *H* 1 250–51/332). This notion of a dream, a nonutopic dream, returns throughout the essay, Derrida speaking later of "new horizons of possibility previously undreamt of by international state law" (*OCF* 8/22). Or else: "We are dreaming of another concept, of another set of rights for the city, of another politics of the city" (*OCF* 8/22; see *H* 1 250/332). But Derrida also speaks of this initiative to develop cities of refuge as a "genuine innovation" in the "history of the right to asylum or the duty to hospitality" (*OCF* 4/12–13; see *H* 1 246/326). We saw earlier this emphasis on innovation or invention in *Of Hospitality* and in the seminar. Hospitality would have to be, as we saw, *neither* completely without rules or limits, like unconditional hospitality, *nor* completely bound by rules or limits, like conditional hospitality. Derrida thus speaks here of "autonomous 'cities of refuge,' each as independent from the other and from the state as possible, but, nevertheless, allied to each other according to forms of solidarity yet to be invented" (*OCF* 4/13; see *H* 1 246–47/326–27)—forms of solidarity that would perhaps take the form of those *intermediary schemata* that Derrida earlier in the seminar said need to be invented between conditional and unconditional hospitality. These cities would thus be independent, autonomous, but linked by various networks. The ways in which the city "belongs to the state" would therefore themselves have to be reformed, transformed, or reinvented (*OCF* 4/14; see *H* 1 246–46/327).

The initiative to form or to designate cities of refuge to address some of the problems of refugees had gained a certain momentum by the time of the conference in Strasbourg because, as Derrida says, "we have given up hope that the state might create a new image for the city" (*OCF* 6/17; see *H* 1 248/329). The notion of a city of refuge would thus be a response to a situation that states, nation-states, were unable or unwilling to respond to adequately at the time. If the nation-state was then, as it is today, one of the principal forms of sovereignty in the West (*OCF* 4/14; see *H* 1 246/326), there were many factors or entities that were threatening it at the end of the twentieth century, everything from terrorist organizations and multinational corporations to international organizations such as the UN, the WHO, or the ICC, as well as, as we saw in Chapter 14, all those rapidly expanding teletechnologies, newly emerging internet companies or social media platforms, so many delocalizations that threaten the power of nation-states. All these things were threatening—and still threaten today—the sovereignty of the nation-state, causing it either to reinvent itself or else to reaffirm itself in more reactionary ways, closing its borders, reasserting its national identity around territory, language, race, or religion. Indeed, it is easy to imagine Derrida linking the rise of various nationalisms throughout the world to the rise of these delocalizing powers, not just because these latter have proven to be effective vehicles for carrying nationalist ideologies but because these same nationalist ideologies are themselves, at least in part, reactions to the growing size and power of entities such as Twitter, with 330 million users today, approximately the population of the United States, TikTok, with 850 million users, and Facebook (aka Meta), with a staggering 2.7 billion users, about the size of China, with 1.4 billion people, and India, with 1.35 billion, combined. The question thus remained open at the time, and still remains open today, whether or to what extent a city could rise above the state, to say nothing of these other trans-state entities, so as to offer hospitality freely and without interference. The question remains open to what extent the city can be an "enclave," as it were, within the nation -state itself.

Derrida goes on to suggest that this new notion or reinscription of the old notion of "cities of refuge" requires them to propose, "simultaneously, beyond the old word, an original concept of hospitality, of the duty (*devoir*) of hospitality, and of the right (*droit*) to hospitality" (*OCF* 5/15; see *H* 1 246/326). What is required is, in the end, a "new charter of hospitality" (*OCF* 5/16; see *H* 1 247/328), one that, I think we can already predict on the basis of these words "duty" and "right," will use Kant, or will be inspired by Kant, but will also attempt to go beyond the kind of limited, conditional hospitality proposed by Kant in *Perpetual Peace*.

Such a project of cities of refuge is, Derrida goes on to say, not only important but *urgent*, because in the mid-1990s tens of thousands of people were knocking at Europe's door asking for asylum or asking for refugee status. This imperative is all the more urgent, he says, insofar as the right to asylum is respected less and less in France (see *H* 1 251–52/333). Derrida speaks here in 1996 of "the foreigner in general, the immigrant, the exiled, the deported, the stateless or the displaced person" (*OCF* 4/14; see *H* 1 247/327), categories of asylum or refugee seekers that, I think we can say, have not only not gone away or been diminished in the past quarter of a century but have only grown.

Derrida here evokes Hannah Arendt's *The Origins of Totalitarianism*, which identifies two moments or movements of upheaval in the recent history of the *Heimatlosen*, that is, in the modern history of stateless, homeless, deported, displaced persons. First, there has been, Arendt underscores, a progressive abolition of a right to asylum, which requires, of course, international charters (*OCF* 6–7/19–20; see *H* 1 249–50/330–31). Though this right, with its origins in the Bible and the Middle Ages, continued to exist, it was considered to be more and more an anachronism in international law. And, of course, this progressive abolition of such a right—an abolition in practice if not in theory—was happening at a time when massive numbers of people were seeking asylum. The second moment or movement, a result of the massive influx of refugees between the two wars, was the abandoning of "the classic recourse to repatriation *or* naturalization" (*OCF* 7–8/21–23; see *H* 1 250/331; my emphasis). Because of the huge numbers of people involved, and because many of these were stateless, host states could no longer resort to this older alternative. Derrida thus asks: "How can the right to asylum be redefined and developed without repatriation and without naturalization?" (*OCF* 7/21–22; see *H* 1 250/331). They must invent a new right of exile beyond that alternative of repatriation and naturalization. The city of refuge had done just that with a handful of writers and intellectuals, but this had so far been, says Derrida, little more than *symbolic*. Some other status or arrangement needs to be invented in order to make this effective on a larger scale.

International law is thus necessary, it seems, but "nowadays international law is limited by treaties between sovereign states" (*OCF* 8/23; see *H* 1 251/332), and those who are without a state are left out. Arendt had written that "a sphere that is above the nations does not exist" (*OCF* 8/24; see *H* 1 251/332). Today there is the United Nations, of course, but it is often ineffectual in trying to regulate the massive movements of people from one part of the globe to another. So the question is whether there is a new role for the *city* in this, one that would elevate the city above nation-states or at least *free it* from them so as to become a *ville franche*, that is, a free city or an open city, a city that would thus appeal to certain "statutes of immunity or exemption" and, "as in the case of the right to asylum, certain places (diplomatic or religious) to which one could retreat in order to escape from the threat of injustice" (*OCF* 9/25; see *H* 1 251/333).

But the challenges for a new notion of a "city of refuge" are enormous, especially since such a notion runs so contrary to current trends. Derrida recalls, in line with Arendt, that the right to political asylum is less and less respected both in France and in Europe, and he cites a recent story from *Le Monde* to this effect (*H* 1 224–25/299–300). Indeed, in France, as elsewhere, it is more and more the case that immigrants must offer something, particularly economically, to the country to which they wish to immigrate (*OCF* 9/26; see *H* 1 252/334). Derrida recalls times in French history when immigrants were accepted at greater rates because the country's birth rate was low and workers were needed to fuel the economy. As for properly political refugees seeking political asylum, this is less and less common. Though the distinction between political and economic immigration regulates the whole field of immigration today, says Derrida, that distinction is often absurd and hypocritical. While the political refugee is supposedly accepted on the basis of criteria that have nothing to do with the economic advantage offered by the refugee to the host country, there is always, Derrida argues, some economic implication, some cost or expense, and, therefore, some reason to accept or deny the application for asylum based on economic reasons (*H* 1 226–27/302–3). In the end, says Derrida, we need to distinguish between the immigrant and the refugee.

If France has thus been more open than other states to asylum, it has been less for "ethical" than for "economic" reasons (see *H* 1 252/334). Even though the Geneva Convention of 1951 gives status to political refugees, Derrida says that "we are still a long way from the idea of cosmopolitanism as defined in Kant's famous text on the right to (*droit de*) universal hospitality" (*OCF* 11/29; see *H* 1 252/334). Writing in agreement with Luc Legoux, the author of a thesis on "The Crisis of Political Asylum in France," Derrida affirms: "There is a still a considerable gap separating the great and generous principles of the right to asylum inherited from the Enlightenment thinkers and from the French Revolution and, on the other hand, the historical reality or the effective implementation of these principles" (*OCF* 11/30; see *H* 1 252/334).

We here see confirmed what we saw earlier in our reading of Derrida on Kant: On the one hand, Derrida is critical of Kant for restricting hospitality as he does, setting conditions for it, while, on the other, he can affirm that the kind of cosmopolitical hospitality Kant *does* promote is one we are still very far from living up to. Derrida says in an oral aside in the eighth session of the seminar:

Despite its failure, the French Revolution signified, gave a sign that progress was possible in the history of humanity, so when I say that this cosmopolitical right of universal hospitality was determined by Kant,

I meant that Kant had formalized the announcement of this universal right as a sign of possible progress in the history of humanity. (*H* 1 220n41/294n1)

Later in "On Cosmopolitanism," Derrida recalls this paradox or tension in the immigration policy that was being implemented just five or six years after the formation of the European Union: "At a time when we claim to be lifting internal borders, we proceed to bolt the external borders of the European Union tightly" (*OCF* 13/34–35; see *H* 1 65/98).[5] There are thus fewer restrictions on the one hand, on the inside, and greater restrictions on the other, on the outside.

Derrida speaks of the need to cultivate an ethics of hospitality even though, as he says, "Hospitality is culture itself and is not simply one ethic amongst others [*L'hospitalité, c'est la culture même et ce n'est pas une éthique parmi d'autres*]" (*OCF* 16/42; see *H* 1 36–37/61). He goes on to explain that insofar as ethics "has to do with the *ethos*," that is, with the notion of a residence, a home, a familiar place of dwelling, the manner in which we relate to ourselves and to others, to others as our own or as foreigners, "ethics is thoroughly coextensive with the experience of hospitality" (*OCF* 16–17/42). In other words, it is not as if there is ethics, a general field of ethics, and the question or the theme of hospitality is located somewhere within that general field. No, the question of hospitality is the question of ethics, and it is coextensive with culture itself, which in its most general sense involves the relation of the self to itself and to others. In an interview with *Le Monde* just after the appearance of *Of Hospitality*, Derrida states: "There is no culture or form of social connection without a principle of hospitality" ("PH" 66).

But Derrida now goes on to argue that we can—that we must—be able to determine or to lay out within this general field of hospitality as culture and as ethics a certain history of hospitality. Hospitality may well be the condition of the possibility of ethics or of culture in general, but there is also a history of hospitality in the restricted sense of the term that must be analyzed for what it might teach us about the project before them in Strasbourg. Derrida thus goes on to recall the biblical and medieval origins of this notion of a "city of refuge." In the case of the latter, it was the city, the medieval city itself, that could "determine the laws of hospitality," an important precedent for what was being attempted in Strasbourg (*OCF* 18/46; see *H* 1 255/338).

As for the biblical origins, cities of refuge were established to offer sanctuary or refuge from those seeking blood vengeance for some crime, usually a crime the sanctuary seeker committed but was not wholly responsible for

(*OCF* 17/44; see *H* 1 254–55/337).[6] Levinas in *Beyond the Verse: Talmudic Readings and Lectures* devotes an entire chapter to commenting on the Talmudic readings of a couple of lines from Deuteronomy where it is a question of establishing such cities. Here is that passage in the New International Version: "Then Moses set aside three cities east of the Jordan, to which anyone who had killed a person could flee if they had unintentionally killed a neighbor without malice aforethought. They could flee into one of these cities and save their life" (Deut. 4.41–42).[7] The idea was to set aside cities of refuge to protect those who have committed involuntary murder of some kind from the "avengers of blood." The example given is that of a woodsman chopping wood and having the head of his axe fly off and kill someone who happens to be nearby. The woodsman clearly did not intend to kill anyone, but his actions, perhaps his negligence, led to the death, and the "anger" (the "heat of the heart," the emotion, the *état d'âme*) of the relatives of the one killed has, as Levinas comments, a certain "right." It is in such cases that a person may go into exile and seek out a city of refuge, which offers both protection for the innocent and punishment for the "objectively" guilty. Levinas writes: "There must be cities of refuge, where these semi-guilty, where these semi-innocent, people, can stay sheltered from vengeance." Levinas speaks of the "humanism or humanitarianism of cities of refuge," and he wonders aloud about this tradition in relationship to our own cities.

Now, much of the Talmudic commentary, and Levinas's comments on it, revolve around the fact that when a master or teacher is exiled he must bring his entire school with him, since one cannot really "live" in exile without study of the Torah, which is itself, perhaps, a "city of refuge" (61). Here is Levinas near the end of his commentary:

> It is precisely in contrast to the cities of refuge that this claim of the Torah through which Jerusalem is defined can be understood. The city of refuge is the city of a civilization or of a humanity which protects subjective innocence and forgives objective guilt and all the denials that acts inflict on intentions. A political civilization, "better" than that of passions and so-called free desires, which, abandoned to the hazards of their eruptions, end up in a world where, according to the expression from Pirque Aboth [a text from the Jewish Rabbinical tradition], "men are ready to swallow each other alive." A civilization of the law, admittedly, but a political civilization whose justice is hypocritical and where, with an undeniable right, the avenger of blood prowls. (*BV* 51–52/69–70)

That is the penultimate paragraph of the chapter of *Beyond the Verse* on "Cities of Refuge." It sounds vaguely reminiscent of what Derrida calls conditional hospitality, the kind of hospitality determined by the law—better, to be sure, than nothing, better than a city or a tradition without such hospitality, but a *conditional* hospitality nonetheless. Here is the final paragraph of that chapter, which is vaguely reminiscent—though with several important caveats—of a sort of unconditional hospitality, though one that is identified here with a "new humanity" and the promise of Jerusalem.

> What is promised in Jerusalem, on the other hand, is a humanity of the Torah. It will have been able to surmount the deep contradictions of the cities of refuge: a new humanity that is better than a Temple. Our text, which began with the cities of refuge, reminds us or teaches us that the longing for Zion, that Zionism, is not one more nationalism or particularlism; nor is it a simple search for a place of refuge. It is the hope of a science of society, and of a society, which are wholly human. And this hope is to be found in Jerusalem, in the earthly Jerusalem, and not outside all places, in pious thoughts. (*BV* 52/70)

In addition to the biblical and medieval traditions of cities of refuge, Derrida also recalls the philosophical heritage of cosmopolitanism, the Stoic, Pauline, and then Kantian heritage. He cites Paul's Letter to the Ephesians, where the term *xenos*, which we have been following throughout this work, is itself transformed in a new world order where there are only fellow citizens, indeed only family members, in a new world city and family, "no longer foreigners [*xenoi*] nor metics [*paroikoi*], but fellow-citizens [*synpolitai*] with God's people, members of God's household [*oikeioi*]" (Eph. 2:19–20) (*OCF* 19/48–49; see *H* 1 257/340).

Derrida more or less ends *Cosmopolites de tous les pays* with an invocation of the *seuil*, of the threshold, the threshold of these cities where the idea of a new cosmopolitanism, or another cosmopolitanism, has not yet arrived. He writes—and then stages a little dialogue in response to what he has written:

> With this experience of cities of asylum, it is a matter of experimenting with new possibilities and new laws, forging new law and putting it to the test, putting the state to the test of this new law. On the threshold of these cities, of these renewed cities, which would be something other than "new cities," a certain idea of cosmopolitanism, *an other idea*, has perhaps not yet arrived.
>   – Yes—it has arrived . . . [*Si—elle est arrivée* . . .]

– . . . then it has perhaps not yet been recognized [. . . *alors, on ne l'a peut-être pas encore reconnue*]. (OCF 23/58; H 1 259/343)

Perhaps it has not yet arrived, or perhaps it has arrived without having been recognized, or recognized as arrived, having not yet attained, we might speculate, the threshold of a phenomenon. In either case, it seems that we remain on the threshold, and that to take a step in either direction is to miss what we have been waiting for without knowing it.

18

Beyond Anthropo-Hospitality: Plants, Animals, Gods, and Clones

> . . . a threshold determinable because self-identical and indivisible, one whose line is traced (the door of a house, a human house, family or house of god, temple or *hôtel-dieu*, hospice, hospital or hospitable hotel, border of a city or a country, or of a language, etc.) (*H 1* 8/27–28)

Very early on in the seminar, Derrida asks, just as he is introducing Kant's cosmopolitical project of hospitality in *Perpetual Peace*, whether one can give hospitality to or receive it from nonhumans—whether animals, plants, or gods (*H 1* 3/22). He poses this question because Kant would seem to leave out, to exclude, all kinds of other living beings from his cosmopolitical project, restricting the scope of that famous Third Definitive Article of a Perpetual Peace to the human alone, indeed, as we saw earlier, to citizens of nation-states. Derrida says during the session:

> Once, stupidly [*bêtement*], or let us say, massively, once hospitality is determined as a human thing, once it is forbidden to speak of hospitality with respect to God, the animal or plants, one can already say that there is something about hospitality that one is not yet thinking. (*H 1* 17n46/38n2)

Derrida elaborates upon this point several weeks later during a discussion session. He there suggests that while we must acknowledge the "great ambition" of Kant's "universal hospitality," the "it is necessary," the *il faut*, of Kant's ambition cannot be restricted simply to the human (*H 1* 133/183). That is, within or according to "the hyperbolic 'it is necessary' of unconditional hospitality, there must be no anthropological restriction, not even at the scale of the human race, in general," for if "every foreigner is human and is therefore entitled to hospitality . . . that excludes many beings and even living ones: gods, animals, plants, etc., and everything that, even in the human, is or can be characterized as divine, animal or vegetal" (*H* 1 133/183–84). Derrida continues:

> Already this idea of human hospitality is a very problematic idea because, just to remain with what is the most plausible—because I imagine that the idea of being hospitable to plants may surprise here or there, in certain cases, perhaps not in every case, but the idea of being hospitable to animals is less surprising—how am I going to justify the fact of welcoming into my house, my domesticity, my very home, even to the extent of feeding it, caring for it, offering it a sepulcher even, some domestic animal or another, rather than some other human? To have a cat, a dog, from birth to death, one that bears a name, that I bury, is that hospitality or not? Is that anthropomorphism or not? And then God, the gods? It is starting from the relations with the gods that hospitality opens up. (*H* 1 133/184)

With regard to this last example, Derrida recounts that the French historian of religions Charles Malamoud once told him that in Indian culture "every stranger one receives, to whom one grants hospitality, under certain conditions, is considered as a god, the guest is god" (*H* 1 133–34/184). Though the extension to gods may seem merely theoretical or rhetorical, or else pertinent only to cultures such as India or, as we saw in Chapter 6, ancient Greece, where hospitality was often offered to the stranger because he or she may have been a god in disguise, Derrida recalls the fact that in the France of his day conflicts would often arise when someone performed some religious ritual that broke with generally accepted norms, for example, sacrificing or slaughtering a sheep in a public housing complex. But, he says, "to welcome the other is to welcome the other also, if not as a god, at least as one bearing a god [*théophore*], so to speak, who carries something divine with him," which means that "it is difficult to think hospitality without religion, without hospitality to the divine" (*H* 1 134/185).

 Hence Derrida asks about this limitation of hospitality, indeed the "limits of cosmopolitanism," as he writes in the margins of his text, in Kant and others, and whether it makes sense to expand or extend hospitality beyond the human to animals, plants, or gods.[1] He thus expands our *thinking* of hospitality, asking about hospitality toward the nonhuman, and he then takes this thinking back to the France of the 1990s and actual problems of cohabitation and hospitality regarding newly arrived immigrants in France with different gods, religions, and practices with regard to animals. Just as Derrida in *The Animal That Therefore I Am* and *The Beast and the Sovereign*, among other texts, asked whether such things as dying, as opposed to perishing, or language or weeping or laughing or having technology, and so on, are the sole province of humans, as philosophers from Plato to Heidegger had assumed, so he asks here whether hospitality really can be restricted to the human, as Kant seems to have assumed.[2]

This extension of hospitality beyond the human to other living beings, assuming that the gods are living, is a recurring theme throughout the seminar. And it continues right up through the end of the second year. Early on in that year, that is, in November 1996, Derrida writes, more or less summarizing questions posed during the first year:

> You recall that at the beginning of the seminar last year and this year
> again, we wondered whether hospitality was proper to the human; in
> other words, whether there was any sense in offering hospitality to the
> non-human, to plants, to what is animal or divine. Does that have any
> meaning? An enormous question. (H 2 27/55)

That's more or less where the question—this enormous question—remains, pretty much unchanged from the first year, when all of a sudden it reemerges some months later, probably to everyone's surprise, including Derrida's, because of a discussion or a debate that was going on at the time around cloning. For it was on February 22, 1997, right in the middle of the second year of the seminar, that the birth of the first mammal ever to have been cloned was announced to the world at large. The animal in question was a sheep named Dolly (apparently after Dolly Parton), which had been cloned by researchers at the Roslin Institute in Scotland. Though Dolly had actually been born some months earlier, on July 5, 1996, her birth was publicly announced only on February 22 of the following year, igniting a media frenzy in France and elsewhere. The question of cloning thus arrives on the scene of the seminar soon thereafter, in the eighth session, of March 5, 1997, though Derrida does not treat the question in any detail before the ninth and tenth sessions (of March 12 and May 7). For that session of March 5, which was a wholly improvised session, transcribed by the editors of the volume from cassette recordings, Derrida had prepared just a half-page of typed notes, which concludes with "outline of the question: cloning and substitution [*esquisse de question: clonage et substitution*]" (H 2 179n3/249n11).

Cloning thus emerges as a theme in the seminar because of the worldwide interest and controversy surrounding the birth of Dolly, along with the prospect and fear that her birth would eventually be followed by the cloning of other kinds of mammals, including humans. It was thus only natural, absolutely to be expected, that Derrida, as a thinker of repetition or itera- tion and of the animal, would want to take up the question of cloning in his seminar, whatever the topic was for that year. But Derrida's note to himself for that eighth session — "outline of the question: cloning and substitution" — indicates that the reception of this question had been, unbeknownst to them all, well prepared by the seminar in the weeks leading up to this discussion. By this point in the seminar, Derrida will have read and quoted at great length both Levinas and Louis Massignon on the topic of substitution, and he will have questioned, not surprisingly, Levinas's assumption that substitution is a uniquely human affair, that the "thou shall not kill" pertains only to humans.

It is, therefore, in the context of a discussion of substitution, ethical substi- tution, that is, ethical as opposed to arithmetical or arithme*thical* (as Derrida calls and spells it) substitution, that the question of cloning comes to find a place in the seminar. Here is Derrida at the beginning of that improvised eighth session announcing the topics he would like to broach and his reasons for wanting to take up the question of cloning:

> I would like us to approach — and don't be surprised by this leap —
> the great question of substitution that we have already approached
> in Levinas and in Massignon, which is at the heart of this thinking
> of the hostage, the host as hostage, and, starting from substitution,
> to pose the problem of cloning, which is, as they say, in the news.
> I would like us to consider what is going on with substitution and
> cloning — it's a very complicated problem as you might imagine. In
> passing — I am coming to the end of my program, but I have not yet
> begun to speak — I would like to evoke, precisely on the subject of the
> pervertibility of hospitality, the polemic going on today on the subject
> of hospitality in our fine country and the accusation launched by the
> head of state against the supposed angelism of those who, today, call
> for civil disobedience of the Debré laws . . . (H 2 180/250–51).

One can see that Derrida is still very much focused on questions of hospitality, many from the previous year having to do with new restrictions on immigra- tion, the Debré laws here being the target of his criticism in much the same way that the Pasqua Laws and the proposed Toubon Law were the previous year. There is even that reference to civil disobedience that emerged several times during the first year. So it is perhaps not surprising that some eighteen pages later in the transcribed seminar Derrida has still not gotten to the ques- tion of cloning. He there says in a parenthetical remark:

No one can be a substitute in my place in the substitution for the other. (This is where I would like gradually to arrive at the question of cloning if we have the time. What is a clone? What is the import of all the rumors circulating recently on the subject of Dolly?) (*H 2* 194/269)

We will return later to this aspect of "rumors circulating" around Dolly, which will be tied to what Derrida will call a "fantasmatic" reaction to cloning in general. For the moment, let me simply note that Derrida has put Dolly on the program, on the agenda, though he is not going to address her or the question of cloning right away. Some nine pages later in this eighth session, Derrida finally returns to the question of cloning through a different though related question in Levinas, not the question of substitution this time, at least not explicitly, but the question raised by Levinas of what makes me me, what makes an ego an ego, that is, whether there is some substantial or unchanging core or *noyau* that makes the ego unique, this word *noyau* being used, interestingly, both in Levinas and in discourses of cloning. In *Otherwise Than Being*, for example, Levinas speaks of "an enucleation of the substantial core [*noyau*] of the ego that is formed in the same," this word enucleation also coming from the discourse of cloning. For what is cloning but the transfer of the nucleus (in French the *noyau*), that is, the nuclear core, from one cell to another that has had its nucleus or its nuclear core removed? It is thus Levinas, notice, who will have brought Derrida back to the question of cloning by speaking of an "enucleation of the substantial core [*noyau*] of the ego," a line that elicits this comment from Derrida:

Here each word obviously deserves a lengthy comment. Let me go back to this. "It is an enucleation of the substantial core [*noyau*] of the ego": the word "noyau" is going to occur twice. In the common tradition that Levinas is taking on, the ego is a *noyau*, a core or a nucleus, the "I" is a core, in other words, a place that is central, substantial, identical to itself, closed on itself, around which are arranged the envelope, flesh, accidents, attributes, etc. It is this core of the ego, of the "I", of identity, of the me equals me, of the same, it is this core that is enucleated, dispossessed of its nuclearity, as it were, a core from which the core of the core has been torn out. It is remarkable that today in the matter of cloning, it is precisely the enucleated core into which cells are introduced that are going to produce what is called a "clone." We will come back to this, I don't want to mix things up here for the moment. (*H 2* 200–1/278)

Four pages later, now near the end of the session, Derrida brings together in an even more explicit way this question of singularity and repetition raised by Levinas with the question of substitution. He says—and interrupts his own train of thought in order to recall what he had wanted to talk about but will not have time for:

> As soon as one thinks pure singularity, outside of concepts, one is in madness. Madness (we are not going to get to cloning, again) is already mad, but it is still more mad when unicity or absolute singularity, which is already madness because it is outside concepts, unthinkable as it were—pure singularity is unthinkable—it becomes madder than madness when this unicity is at the same time substitution, when it gets itself replaced in its very irreplaceability, that is, when one wants to think together the unique and the replaceable. (*H 2* 204/282–83)

That is all that is said about cloning in the eighth session, that of March 5, 1997. The following week, the ninth session, Derrida again raises the question of cloning, but from a seemingly very different and more elliptical direction. Indeed it could not have been altogether obvious how his comments on Levinas's *Humanism of the Other*, the French title of which is *Humanisme de l'autre homme*, suggest the topic of cloning. Derrida reads a passage from this work by Levinas and comments:

> I translate: Do we have in the two lineages of inheritance that are ours, that cross in us, the biblical and the Greek, is it that in these two lineages, one line, one filiation has simply inflected the other, imprinting it with a particular inclination or declension or *clinamen*, causing it simply to leave its path? One filiation that makes another one deviate? Or else monstrosity, teratology, these two filiations produced in us some monstrosity? I insist on this because we are later going to address the question of cloning [*Laughter*], which I set aside last time: "or are they united only teratologically?" It is indeed a matter of nuptials, of sexual union. Do Greek philosophy and the Bible form a monstrous couple? For Levinas, I believe it is neither the one nor the other. It is not monstrous because he loves them both. (*H 2* 215/297–98)

We will see in what follows that what makes Derrida think of cloning after this reference to monstrosity in Levinas is the fear, the fantasmatic fear, according to Derrida, that cloning will produce monsters, not unlike what we saw in Chapter 14 regarding the fear of what is called the xenograft, the fear that transplants from other species into humans will produce some kind of monstrosity. But he is not quite ready to take that step. Two pages later, he again mentions cloning, this time again, as we saw earlier, in relation to substitution:

> Obviously, since the hostage is in substitution, it is about this sub-
> stitution that he is speaking here. Once again, I am insisting on this
> because, with the question of cloning that awaits us, we are going to
> return to this paradox of substitution. (*H* 2 217/300)

Now, I have been following Derrida here not quite step by step but di-gression by digression, some might even say tease by tease, because it seems that Derrida is engaging in a rather elaborate negotiation of the threshold, approaching the question of cloning and then backing off, announcing it and then deferring it. For if the "question of cloning," as Derrida says, "awaits us," it is only because Derrida has in some sense *made* it await them, referring to it now multiple times but then putting it off, trying to find the right way or the right time to improvise some comments about it.

Some eighteen pages later, he is at it again, this time speaking of cloning in the same breath as improvisation—improvisation itself being, we might say, a break with the preestablished program, a break with what has been prepro-grammed, a break with merely imitative, repetitive, clone-like behavior, if you will, an attempt—not unlike what we saw with the poetics of hospitality—to respond in a unique way to a unique situation. Derrida says:

> We haven't got to cloning, once again. I was going to broach it, but we
> don't have time. We are going to return to it in the restricted seminar,
> but I would like to say a few words because we are not going to see
> one another for a while. In the momentum gained today, I wanted to
> connect to what we have said about the question of improvisation, de-
> viation and improvisation. To what extent does hospitality presuppose
> improvisation? It must not be calculated. If there is visitation, there
> is thus surprise and there is improvisation. One must improvise, but
> not too much. One must be ready to improvise. And so a question of
> the unforeseen, of providential hospitality, of the "à l'improviste," the
> visitor comes *à l'improviste*, off the cuff. Hospitality is messianic in this
> sense. (*H* 2 231–32/318)

Still improvising in this ninth session, Derrida both does and does not want, it seems, to take up the question of cloning. He needs more time, but because, as he says, they will not be seeing one another for a while—the next ses-sion of the seminar being scheduled for May 7, some seven weeks away—he seems inclined to want to broach the question nonetheless. What comes next,

however, is *not* that question of cloning but the question of the greeting in
hospitality, the "salut," the "hello" (in English in the seminar)—not "hello,
Dolly," as one might be thinking here, but simply "hello," "salut." Spurred
on by a comment that then comes from a seminar member about Mallarmé's
poem "Salut," Derrida recalls, just as he will in *Rogues* some five years later,
the two meanings of *salut*, that is, "health," on the one hand, and "hello" or
"goodbye," *adieu*, on the other, the one *salut* a noun and the other a performative greeting. This then leads him to say:

> Starting from this logic of repetition, of substitution, of the *adieu* in
> Levinas, I would have liked to open the question of cloning, of what
> is happening in the debate around cloning today in relation to repeti-
> tion, of series, and irreplaceability. What is a clone? Is it identical or
> different merely numerically? But here I can't. It's in this direction that
> I would have liked to go. We will come back to it. (*H* 2 232/319)

Derrida thus says that he will not go any further in this direction but will
return to it at some other time. But rather than dropping the subject, as he
seems to have said he would, he continues on for a bit, raising, first—talk
about enormous questions—the question of where life begins and then, just
after, the only slightly less enormous question of the human. "We will come
back to it," he says, and then he continues:

> To let be, to let be born, or to let die. And then two fundamental
> questions: where and when does the living being begin? And what
> does "to let live" mean, because the whole complexity of the network
> around "tenir" can be carried over to the network of "laisser, lassen,
> let, lâcher," etc.? (*H* 2 232/319)

All this is an improvised response to a question, a preface, it seems, to a future
discussion of cloning. But then all of a sudden that discussion begins in some
earnest as Derrida begins to address the question of the human. And let me
simply mention that it will be right at this point that that word I mentioned
earlier, "fantasmatic" (*fantasmatique*), will emerge. He continues:

> And then, second question: where does the human begin? Because
> what arouses fear in the ideological, phantasmatic discourses [*discours
> idéologiques, fantasmatiques*] on the subject of cloning today is that,
> okay, cloning, that's fine for corn or sheep, but definitely not for hu-
> mans. Why? "Thou shalt not kill," which is for Levinas the law of laws,
> does not concern living beings, it concerns the human, the fellow hu-
> man. One doesn't say "Thou shalt not kill" about living beings, about

animals, but about humans. So, the question is that of the human in
the logic of cloning. But here, we don't have the time to look into,
let us say, the scientific reality and then the metaphysico-ideological
discourses that are being developed on the subject of cloning and what
is happening to humanity in the form [*sous l'espèce*] of the clone. (*H 2*
232–33/319–20).

Derrida says he is interested—as he was, recall, with the question of the xenograft—in both the scientific reality of the phenomenon, in this case the
phenomenon of cloning, and in the discourses, popular or otherwise, *fan-*
tasmatique or otherwise, that have developed around it. What is at issue in
these latter, it seems, is precisely the question of replaceability, of repetition
or substitution, that he has been investigating in the seminar through the dual
or hybrid reading of Levinas and Massignon. Here is the end of the passage,
which I quote at some length:

But clearly a guiding thread for the question could be precisely that of
repetition, substitution. As if a clone, presuming that this is a rigorous
concept, were a repetition of the same. Because what causes anxiety in
all of these discourses is not only that the generation of the clone happens without sexual relation and thus without a father—and I would
have liked to compare the concept of paternity in Levinas to this story,
to this perspective of cloning without father—but also the idea that, as
it appears in the newspaper articles and political articles that I would
have liked to read with you, my clone is myself immortalized; I am
going to repeat myself indefinitely, and thus my clone is another me.
The question is, then, that of what the "me" is, what the irreplaceable
is. Assuming this is possible, otherwise than in a genetic fashion—
because people are always confusing the properly genetic question
and the question of history. Even two clones, two absolutely identical
individuals, with exactly the same genetic material, if they have a
history, just as with identical twins, become very different individuals.
And so the hypothesis is that two individuals with perfectly identical
genetic programs, engendered without insemination, without embry-
onic process, are the same and differ only arithmetically. The question this raises is that of whether what makes the self, subjectivity in
Levinas's sense, the substitutable and irreplaceable self, where there is
no difference in the determination of the self or the "me," are exactly
the same except there are two of them. The substitution that can be
made to operate between the two, in the logic of cloning, in the ideo-
logic of cloning, has nothing to do with the substitution that Levinas

speaks of, obviously. Because the substitution Levinas is talking about presumes that I take the other's place where I am absolutely irreplaceable. I am not in a series of clones. In other words, we are dealing with two replaceabilities, two hypotheses of replaceability that belong to absolutely different logics and ethics. Can one say that and up to what point? What are the presuppositions at work that allow one to distinguish between substitution in the sense of Massignon or Levinas and substitution in the serial logic of the hypothesis of cloning? I am not engaging here seriously in the scientific content of the thing, which would pose many problems. I am speaking of the discourse that is held on this subject today.

We don't have time really to develop these questions. I merely wanted to indicate the direction. (*H 2* 233/320–21).

Derrida is clear that he is speaking here not so much about the science behind cloning but about the discourses surrounding it, indeed the anxiety or the fear regarding it. Derrida's response to that fear seems to be to remind us that as long as two beings, even two genetically identical beings, "have a history," they will develop into very different, irreplaceable beings. What makes a thing irreplaceable, it seems, is "having a history," not being *in* history, exactly, but having a history, that is, it would seem, having a certain relationship to time, to the future. This will become crucial when Derrida in the next and final session of the seminar begins to distinguish, as we will see, two different kinds of irreplaceability.

This, then, will prove to have been Derrida's most complete treatment of the clone in the seminar, though he will return to it again, in a much more abbreviated form, in the following session. But before turning to that session, it will be worth our while to engage briefly in a terminological question, initially a simple spelling question that nonetheless has the potential to shed light on several of the questions at issue here (e.g., replaceability, life, fear, phantasm) all at once. I am referring to the term *fantasm* or *fantasmatic*, which Derrida systematically spells with an "f" in the seminar when it is a question of cloning, and its relation to *phantasm* or the *phantasmatic*, spelled with a "ph," a term or a notion that also appears in the second year of the seminar. Indeed, up until these pages from *Hospitality 2*, it might have seemed that the two terms were synonymous, indeed identical, interchangeable, clones of a sort, the use of one rather than the other more a matter of whim or fantasy/phantasy on Derrida's part rather than an attempt to say two different things. And that may indeed be the case elsewhere in Derrida's work, though it here seems that they begin to mean two very different things. At the very least, the two spellings seem to suggest that there are two very different valences or aspects of the phantasm/fantasm, two aspects that seem to oppose each other in the same logic, two aspects that must thus be understood together if we are to understand Derrida's rethinking of the clone, life and death, difference and repetition, and so on.

Let me begin by recalling very briefly what the phantasm (with a "ph") seems to have meant in Derrida before these passages on the fantasm (with an "f") of cloning. First, the phantasm always seems to involve the coincidence or the assumed coincidence of the self with itself, a self that would be indivisible and inviolable. That is why auto-affection as hearing-oneself-speak is often related to phantasm, as we saw in Chapter 16. This self-coincidence or self-identity, what Derrida calls in several later texts, including *Hospitality*, as we have seen, "ipseity," leads to the phantasm of a self-same self that can act, that has power, in a word, that is *sovereign*—a second characteristic of the phantasm. The phantasm is always a phantasm of power or sovereignty, and power or sovereignty—as opposed to force—is itself always a phantasm. Derrida will thus speak frequently of the *force* of an event, or the *force* of thinking or critique or of the unconditional university, but not of its *power*. Third, this phantasm of identity, of sovereignty, this phantasm of a sovereign power, often tends to present itself as natural or organic, as excluding the machine or the artifact, even if, as Derrida shows, it is always the *effect* of an artifact or machine. It thus always presents itself, a fourth characteristic, as pure or as a call to purity, particularly in a political context, a call to return to some original state by purging the body politic of all foreignness and artificiality. Fifth and finally, the phantasm, though always historically conditioned and linguistically coded, appears or presents itself as *ahistorical* and *nonlinguistic*, as having a nonconventional origin. It is thus in the nature of the phantasm not to appear as what it "is." It is in its nature as phantasmatic projection to appear natural or in nature even though it is not.

Now, the word *phantasm* is used a few times in the *Hospitality* seminar in ways that more or less conform to what has just been laid out. It seems to be a quasi-substitute, a loose synonym, for what is "dreamed" or "imagined" or "mythical," a "phantasmatic" justice in Kafka, for example, or a "phantasmatic" notion of original sin (*H* 2 141/199).[3] Elsewhere, it appears related to the spectral, as in the "spectral and phantasmatic" survival of the other in me in a process of forgiveness (*H* 2 174/242). But then in the eighth session there is a use of the term that coincides precisely with the political orientation of phantasm just outlined, though it should be noted that because this is a *transcribed* session the spelling of "phantasmatics" with a "ph" is a decision of the editors. Speaking of the various discourses around immigration and immigrants in France, Derrida asks:

> What is to be done with those who are already there? Every politics can exhaust itself throwing them out. There will always be some within, who got there before Le Pen, they were already there for a long time. That's the problem. It's to this trauma that the phantasmatics [*la phantasmatique*] of reappropriation desperately tries to react. Because, whatever one does, whatever policies one adopts, the other is already there and will always already be there. This is why there is an inexhaustible political problem, one that the politics of identification, of reappropriation, of ethnic cleansing, and so forth do not want to acknowledge. (*H* 2 199/276)

This is exactly the use of *phantasm* one finds in many other places in Derrida: a phantasmatic formation of self on the individual or societal level that comes as a reaction to an even more originary exappropriation.

Finally, there are two more uses of the term *phantasm* or *phantasmatic* that bring us back to that first sense, that is, to a phantasm of self or self-identity. They bring us back to that more common sense in Derrida, but with a nuance or a caveat that might change a great deal depending on how we understand and translate the word "*sens*." The first of the two times occurs in an oral aside (so that the spelling is again a matter of an editorial decision) as Derrida is explicating Levinas and a certain "as if," an "as if" that seems to lead to a phantasmic substitution for the other, that is, still, a somewhat unreal or fictive substitution for the other—not an identification with the other, of course, but a substitution of or for them. The phantasmatic is here still identified with the fictive or the unreal but, in the case of substitution, it is that which gives me a sense of being me. Derrida says in an oral aside:

> Thus, I bear the other's misfortune, I take it on myself through substitution *as if* I were guilty of it; not only do I suffer in your place, but I accuse myself of the suffering, your suffering by taking it on myself. I accuse myself: Levinas often plays on the accusative. To say "Here I am [*Me voici*]," I have to put myself in the accusative, be put in the accusative before any nominative. This "as if" bears all the force of this play. It is not a fiction and yet, and yet, the substitution plays out in what is also not an empirical reality. It is as if it were I who suffers from your suffering still more than you or as you, but this "as if" is both phantasmatic [*phantasmatique*] or unreal or fictive and yet it is the

most serious thing in the world because it is the condition for me to be me. (*H* 2 133n17/189n1)

Though the word "phantasmatic/*phantasmatique*" (with a "ph" and not an "f") is, again, a transcription choice on the part of the editors, everything we have seen thus far regarding the "phantasmatic" confirms this choice. The phantasmatic is, once again, linked to the unreal or the fictive, to a kind of imagined "as if," to putting myself in the place of the other, though it is also that which leads to me being me, to me having a sense of being me. This then leads, just two pages later, to one of the most interesting yet enigmatic uses of this term "phantasmatic." This time it is Derrida's own spelling. Very much in conformity with his use of the term elsewhere, Derrida suggests that it is through feeling responsible for the death of the other that I come to have a phantasmatic sense of myself, or at least a sense of those who are "mine" or "ours." In other words, I come to have a sense, a phantasmatic sense, of those who are close to me, who belong to me, through this notion of an originary responsibility for the other. The passage then ends with a reference not to the origin of the world, or to "the chaos at the origin of the world,"[4] which one could have imagined Derrida saying here, but to an origin of "*sens*," which has to mean, as Peggy Kamuf has translated it, "meaning," though the word "*sens*" seems to open the door to the question of the relationship between the human and sensing or sentient beings more generally.

> When I feel responsible for a death it is because I interpret it as a murder. There is always, at least, some failure to aid a person in danger in the phantasm that relates us to the death of those near to us [*des nôtres*]. I say "those near to us" not because I know and can determine first of all what that means (loved ones, family, compatriots, etc.). No, just the reverse: my nearest, our nearest, are those who never die a natural death since I accuse myself of having killed them or let them die. Those near to me are the victims of murder, those who do not die a natural death, since actively or passively, I feel [*je me sens*] I've had a hand in it. This is also what is called "love." This is how I would define those near to me, those I am attached to: those who always die by my fault, those from whom I ask forgiveness for their death which is my fault. Such is at least the ineluctable empire of the phantasm [*phantasme*] at the origin of meaning [*sens*]. (*H* 2 134–35/191)

But one might want to ask: Why "*sens*"? Is it because I begin to "define" or to identify those whom I "love" or those to whom I am attached from within this phantasm of meaning, this phantasm of self and other, of what is mine and what is other? No doubt, but note that right where Derrida says "I feel"—*je me sens*—he breaks away from his text in order to say "It is an absolutely implacable and necessary phantasm [*phantasme*]" (H 2 134n23/191n1) (the transcription "phantasm/*phantasme*" in this oral aside being here more or less determined by the context provided by the written text). Hence, this self-feeling, this feeling of responsibility for the death of the other, and thus the constitution of those who are "mine" or "ours," is necessary—even though it is a phantasm. It is a phantasm we cannot do without. It is a feeling or self-feeling that seems to be at the origin of me being me—a phantasm of self that seems to be born of the feeling that I have had a hand in the death of those close to me, those "close to me" being defined, it seems, by this feeling of having had a hand in their deaths. The origin of meaning, perhaps the origin of the world, would thus come not with my birth but with the death of the other, which would then be, each time unique, the end of the world and/or the beginning of sense.

But let me now turn to Derrida's use of *fantasme* (with an "f") in the seminar, which, as I have suggested, appears to mean something quite different than *phantasme* (with a "ph"), almost as if it were its corollary or other side. Instead of the phantasmatic projection of an identity that protects one from an originary trauma or dispossession, an originary ex-appropriation, "fantasmatic" would seem to designate something like the *fear* associated with that dispossession, a fear of the lack of purity, organicity, a secure and meaningful origin, and so on. Whereas the *phantasme* is thus something one desires or desires to identify with, a desire formed in reaction to a fear—a desire for purity, for a pure origin, for a nation-state founded in natural law or by God, the desire, in short, for some self-identical, organic whole that would be untouched by the machine, etc.—the *fantasme* or the fantasmatic characterizes the fear itself.[5] It may be that, in the case of cloning, this fear is a response to one of these phantasms, a response to an imagined or fantasized threat against the phantasm of some purely organic or truly living being, but it is clearly not the same thing as that desired phantasm. It is in many ways the inverse of it, as Derrida's discussion of the clone would seem to suggest.

The first conjunction of these two terms—"cloning" and *fantasme*—occurs, as we saw, in the ninth session, though everything seems to come to a head right at the end of the tenth session, when, after deferring and then treating, or treating while deferring, the discussion of clones, Derrida takes it up again, though again rather briefly. It comes in the context of the discussion of substitution:

What can that mean, an autosubstitution? Can one, must one substitute oneself for oneself? What then does "oneself" mean in that
case? Obviously, just as the "race" in question, as place of substitution,
defines a space of inheritance, as space of the same, so simple reproduction by autosubstitution of the identical (the phantasm [*fantasme*]
of cloning) prohibits the inheritance that it seems on the other hand
to make possible, interrupts the parental filiation that seemed to be
announced with the substitution. (*H* 2 238–39/329)

And these words lead to an oral comment:

That's what is frightening about cloning, in the phantasm [*fantasme?*
MN] of cloning, this perfect filiation: X engenders X that engenders
X that engenders X. But obviously there is no longer either a father or
mother, so there is no longer filiation. Thus, it provokes dreams and
fear, assuming that there might be something that ever corresponds to
this phantasm [*fantasme?* MN]. (*H* 2 239n10/329n1)

But why, we might ask, does Derrida resort to this language of *fantasme*? Is
it not enough to say that the fear is the result of some "misunderstanding" or
"misinterpretation" of what a clone actually is? It seems not, and I would suggest that this is because this *fantasme* or this aspect of the *fantasme* is very different from the notion of *phantasme* we saw earlier, even if it remains closely
tied to it.[6] Whereas the *phantasme* usually tries to elide history, to present
what is historical as ahistorical, the *fantasme*, or the fantasmatic fear related
to cloning, is that the clone will bring about this very elision of history or of
historicity, or at least of identifiable origins, a mother and a father, and so on.
So while the *phantasme* desires this elision of origins or is in fact the desire
for such an elision, the *fantasme* fears it or is itself nothing other than the fear
of a living being without any history.

What links the two notions, despite all the differences between them, thus
seems to be the securing of some kind of *natural* origin in the name of *life*.
In the case of *phantasme*, an attempt is made to elide human institutions,
language, and so on in order to secure an origin in nature or in God, in what
is thought to be a more natural, living origin. In the case of the *fantasme*, there
is the fear of an elision of a supposedly natural origin, mother, father, etc. and
the substitution of an endless technological process for a natural one. Note
that Derrida speaks just a few pages later of passivity in substitution as being
anything but "a mechanical reproduction" or "the bio-technical reproducibil-
ity of phantasmatic cloning [*clonage fantasmatique*]" (*H* 2 244/336).

Derrida himself would no doubt answer this fear, this fear of those who oppose cloning, not, of course, by claiming that the clone really has a mother or father or some other filiation of a natural order. He would not answer the fantasmatic fears of cloning by restituting or restoring a phantasm of the natural. He would instead argue that no clone is identical to another because it remains in history, because it *has* a history, with all the difference and chance that such a history or historicity brings to a living being. The *fantasme* is thus related to the fear caused by a threat or a perceived threat to the *phantasme*, the threat to some natural rather than artificial or technical origin (a mother, a father, the so-called nuclear family, etc.), the threat to a natural origin that, while in time or in history, would *seem* to escape the historicity of human institutions. For that is the very nature of the *phantasme*.

This reference to the human, to institutions, is perhaps crucial, because it points to a supposed unicity of the human, of the human as opposed to the machine, on the one hand, and the animal, on the other, a uniquely human filiation that cloning would threaten. That seems to be what Derrida means by "ideological"—a *fantasme idéologique*—in another passage from the tenth session:

> Substitution is not the indifferent replacement of an equal thing by another equal or identical thing, the way, for example, one can imagine (an ideological phantasm [*fantasme idéologique*]) that a clone can replace the individual from which it comes or another identical clone, the difference being nil between the two individuals, except numerically, the difference between them being only that of number, *solo numero*, as one says. (H 2 244/336)

It is, admittedly, rather difficult to understand what Derrida means by "ideological" from this passage alone, but it becomes clearer when set alongside a passage from the preceding session that we cited earlier: "And then, second question: where does the human begin? Because what arouses fear in the ideological, phantasmatic discourses [*les discours idéologiques, fantasmatiques*] on the subject of cloning today is that, okay, cloning, that's fine for corn or sheep, but definitely not for humans" (H 2 232/319). What Derrida seems to be suggesting here is that this *fantasme* regarding the clone is related to a fear of the erasure of putatively natural origins, as well as a fear of the erasure of that supposedly indelible metaphysical line between the human and the animal. It is an ideological fear, a fantasmatic fear related to an effacement of origins and an erasure of lines, of borders, an erasure of those very identity formations that the *phantasme* was there to support or to maintain.

Finally, in one last use of the term, Derrida relates the fantasmatic substitution of cloning to what Levinas calls the third, that is, to the whole regime of equivalence and symmetry that substitutes itself for the substitution of irreplaceables in the face to face. Derrida says in an oral aside:

> You see that the third and justice introduce here another type of substitution that is going to substitute itself for the first, that is going to combine with the first, that is going to correct the first. Now one has to say one substitution for another, with symmetry, calculation, equivalence, and thus already a certain logic of cloning, what is phantasmatically interpreted as cloning [ce qu'on interprète fantasmatiquement comme le clonage]. (H 2 257/352–53)

It seems that both aspects of the "phantasm," both *phantasme* and *fantasme*, are, for Derrida, if not necessary at least ineluctable, the phantasm of a self, of a self-identical self, and the fantasmatic fear that this unique, human, self-identical, organic, and natural self is, in the end, comparable in some sense to others, equivalent to others, and that it can be measured against others by institutions that are not at all natural, that are historically determined, and so on. What is at issue here is perhaps two different notions of substitution related to two different aspects of the *phantasme/fantasme*.

This leads us, finally, to the tenth session of the seminar, the final one of the two-year seminar on hospitality. We are just a couple of pages from the end of the seminar—at least as it appears in its published version, since there were a couple more weeks of student presentations, no doubt preceded and followed by remarks from Derrida. This is, in any case, the last of Derrida's fully prepared sessions. Having returned, via Levinas and Massignon, to the question of substitution and to the apparent difference between two kinds of substitution, that is, an "ethical" substitution of irreplaceables and an "arithmet*h*ical" substitution of equivalents, a substitution of heteronomy and a substitution of equivalence, Derrida goes on to question this opposition, suggesting that *no* two things, *whatever* they are, are ever the same. He writes:

> It would be necessary now to take a further step by displacing in a certain manner an axiomatic assurance on the basis of which we opposed an ethical substitution as it were to arithmet*h*ic substitution. The criterion of exceptionality, of irreplaceable singularity, of uniqueness seems to me insufficient for this.
>
> Basically, in every substitution, whatever its terms may be, the units or identities, the conceptual equivalence of the contents, the homogeneity of the seriality, in every substitution there are singularity and exceptionality of the substituted units. Even if I replace a grain of sand

by a grain of sand, one hour by another, one hand by another (to take
up again the Kantian example of dissymmetry . . .). Each unity, each
identity, each singularity is irreplaceable in its factual existence, and
is even elected in a certain way, even if this election is by chance or
unconscious. (*H* 2 257/353)

This might seem to be a real departure for Derrida, not only in the *Hospitality* seminar but in his work more generally, an extension of irreplaceability
to all things, inanimate as well as animate. While there are places in Derrida's
work that could be read as tending in this direction, Derrida very consistently
restricts a certain irreplaceability—death as the end of the world, the other as
an origin of the world—to animate things. Even if, in texts such as *Aporias*,
Derrida will speak of a hospitality to the event, this does not mean that he is
extending hospitality, irreplaceability, and so on to inanimate beings.[7] There
may be a certain hospitality to the event, which can be at once a "who" or a
"what," but this does not seem to mean that hospitality is or can be granted
to inanimate things, as Derrida in this singular passage would *seem* to be
suggesting.

In this one passage, near the very end of the second year of the *Hospitality*
seminar, we are forced, it seems, to rethink not only the relation between
the human and the animal but that between the living and nonliving. That
is what *seems* to be suggested by that comment questioning the difference
between the ethical irreplaceability of living beings and the supposedly arithmetical replaceability of nonliving ones. But after having thereby erased
one line, or resituated one threshold, Derrida goes on almost immediately
thereafter to redraw or reestablish another, this time within the more general
field of an irreplaceability that covers both animate and inanimate things. He
goes on to distinguish one kind of irreplaceability from another, speaking of
an irreplaceable being that *se sent*, that is, "senses itself" or "feels itself." Writing in the context of the discussion of cloning that took place in the seminar
several weeks before, and perhaps also already thinking about—and perhaps
even already writing—his essay on the animal that he would deliver in just
a couple of months, in July 1997, at the Cerisy-la-Salle conference that went
under the title "The Autobiographical Animal," Derrida begins:

> It is not, then, the criterion of irreplaceability, of singularity, of unique-
> ness (*solo numero*) that distinguishes "ethical" substitution, let us call
> it that to go quickly, from simple arithmetic substitution. One must
> take into account, so to speak, along with these values of compassion,
> expiation, and sacrifice, another set of factors. And with these other

factors, we are immediately going to find ourselves again at the heart of the question of hospitality, of hostipitality.

This is because it is not enough that the subject of the substitution (the term, the X subject to substitution) be unique, irreplaceable, elected for it to come or to offer itself in place of the other, irreplaceable so as to be replaced; it's also necessary that this irreplaceable feel *itself* to be irreplaceable, that it feel [*sente*] and feel itself [*se sente*], and thus that it be a self having a relation to itself, which is not the case of every being that is unique and irreplaceable in its existence. This self, this ipseity, is the condition of ethical substitution as compassion, sacrifice, expiation, etc. (*H* 2 257–58/353–54)[8]

And Derrida continues:

The question is then, once again: what is a self, an ipseity? If auto-affection, auto-mobility, the fact of being able to move oneself [*se mouvoir*], stir oneself [*s'émouvoir*], and affect oneself is its condition and in truth its definition, it is the proper trait of what can be called the living in general, and not only the human, but also the animal, of compassion with the animal. The question then to which we return is that of "ipseity," with the whole charge that we have recognized in this word where ipseity is also the master, the host, etc. We have already identified the question of ipseity as the question of hospitality from the start. (*H* 2 258/354)[9]

The difference Derrida is trying to define here is thus not between irreplaceable living things and replaceable nonliving ones. Since all things, whatever the terms, are irreplaceable, irreplaceable, we might speculate, because of their unique taking-place, their bodily difference from other bodies, and so on, the difference Derrida is trying to define is between the irreplaceability of things that do not "feel" or "sense themselves" and those that do. Such emphasis on "feeling oneself," "sensing oneself," or "affecting oneself" can be read as an expansion of the category of auto-affection in *Of Grammatology*, *Voice and Phenomenon*, and elsewhere, an auto-affection that, as we saw in Chapter 16, is most evident in hearing-oneself-speak, in the *s'entendre parler*, an auto-affection that Derrida typically relates to the generation of the phantasm of self, the phantasm of a self that is self-identical, and so on. But here, instead of *s'entendre parler*, we have *se sentir*, as if Derrida wanted to enlarge the basis for thinking this kind of irreplaceability to include other sentient beings, but without going so far as to attribute *this kind* of irreplaceability or uniqueness to every*thing*, that is, to every rock, grain of sand, or inanimate being, even if these too are, as Derrida says, in a certain sense "elected." It is this irreplaceability, and this one alone, that is to be identified with "the values of compassion, expiation, and sacrifice." It is, it seems, this capacity for being "moved" (*se mouvoir, s'émouvoir*), that is, for moving oneself and being moved by others, bestirring oneself and being bestirred by others, that is or that leads to compassion, expiation, sacrifice, and, thus, ethical irreplaceability in substitution.

Every human and, perhaps, every sheep—every animal that feels or senses itself—would thus be irreplaceable, not just arithmetically but ethically, and so is capable of that strange kind of substitution of irreplaceables of which Levinas speaks. But then what about every stalk of corn? I use the examples of sheep and corn because those are, as we saw earlier, Derrida's examples in the ninth session, examples inspired, clearly, by the question of "cloning" that had emerged in the seminar just a couple of weeks before. Humans, sheep, and corn: These are three examples of living beings that were commonly talked about at the time in terms of cloning or genetic modification. While the human would be both living and subject to auto-affection and sensing itself, the sheep, arguably, would be living and able to sense itself but not able to hear-itself-speak in the form of a *vouloir-dire*. But then what about the corn? It is alive, to be sure, but it is hard to attribute to it the ability to hear-itself-speak (no matter how many "ears" a stalk may have). But then what about "sensing itself"? Derrida provides no answers to these questions. He initially opens up the door completely, as it were, by extending the category of "irreplaceability" to all things, inanimate as well as animate, but he then quickly distinguishes between *two types* of irreplaceability, the irreplaceability of those beings that can "sense themselves"—humans, sheep, and, perhaps, corn, in a word, animate things—and the irreplaceability of those that cannot "sense themselves," inanimate things.

But then what about clones—living beings that would, it seems, "sense themselves," perhaps even, in some cases, hear-themselves-speak, but that, as commonly understood, as commonly feared, would seem to lack the kind of irreplaceability that Derrida has been attributing to beings that are able to "sense themselves"? The question of the relationship between the clone as opposed to the naturally born animal is obviously not the same as the question of the relationship between animate and inanimate things, but they cross or coincide in the question of replaceability. Though Derrida does not pose it in exactly this way, one might begin by asking whether the death of a clone is each time the end of the world or something less than that, something like the destruction, though not the death, of an inanimate being. The fear, what

Derrida characterizes as the *fantasmatic* fear, on the part of opponents of cloning would be that, no, the death of the clone is *not* exactly the end of the world because the clone, unlike the irreplaceable offspring with living parents, is a non-natural technological monstrosity without mother or father and thus without any kind of true or genuine or authentic life, and so, without that life, it would be unable truly to die. For Derrida, as we have already suggested, such a prejudice, such a rumor, such a fantasmatic fear, is the result of a phantasm that draws a single, indivisible line not only between the human and all other living things but between naturally born living beings and their clones, an indivisible line, a threshold, for which Derrida finds no justification.

Let me conclude this brief analysis of Derrida's brief look at the clone in *Hospitality* 2 with a passage that would come a few years later, in Derrida's final seminar, the second year of *The Beast and the Sovereign* (2002–2003). We will see the term "clone" deployed once again in relation to "fantasmatics" and "ideology," as well as to the question of reproduction, two different conceptions of repetition or reproduction, and the question of the living:

> What I call iterability, which repeats the same while displacing or altering it, is all at once a resource, a decisive power, and a catastrophe of repetition or reproduction. In this logic of iterability are found the resources both to cast into doubt oppositions of the type *physis/ tekhne* (and therefore also *physis/nomos*, *physis/thesis*) and to begin to analyze, in a different domain, all the fantasmatics, all the ideologies or metaphysics that today encumber so many discourses on cloning, discourses both for and against cloning. *Klôn* is moreover, in Greek, like *clonos* in Latin, a phenomenon of *physis* like that young sprout or that (primarily vegetable) growth, that parthenogenetic emergence we talked about when we were marking the fact that, before allowing itself to be opposed as nature or natural or biological life to its others, the extension of *physis* included all its others. There again, it appears symptomatic that Heidegger does not speak of the plant, not directly, not actively: for it seems to me that although he mentions it of course, he does not take it as seriously, *qua* life, as he does animality. I always think of the ranunculus [*la renoncule*] (*clonos* in Latin), a marsh or aquatic flower whose name comes from *renonculus*, little frog or froglet. (*BS* 2 75–76/120)

The word "clone," which was used in 1996–1997 to characterize Dolly, the Scottish sheep, and which is used today in fear, no doubt fantasmatic fear, of the first human clone, the first human iteration, would thus be related etymologically, Derrida reminds us, to plants, and it was used from the beginning of the twentieth century to refer to the cloning, precisely, of plants. But Derrida's association of cloning with "iterability" is no doubt also telling, for iterability—which, as Derrida reminds us in "Signature Event Context"—comes from the Sanskrit "iter," meaning *other*—suggests that cloning would always be a repetition with a difference, a repetition that refers always to the other, in other words, a repetition that is not simply subject to time but is responsible for opening it.

Conclusion
From Threshold to Threshold—Derrida's **Démarche**

As reaffirmation of mastery and of being oneself at home, hospitality
limits itself already from the threshold on its own threshold [*dès le
seuil sur le seuil d'elle-même*], it remains always on the threshold of
itself, it commands the threshold—and to that very extent it forbids in
a certain way crossing the threshold whose crossing it seems to permit.
Hospitality becomes the threshold. (*H* 1 24–25/46)

Pas d'hospitalité: We have referred to this phrase and discussed it more than
once. But we are perhaps only now beginning to understand it, to experience
it, to see what it means to return perpetually to the threshold. For while we
have, I hope, made progress in thinking along with Derrida the question of
hospitality, looking, for example, at the figure of the threshold in Homer and
Sophocles and its relation to hospitality, the question of language, including
that of translation, in the offering of translation, as well as the translation of
certain key words like *hôte*, *étranger*, and *xenos*, the question of the stranger
in Plato, Kant's cosmopolitical project of hospitality, the two regimes of hospitality that Derrida claims to be essential to think together, the rapidly changing relationship between hospitality and contemporary teletechnologies, the
whole notion of a mother tongue, the traditional restriction of hospitality to
the human—to name just some of the central themes and questions addressed
here—we have been forced each time to begin again, to start out from a different perspective, in a word, to return to the threshold for a new departure. No
matter how many steps we will have taken, no matter how far we will have
advanced, we have been perpetually sent back to the threshold, to the *odos*,
the *seuil*, from which we set out.

Were one to gather together the epigraphs to all twenty of this work's sections (its eighteen chapters, the introduction and conclusion)—all of them drawn from the *Hospitality* seminar or a related text and all of them containing the word "threshold"—one might come to the conclusion that Derrida's seminar is as much about that notion of the threshold, the threshold from which one sets out and to which one perpetually returns, as it is about hospitality. And one might then be tempted to conclude that that is because Derrida's other ambition in the *Hospitality* seminar, besides trying to understand the "concept" of hospitality and all those issues identified with it, is to try to develop in this work the "threshold," the *seuil*, as another way of saying and thinking such notions as trace, margin, hymen, or *différance*, names that all seem to call for their supplementation by other names. While a *seuil* might thus initially appear to be a determinable, identifiable, and indivisible line of demarcation, whether public or private, on a micro or macro level, that is, a line or boundary separating the inside from the outside of a house or a nation-state, separating those who are inside the family or the nation-state from those who are outside it, the threshold between inside and out is, in fact, as anyone who has ever offered private or public hospitality well knows, drawn and re-drawn throughout the "inside," perpetually renegotiated and recast.

Indeed, it could be said that Derrida's work has always been about criticizing or calling into question the assumption of an *indivisible threshold* separating, for example, speech and writing, life and death, and, perhaps especially, inside and outside. For it is on the basis of such an assumption that ownness and propriety, what we take to be a certain "interiority," is typically constructed. As we saw in Chapters 16 and 18, Derrida argues that such a notion of interiority—and the conceptions of self, property, and propriety that are always associated with it—is but a *phantasm*, an unbreakable, unburstable, undeflatable, ineluctable phantasm, but a phantasm nonetheless. Whether he is rethinking hospitality or anything else, there is no absolute interior, no pure inside that is not already in communication with its outside. In a word, in an untranslatable French word, the inside is always already and from the beginning *entamé*, that is, broached, breached, compromised, opened. The only question, then, is *how* that inside is opened, what kinds of negotiations are allowed to take place between inside and outside, and, perhaps finally, whether the inside has become a *phantasm* of interiority, a phantasm of what remains pure, unbreached, uncontaminated, proper, or whether it is understood as being already compromised, as having a threshold not only at its edges but always already within.

That is why the term "threshold," *seuil*, becomes throughout the *Hospitality* seminar a quasi-synonym of *différance*, as the place or nonplace between binary oppositions, beginning with inside and outside, the place or nonplace where identities are perpetually determined and deferred, in a word, deconstructed. One thus hears Derrida not only mentioning the term "threshold" but using it, not only referring to it but deploying it in a series of speech acts, the traces of which have been retained in many of this book's epigraphs. It is as if the seminar were not just a theoretical investigation into the topic of hospitality but something like a performative enactment of it, as if it were or could be a place, perhaps even an exemplary place, for hospitality.

In Chapter 2 we looked in some detail at that notion of a threshold, *odos*, in Homer, contrasting it with the very similar word *hodos*, meaning "path," "way," *chemin*, the word at the root of our word for "method." We did this in order to suggest that Derrida's approach to hospitality is more a thinking of the threshold than it is a method. It entails always a departure from and a perpetual return to a threshold rather than a step-by-step methodical process that takes us from a beginning to an end, according to some preestablished plan, goal, or *telos*. But this description can also be misleading. It can suggest that the threshold is not a point of departure to which we inevitably return but an origin from which we never depart, at which we remain paralyzed, whereas the threshold that we have been following is what *motivates*, I would suggest—not unlike that unconditional hospitality we spoke of in Chapters 8 and 9—all of Derrida's thinking. As the place from which hospitality is offered and the place from which the concept of hospitality must be thought, the threshold would be that which moves and motivates the very movement for the search for hospitality. No thinking of hospitality, then, without a thinking of the threshold.

And perhaps no *teaching* about hospitality without a teaching from and about the threshold. It is this thinking and teaching from the threshold that will have perhaps dictated—dictated but in a nonmethodological, nonteleological way—the very movement of the seminar. As Derrida remarks near the middle of the seminar on his own back-and-forth between classical texts from the history of philosophy and literature, between an abstract formalism that comes out of these readings and contemporary examples of laws or teletechnologies that are radically changing the nature of hospitality: "Perhaps you have already sensed or anticipated the strangeness of the approach I am attempting or to which I see myself constrained here by a sort of law" (*H* 1 121/166; see *OH* 139/123). The suggestion here seems to be that Derrida's going back and forth between a formal logic or structure developed out of the history of Western thought and contemporary examples is dictated by a kind of law that puts that formal structure to the test of contemporary examples, contemporary examples that perhaps resist or contest the very definition of hospitality they are supposed to exemplify. As Derrida argues: "It is often techno-political-scientific mutation that obliges us to deconstruct; really, such mutation itself deconstructs what are claimed as these naturally obvious things or these untouchable axioms. For instance, from the Latin or Greek tradition that we have just mentioned" (*OH* 45/45; see *H 1* 91/129). Derrida is thus suggesting a back-and-forth, a perpetual crossing of the threshold, as it were, between a close reading of texts in the history of philosophy and literature and analyses of "things, phenomena, that are to my mind irreducible today, like tele-technological mutation, like what is happening in politics today" (*H 1* 140/192).

This is not, therefore, a merely "academic exercise." Everything is being done to multiply the thresholds and the crossings between the "matters of urgency that assail us," on the one hand, and, on the other, "the tradition from which we receive the concepts, the vocabulary, the axioms that are ele-mentary and presumed natural or untouchable" (*OH* 45/45; see *H 1* 91/129). Derrida is suggesting that these urgencies actually *require* us to read and to return to the tradition, that is, to the tradition and to the *seemingly indivisible thresholds* (between the human and the animal, for example) it seems to in-scribe. For these thresholds are embedded in our language and our concepts, and perhaps especially our language and concepts about hospitality, where the relationship between inside and outside, self and other, purity and impu-rity, and so on informs so many of our assumptions and concepts, so much of our language and vocabulary. Derrida is interested in asking what happens to both the concepts and the language of hospitality that we have inherited from the Greeks and from the Bible when they are put to the test of today's urgen-cies, or else, especially during the second year, when these concepts and this language are read against other traditions—the Talmudic readings of Levinas, for example, on "cities of refuge" or the notion of substitution in the works of the French Catholic scholar of Islamic religion and culture Louis Massignon. The seminar thus tries to perform that back-and-forth in order to ask "what must be done." That, says Derrida, is "the horizon of the seminar," and it will have been the horizon from the very beginning (*H 1* 140/193).

Derrida writes in the very first session of the seminar, "Now we begin, or we pretend to open the door of the seminar. We are on the threshold [*le seuil*]" (*H 1* 7/26). Derrida is here suggesting that the seminar itself is a place or can be a place of hospitality, that it has a door, with an opening, and a threshold. It is or can be a place of hospitality even though we do not yet know what hospitality *is*, even though we are not yet able, and perhaps will forever remain unable, to answer the *ti esti* question with regard to it. Derrida thus approaches the question of hospitality with a kind of teaching that he will have been practicing for more than three decades before the seminar on *Hospitality* and that he would continue to practice for several years thereafter. And yet that teaching seems to have been, perhaps from the very beginning, motivated and inflected by the very notion of hospitality that would be the explicit theme of this seminar that ran from November 1995 to May 1997. At the very least it will have been motivated, as we suggested in the previous chapter, by a certain "improvisation" that is perhaps central to any art or poetics of hospitality, an "improvisation" that is perhaps central as well to a certain conception of teaching. Here is Derrida speaking, improvising, during that penultimate seminar session of *Hospitality* 2 about improvisation, as if to suggest that teaching or pedagogy too involves a certain improvisation, a combination, it seems, of planning and inventiveness, preparation and attentiveness to the situation, programmation and the chance mutation that comes to change the program:

> To what extent does hospitality presuppose improvisation? It must not be calculated. If there is visitation, there is thus surprise and there is improvisation. One must improvise, but not too much. One must be ready to improvise. And so a question of the unforeseen, of providential hospitality, of the "à l'improviste," the visitor comes *à l'improviste* . . . (H 2 231–32/318)

Derrida is speaking here about hospitality, but it is hard not to think that he is also speaking about teaching. In a transcribed discussion session of January 31, 1996, that is, midway through the first year of seminar, Derrida makes a series of remarks about the topic of their seminar, hospitality, and about their previous analyses of it. But then he makes a remark that addresses specifically *teaching*, the necessity of paying attention to what is explicitly said and what is not, what is said and what remains silent, what is thought and what remains unthought, what is explicit, conscious, and "what is enclaved and unconscious [*l'enclavé inconscient*], etc." (H 1 198/266). It is a necessity that Derrida himself seems to follow when he reads others, and it is one he suggests others follow when listening to or reading him. It is the kind of attention that might lead one to ask exactly why a seminar went in the unexpected direction it did, why it sometimes allowed itself, for example, "the time for a long detour"—the detour often being the best or most powerful way of advancing, the most pedagogical way of returning to the threshold, or else the most visible sign of what is "enclaved and unconscious."

"The time for a long detour": This phrase, which is not in the seminar but was later added to *Of Hospitality*, is a good way to characterize Derrida's way of proceeding in the seminar (*OH* 85/79; see H 1 105/149). He goes, in fact, from detour to detour, oftentimes with detours within each detour. He begins the fifth session by remarking, "We are going not only from transgression to transgression but also from digression to digression. . . . What do these strange steps of hospitality mean, these interminable thresholds and these aporias of hospitality?" (*H* 1 102/145; see *OH* 75/71). Just a few pages later, Derrida returns to this notion of digression, saying—or wanting to say—"You remember—and you see I am going from digression to digression . . ." (*H* 1 105/149). I say that that is what Derrida *wanted* to say because the editors note that what Derrida *actually* said, misreading his own text, was "you see I am going from transgression to transgression" before correcting himself, substituting "digression" for "transgression" but then adding, "it's the same thing < *Laughter* >, for a professor at any rate" (*H* 1 105n8/149n1). It's a telling lapsus and an even more telling comment about that lapsus. From the point of view of a certain, more traditional pedagogy, to go from digression to digression like he has been doing is indeed a transgression. As he writes much earlier in the seminar, "The passage across the threshold of hospitality is always a step of transgression" (*H* 1 102/145).[1]

But this is Derrida's approach to the question of hospitality. This is his *démarche*, which, as I have tried to suggest, is not exactly his *method*. It is his way of negotiating the threshold between the unbreachable wall and the open door, his way of stepping over a threshold, an *odos*, and then returning to it, drawing and redrawing it, marking and remarking it, both in a certain practice of hospitality and in his way of thinking about it. During the second year of the seminar, Derrida will actually relate the very notion of the stranger, which is, as we have seen, at the center of the *Hospitality* seminar, to digression itself. "The stranger is always in digression, a digression, a step to the side that risks misleading, that is, corrupting the proximity to itself of the proper" (*H* 2 210/290). It is the stranger, it seems, who opens up the way to thinking about the stranger and about hospitality, the stranger who interrupts the proximity of the host to himself and, in so doing, opens up the time for teaching.

But of course, if the seminar really is a place of hospitality as Derrida has tried to understand or practice it, if it really is or could be a place that negotiates between conditional hospitality, where the master holds all the power and all the keys, and unconditional hospitality, where host and guest—and perhaps teacher and student—can no longer be identified, then perhaps this too must be risked in any seminar worthy of the name. Derrida asks himself in the seventh session of the seminar:

And if the whole question of hospitality comes down to a question of the key, the threshold and the door insofar as it involves a key, the old question of the keys to the city or keys to the house—the guest (*Gast*) is the one to whom the host (*Gastgeber*) gives the keys (one can give the other nothing more precious than keys) . . . (H 1 187/252)[2]

Just a few pages later in the same session, Derrida seems to return to this dream of giving the keys over to the other, the dream, perhaps, of a form of teaching where the teacher would renounce all forms of sovereignty over his or her teaching, giving over the keys of the seminar to those who had just come in over the threshold—perhaps invited, perhaps not, perhaps officially enrolled in the seminar, perhaps not, perhaps just "sitting in." He says, suggesting a kind of teaching that—echoing the language of *khōra*—would "give rise to place," or "make place for a place":

> However one settles this question of the question, between the hospitality we have called just and the hospitality of rights, between the law and the laws of hospitality, we can dream of what a teaching would be, and whether it would still be teaching, if it were dispensed by someone who would say that they did not hold the keys to what they say, in the final instance, did not have them or know them, so would dispense neither knowledge nor questioning, but would give rise to the place [*donnerait lieu au lieu*] by leaving the keys to the other, by saying to them: "Here, you have the keys, it's up to you to decipher if not unlock [*désenclaver*], if you like . . . without losing sight of the fact that one enclave can always hide another *en abyme*. (H 1 199/266–67)

In other words, I think he is saying, "The seminar is open. Now be my guest."

Acknowledgments

This work owes a great deal to many people, first among them my friends and colleagues in the Derrida Seminar Translation Project (DSTP), which (pandemic permitting) meets every summer at the IMEC archives in Normandy to discuss the editing and translation of Derrida seminars. It was during our recent gatherings devoted to the two years of *Hospitality* that many of the ideas in this work came into focus. My deep thanks to my fellow DSTP members, Geoffrey Bennington, Pascale-Anne Brault (coeditor of *Hospitality* 1 & 2), Ellen Burt (translator of *Hospitality* 1), Katie Chenoweth, Peggy Kamuf (coeditor of *Hospitality* 1 & 2 and translator of *Hospitality* 2), Kir Kuiken, Elizabeth Rottenberg, and David Wills. I am also very grateful to the students at DePaul who attended my graduate seminar on Derrida's works on hospitality in autumn 2021. Their comments, questions, and suggestions informed almost every page of this work.

But this work would have never gone beyond the stage of informal presentations and class lecture notes were it not for several invitations to discuss Derrida's work on hospitality. Early versions of Chapters 1, 8, and 9 were thus first presented at Penn State University and at Salisbury University under the title "The Wall, the Door, the Threshold: Derrida and the Question of Hospitality." My heartfelt thanks to Nancy Tuana and Charles Scott at Penn State for their generous invitation and to Len Lawlor, Robert Bernasconi, and Jeff Nealon for their exemplary hospitality during my stay. My thanks as well to Tim Stock, his colleagues, and the alumni at Salisbury for their kind and stimulating reception. I am also grateful to Kristian Olesen Toft for his invitation to present much of this work during a two-day seminar at the University of Copenhagen in November 2022. His comments and questions, as well as those from other doctoral students in attendance (from Denmark but also from Belgium, France, Germany, the Netherlands, and Sweden), were invaluable as I tried to think some of the larger issues raised by the seminar. The same is true of Fernanda Bernardo and her extraordinary students at the University of Coimbra, in Portugal, where I presented large parts of this work in March 2023. I also very grateful to Sam Weber and the students in the Northwestern University program in Paris for inviting me in autumn 2022 to present parts of Chapter 18 on the relationship between humans and animals in Derrida's work and the question of cloning.

Finally, I would like to thank Rick Lee, my colleague at DePaul, for his invitation in September 2022 to speak about Derrida and hospitality on the podcast *Hotel Bar Sessions* with him, Leigh Johnson, and Jason Read. It was that virtual discussion and accompanying drink (in my case a virtual glass of Côte du Rhone) that first gave me the idea of pulling together into a single work the various pieces I had written on the topic of hospitality.

Chapters 17 and 18 were initially published together as "Mother Tongues, Mobile Phones, and the Soil on the Soles of One's Shoes: Jacques Derrida and the Phantasms of Language," *Journal of Continental Philosophy* 3, no. 1 (2023): 1–18. My deep thanks to the editor of that journal, Dennis Schmidt, for allowing me to publish a revised version of that essay here.

Appendix
Two Regimes of Hospitality

Conditional Hospitality	Unconditional Hospitality
Limited, concrete, effective	Absolute, hyperbolic, pure, unlimited
Invitation	Visitation
Laws of hospitality (n + n + n)	The (One) Law of hospitality
Hospitality of Law	Hospitality of Justice (*an anomos nomos*)
Economy, reciprocity, circle of exchange	Gift, irreciprocity
Vision, calculation, reason	Blindness, incalculability, madness
Norms, proportion	Absolute respect, desire
Offered by a host with power over guest	Host and guest are indistinguishable
Guest as a virtual enemy	Guest can be loved or hated
Offered to someone with a name, family, etc.	Offered to the absolute, anonymous other
Offered by a sovereign who selects, filters	Offered without selection to the *arrivant*
The host questions the guest	The guest puts the host in question
Entails laws, rights, duties, debts	Justice before the law, rights, and debts
Offered to other humans (from nation-states?)	Offered to humans, gods, animals, plants?
Offered on the basis of birth (rights)	Offered on the basis of death
Historical laws	Quasi-transcendental (historicity)

< contradictory, antinomic >
< heterogeneous but inseparable >
< nondialectizable antinomy >

Mediating Schemata

The (One) Law of hospitality + the many conditional Laws of hospitality
(1 + a multiplicity: Un + n)
"Civil Disobedience"

The Becoming-Law of Justice

Conditional Hospitality "inspired," "guided," "drawn," "motivated," "required"
by Unconditional Hospitality

Grace, Politesse, Art, Poetics

Notes

Introduction. Fist Bumps and Pandemic Bubbles

1. Among the many excellent books written in the wake of the COVID-19 pandemic, see Samuel Weber, *Preexisting Conditions: Recounting the Plague* (New York: Zone, 2022), which includes readings of literary and historical works on the plague from Artaud and Camus all the way back to Sophocles and Thucydides.

2. The little book *Of Hospitality*, written together with Anne Dufourmantelle and published in 1997 (and in English translation in 2000), essentially reproduces, with some modifications, two sessions from the first year of Derrida's two-year seminar *Hospitality*, the fourth session (January 10, 1996) and the fifth (January 17). When quoting from those two seminar sessions, I will use throughout, except where otherwise noted, the version published in *Of Hospitality*. Since Derrida had a chance to review and rework those sessions for that volume, they can be considered more "authoritative" than the two corresponding seminar sessions. I will also occasionally remark on the *differences* between the two versions. While most of these are little more than editorial tweaks, some are more significant, among these a number of passages having to do with the *phantasm*. Though the theme is hardly absent from the original seminar, it takes on even greater significance in *Of Hospitality*. To highlight this theme and for the sake of consistency, I have, in what follows, replaced Rachel Bowlby's perfectly legitimate translation of the French *phantasme* as "fantasy" by "phantasm."

It should also be noted that the first session of the seminar was also previously published in French in its near entirety, including oral additions (17–44) and with an accompanying Turkish translation (45–71), as "Hostipitalité," in *Cogito*, ed. Ferda Keskin and Önay Sözer, no. 85, *Pera Peras Poros: Atelier interdisciplinaire avec et autour de Jacques Derrida* (Istanbul: YKY, 1999). It was also translated into English by Barry Stocker and Forbes Morlock as *"Hostipitality,"* *Angelaki* 5, no. 3 (December 2000): 3–18.

3. Derrida recalls in many places the ways in which "the nationalist phantasm, as with its politicking rhetoric, often passes by way of . . . organicist analogies" (N 102). As a critique of this "phantasm or of the axiom of purity," deconstruction would call into question all such organicist analogies, all calls to purify the body politic—in deed or in word—by purging it of what threatens its putatively natural health and integrity. It is with this in mind that it is perhaps worth recalling here that at a conference held at the Sorbonne on January 7, 2022, one of these "organicist analogies" was used by none other than the French minister of education, Jean-Michel Blanquer, to describe the thought of Derrida, Deleuze, and Foucault. The occasion was a conference on "cancel culture" and "wokeism" at the Sorbonne at which Blanquer participated, to the dismay of many of his colleagues, as *Le Monde* reported. Blanquer apparently said during his remarks that "we must deconstruct deconstruction," describing France as being "under attack" from a strain of thought coming from the United States. It is a "virus," he is reported as saying, whose source would be the so-called French Theory (in English) of the 1970s, in particular, the thinking of Derrida, Deleuze, and Foucault. Blanquer is reported to have gone on to say that "having provided the virus, we must provide the vaccine." See Soazig Le Nevé, "Le 'wokisme' sur le banc des accusés lors d'un colloque à la Sorbonne," *Le Monde*, January 8, 2022.

So here you have a minister of education using the language of viruses, and during a global pandemic, no less, to describe the thinking of Derrida, Deleuze, and Foucault. Though he does not spell it out, the idea would seem to be that the so-called virus originated in France, in Derrida, Deleuze, and Foucault (who would be patients 0, 1, and 2), and was then exported abroad, particularly to the United States, where it mutated into "French Theory" and other even more dangerous variants such as cancel culture and wokeism, before being imported *back* to France, where it is now "attacking," we are to assume, the good and noble values of reason, truth, freedom of thought and expression, and so on that would be hallmarks of French culture and education. The "vaccine" would thus consist, it seems, in stopping the transmission of this dangerous thought, either by discouraging the propagation of "French Theory" or by inoculating the populace against it through a return to those traditional French values.

It is hardly necessary to spell out all the reasons why such claims are misguided, at once silly and dangerous, and why they need to be at once ignored and taken seriously, at the very least for their rhetoric. For while a certain credit can, perhaps, be given to a minister who knows who Derrida, Deleuze, and Foucault are and what "French Theory" is, to espouse this unnuanced and politically motivated characterization of them is, at the very least, worrisome, and to use the language of viruses and vaccination, "organicist analogies" if ever there were any, and in the midst of a pandemic, the height of irresponsibility. One should certainly expect better from a French minister of *education*.

4. Pierre Klossowski, *Roberte ce soir* (Paris: Minuit, 1953). English translation in *Roberte Ce Soir and The Revocation of the Edict of Nantes*, trans. Austryn Wainhouse (London: Dalkey Archive, 2002). Let me add here that Derrida's strategy is complex and intentionally multipronged from the start, though also open to change and improvisation. This becomes evident in the seventh session when Derrida reads, at the suggestion of a seminar member the week before, it seems, La Bruyère's "Le Distrait," "The Absent-Minded."

5. Emile Benveniste, *Indo-European Language and Society*, trans. Elizabeth Palmer (London: Farber and Farber, 1973), esp. chap. 7 of vol. 1 on hospitality. *Vocabulaire des institutions indo-européennes* (Paris: Minuit, l969).

6. This can be seen in the way Derrida labeled on his computer the nine documents corresponding to the nine prepared sessions of the seminar: "H (un), HO (deux), Hos (3), Host (4), Hosti (5), Hostip (6), Hostipi (7), Hostipit (8), Hostipita (9)." In their preface to *Hospitality 1*, the editors explain their decision to give the seminar the general title "Hospitality [*Hospitalité*]" rather than "Hostipitalité [*Hostipitalité*]." They point out that Derrida uses the latter only twice in the first year of the seminar (both times in the seventh session) and only seven times during the second year, as compared to the more than four hundred times he uses the term "hospitality." Moreover, the fact that Derrida never announced his seminar at the École des Hautes Études under this title, coupled with the fact that two of the seminar's sessions were published during his lifetime under the title "Of Hospitality," suggest a certain reticence on Derrida's part to retain the neologism "hostipitality" as a general title. See "Editors' Introduction," *H* 1 xv/14.

7. Four sessions of the second year had also previously been published, though without Derrida's oral comments included and sometimes with significant variations, as "Hostipitality," in the translation of Gil Anidjar, in *Acts of Religion*, ed. Gil Anidjar (New York: Routledge, 2002), 356–420. These are the EHESS seminar sessions of January 8, 1997, February 12, 1997, March 5, 1997, and May 7, 1997, of *Hospitality* 2.

8. This book owes a great deal to Judith Still's remarkable work *Derrida and Hospitality: Theory and Practice* (Edinburgh: Edinburgh University Press, 2013). While the title of Still's book is not inaccurate, for Derrida's thinking of hospitality is central from beginning to end, the book is really much wider in scope than that title would suggest, with many pages devoted to Homer, the Old Testament, Levinas, Cixous, and Irigaray, as well as Tahar Ben Jelloun, Albert Camus (his short story "The Guest"), J. M. Coetzee, André Gide, and Jean-Jacques Rousseau, among others. There is also an entire chapter devoted to friendship and sexual difference; one on Derrida's, Cixous's, and Irigaray's respective treatments of animals, particularly with regard to hospitality; and another that takes up questions of "post-colonial hospitality" and "cultural differences" in hospitality between France and the Maghreb, particularly Algeria, themes I touch on only in the context of Derrida's seminar. If Still's focus is thus more on the theme of hospitality as such than on Derrida, though Derrida remains central to her thinking, this work has the narrower

and admittedly less ambitious goal of trying to illuminate questions of hospitality only within the context of Derrida's *Hospitality* seminar of 1995–1997 and the series of texts he wrote on hospitality around the same time.

I also learned a great deal from the terrific book by Jacques de Ville, *Jacques Derrida: Law as Absolute Hospitality* (New York: Routledge, 2011), especially the chapter "Hospitality towards the Future," which puts Derrida's work into the context of legal studies and details the kind of reforms within the law that Derrida's work demands. I also took my bearings from the excellent essay by Mark W. Westmoreland, "Interruptions: Derrida and Hospitality," *Kritike* 2, no. 1 (June 2008): 1–10; and, once again, from the final chapter of Hent de Vries, *Religion and Violence: Philosophical Perspectives from Kant to Derrida* (Baltimore, MD: Johns Hopkins University Press, 2002), which has an excellent analysis of hospitality in Derrida's work and of deconstruction as a hospitable form of thought.

Focusing on the first volume of *Hospitality* as I have, I benefited enormously from David Krell's very helpful review and analysis of the seminar in *Philosophy Today* 67, no. 3 (Summer 2023): 715–32. He writes near the beginning of his review: "The published transcript—containing nine sessions along with two annexes and other manuscript material—is beautifully edited, eminently readable, perfectly straightforward and impossibly complex" (716). No one could have said that any better. Krell is also attuned to all the ways in which "Derrida's seminar forces us to think of hospitality—and hostility—in the here and now" (716). Writing in the summer of 2022, Krell feels compelled to note how this seminar from more than a quarter of a century ago seems to be addressing our own troubled times: "Derrida cites as examples of singular events the first and second world wars, but also the breakup of the Soviet Union, the wars and genocides in the former Yugoslavia, the influx of African immigrants into France and Europe generally; today we would add the influx of Syrian refugees into Europe, the stream of persons from Central America and the Caribbean seeking refuge in the United States, the flow of millions of Ukrainians into the rest of Europe, and so on, without end" (724–25). There are also enlightening comments throughout his review on Arendt; on Derrida's two "grandfathers," Heidegger and Freud; on the question of mourning; datability; cruelty (a word I hardly mention); among so much else. Krell ends his lengthy review of the first volume of *Hospitality* with yet another reference to our own contemporary situation, concluding with words that could serve as the epigraph to *Threshold Phenomena*: "We recognize the echoes of all this in our own time and place, our own policed place on this spherical Earth. Yet each act of hospitality is singular, directed to a particular person at a particular time and location. And each act of hospitality remains suspended between the ideal of an unconditional hospitality and a host of reservations that both frustrate and sustain that ideal. Zarathustra says that we stand in the gateway of the moment, the gateway called 'Blink of an Eye.' Each time we try to cross over the doorstep of the moment, the gateway moves with us. We remain on the threshold. Hospitality is like that" (728).

Finally, there is the magnificent edited collection *Le livre de l'hospitalité: Accueil de l'étranger dans l'histoire et des cultures*, ed. Alain Montandon (Montrouge: Bayard, 2004), which contains an invaluable entry by Ginette Michaud on hospitality in Derrida. Michaud refers to almost all of Derrida's major works on hospitality, including what was at that time the still unpublished seminar of 1995–1997, referred to under the title "Hostipitality." See, too, her essay "Politique et poétique de l'hospitalité," in *Lire dans la nuit et autres essais. Pour Jacques Derrida* (Montréal: Les Presses de l'Université de Montréal, 2020), 187–214.

9. To briefly recall the seminars and courses that have been published in French over the past decade or so, there are the two volumes of the *Beast and the Sovereign* (seminars of 2001–2002 and 2002–2003), the two on *The Death Penalty* (seminars of 1999–2000 and 2000–2001), and then the single-year courses on *Heidegger and the Question of History* (course of 1964–1965) and *Theory and Practice* (course of 1976–1977), all of which were published with Éditions Galilée. The single-year course *Life Death* (1975–1976), the two years of *Perjury and Pardon* (seminars of 1997–1998 and 1998–1999), and, now, the two years of *Hospitality* (seminars of 1995–1996 and 1996–1997) have been published with Éditions du Seuil.

10. Though the threshold may look like a nonplace between places and Plato's *khōra* a nonplace that gives rise or gives space to space, the two might be thought together, since the threshold is also described in the *Timaeus* as a *plokanon*, that is, a sieve or winnower that separates particles of fire, air, water, and earth before they have become separate, identifiable elements (see 52e–53a, 78c).

1. *Hodos* and *Odos* (Homeric Hospitality 1)

1. I offer this brief analysis of the "threshold" in Homer as a friendly supplement to the excellent chapter of Judith Still's *Derrida and Hospitality: Theory and Practice* (Edinburgh: Edinburgh University Press, 2013) devoted to Homer and the Old Testament (51–92).

2. As Judith Still nicely puts it in *Derrida and Hospitality*, "Zeus is the god who presides over hospitality while some inhuman male hosts (notably Polyphemus) are the antithesis of hospitality" (66).

3. For example, Hector in the *Iliad* inquires of the serving women about Andromache as he stands on a threshold (*Iliad* 6.375), while Penelope sits on the threshold of her own chamber mourning Odysseus, having no more "the heart to sit upon one of the many seats that were in the room" (*Odyssey* 4.718; see 4.480, 17.575).

4. The expression can also be found in Hesiod (*Works and Days* 331) and Herodotus (*Persian Wars* 3.14).

2. Translating Hospitality

1. These problems of translation, intelligibility, and understanding are not restricted to what we typically mean by a "language." Derrida distinguishes in the seminar and in *Of Hospitality* between a strict (linguistic) sense of the term

"language" and a larger (cultural) sense. He does this to point out that one can be closer to someone whose language one does not speak but whose culture, class, and values one shares than to someone who speaks the same language but has a very different culture, class, values, and so on. And one can sometimes feel closer to someone in another country because they speak the same language than to someone who does not speak the same language but is living next door (*OH* 131–33/117–19; see *H* 1 118–19/164–65; see also *OH* 158n1/23).

2. In "The Principle of Hospitality," Derrida again takes up this notion of a "first violence" being inflicted upon the foreigner by asking them "to assert their rights in a language they don't speak." He there concludes that this requires a "formidable duty to translate" and a "transformation of law" ("PH" 68). In an interview published in *Sur Parole*, Derrida says this about the question of addressing the other in his or her language or not: "Welcoming someone in their language is, obviously, taking into consideration their idiom, culture, etc. But nation-states, France, for example, on both the Right and Left, say that it's good to welcome the other but only on condition that they recognize the values of secularism, or republicanism, the French language and culture. The right decision [*décision juste*] must be found, here again, between the integrationist model, which would end up simply erasing all alterity, in asking the other to forget, as soon as they arrive, their entire memory, their language, their entire culture, and the opposite model that would consist in giving up on requiring that the one who comes [*arrivant*] learn our language" (*S* 73).

3. It is in recognition of this fact that universities around the country, DePaul University included, have often put at the disposal of immigrants or asylum seekers the expertise of those working in their Modern Language departments and elsewhere throughout the university. In addition, then, to DePaul's academic program in Refugee and Forced Migration Studies and the DePaul Migration Collaborative, there is the Translators and Interpreters Corps (TIC), a group of students, mostly from the Law School and Modern Languages, who help with the translation of texts and documents of people seeking asylum and offer interpreting services during official judicial hearings and immigration interviews.

4. See *The Dictionary of Untranslatables*, ed. Barbara Cassin, Emily Apter, Jacques Lezra, and Michael Wood (Princeton, NJ: Princeton University Press, 2014).

5. Derrida himself refers (at *H* 1 176–77/239) to an essay of Samuel Weber titled "Reading and Writing—chez Derrida," in *Institution and Interpretation* (Minneapolis: University of Minnesota Press, 1984; reedited, Stanford, CA: Stanford University Press, 2001), an essay that is as much about the *chez* as it is about reading and writing.

6. One might say, citing *Aporias*, that *il y va d'un certain pas*, that is, that the phrase itself is a matter of a certain "pas," a matter of a certain "step," but also of a certain negation, and that it goes at a certain "pas," that is, at a certain step, a certain pace, a pace determined, it could be said, by the necessity of returning to the threshold, since this phrase has to be read in *at least* two times, in two different registers.

There are several references to "hospitality" in *Aporias*, which was first presented at a conference at Cerisy la Salle titled "Le passage des frontières," that is, "Border Passage" or "Border Crossing." Though much of that work is devoted to the question of being-towards-death in Heidegger, it is framed by sociopolitical and ethical questions regarding frontiers or borders, political thresholds, as it were. I would like to thank Sam Rome, who was attending my graduate seminar on Derrida and hospitality at DePaul in the autumn of 2021, for reminding me of these connections.

7. Elsewhere, it will be a question of the French idiom or phrase *tout de même*, meaning "all the same" (*H* 1 32/55), an expression with *même*, that is, "self" or "same," within it, a very common, everyday French word that is nonetheless found at the center of French philosophical language and thus, inevitably, at the center of Derrida's analyses. An analysis of *même* and *tout de même* will thus lead to *à même* and even to the homophone *m'aime* (loves me)—all these French idioms imprinting an indelible and ineradicable *difference* onto this lexicon of *sameness* (*H* 1 38/62).

3. Masters of the House: Hospitality and Sovereignty

1. Emily Apter in an interesting YouTube video filmed in Berlin speaks about programs designed to evaluate the accents of immigrants and asylum seekers so that authorities can confirm whether the accents match the place the immigrants or asylum seekers say they are from. One might also mention the controversial use of bone density scans to determine the age of asylum seekers and, thus, in the absence of any official documentation of their birth, whether they should be granted the advantageous status of "minor."

2. This reference to the *Beiträge* is in fact already beginning to attract the interest of both Heidegger and Derrida scholars. For an excellent reading of Derrida's seminar on the questions of sovereignty and selfhood, particularly in relation to Heidegger, see Benjamin Brewer and Ronald Mendoza-de Jesús, "The Hidden Law of Selfhood: Reading Heidegger's Ipseity after Derrida's *Hospitality*," *Oxford Literary Review* 43, no. 2 (2021): 268–89. While Heidegger plays a leading role in many other Derrida seminars, his presence here is somewhat limited. Beyond this long passage on *Selbstheit*, Derrida speaks in the first session of Heidegger's *Was heisst denken?*, that is, of what calls for thinking, what gives thinking, what promises or indeed *invites* thinking (*H* 1 18–19/39–40), and he recounts having just recently returned from visiting Heidegger's hut in Germany (*H* 1 20/41). In the eighth session there is reference to the *Unheimlich*, that is, the uncanny or the unhomely, in Heidegger (as well as Freud) (*H* 1 218/291). Finally, Derrida evokes in the same session a few texts of Heidegger's, including the essays "Poetically Man Dwells" and, especially, "Building Dwelling Thinking" (1951), where Heidegger speaks of an *originary Heimatlosigkeit*, that is, an originary homelessness that must be thought before we can understand what it means to inhabit (*H* 1 223/297; see also 236–38/314–16, 242/321–22).

4. *Xenos* and *Xenia* (Homeric Hospitality 2)

1. Judith Still briefly mentions this scene in her *Derrida and Hospitality: Theory and Practice* (Edinburgh: Edinburgh University Press, 2013), 87n13.

5. On Dying Abroad: Oedipus (on the Threshold) at Colonus

1. There is some debate about whether the Greek here is in fact *hodos* or *odos*, road or threshold, a difference that, for the reading I am purposing here, is obviously crucial (56). Jebb translates: "as for the spot on which you tread, it is called the bronze threshold of this land, the support of Athens."

2. I note in passing that in his comments on Oedipus's exchange with the Chorus and his blaming the city of Thebes for his plight, Derrida raises the question of *forgiveness*. Derrida asks, "How can the unforgiveable be forgiven? But what else can be forgiven?" (*OH* 39/41; see *H* 1 89/126). This reference to forgiveness, which is not in the seminar, was apparently added to *Of Hospitality*, as Derrida was no doubt at once reviewing this session of the seminar for publication and preparing, if not already teaching, the first year of his two-year seminar *Perjury and Pardon*, the seminar that directly followed the *Hospitality* seminar and that would run from autumn 1997 through the spring of 1999.

3. These are, of course, all male couples, in the phallocentric-fraternalistic model of friendship that Derrida is trying to rethink and contest in *Politics of Friendship*. See the subchapter "The Model of Perfect Friendship among Men and the Question of Mourning" in Judith Still, *Derrida and Hospitality: Theory and Practice* (Edinburgh: Edinburgh University Press, 2013), 101–6.

4. See the editors' note on the funeral and Mitterrand's own "two families" (*H* 1 107n12/151n1). An Associated Press article by Christopher Burns dated January 11, 1996, recounted the event this way: "Widow Danielle Mitterrand, in a black overcoat and white scarf blowing in the wind, looked on stoically and a military band played somberly. She was joined by her sons, Gilbert and Jean-Christophe, and her grandchildren. Mitterrand's longtime mistress, Anne Pingeot, and their 21-year-old daughter, Mazarine, stood next to them." https://apnews.com/article/fde0b1870af16f3b21c3151e7bd12fb2.

5. All this was written, let me recall, in January 1996. In October of the same year, Derrida came to DePaul University for a conference on politics and mourning, a conference that was at the origin of the volume *The Work of Mourning*, published in English in 2001. As for the ambiguous mourning being described here, many have noted how mourning during the COVID pandemic was compounded by the fact that people were often unable to visit their loved ones in the hospital as they lay dying or hold the kind of funeral service or memorial ceremony they would have liked, condemning them to a mourning that was even more "ambiguous" or "incomplete" than usual.

6. Derrida recalls, for example, Montaigne on different ways of dying, on dying

abroad, for example, on a trip, "en voyage," or dying with another, together, co-diers, *commourans*, like Romeo and Juliet or Anthony and Cleopatra (*H* 1 24–25/47).

6. Plato's *Xenoi*

1. Derrida here recalls the famous opening of *Being and Time* with its reference to the *Sophist* (*OH* 9/15; see *H* 1 78/114).

2. In book 24, however, it is suggested that one should not entertain a god knowing that he or she is a god, that is, entertain a god *openly*. Hermes says to Priam as this latter approaches the tent of Achilles to ransom back the body of Hector, "good cause for wrath would it be that an immortal god should thus openly be entertained [*agapazemen*] of mortals" (24.462–64). As for hospitality *among* the gods, see, for example, *Iliad* 15.86.

3. Recalling the motif of blindness in *Sophist* ("obvious, *even to a blind person*"), Derrida forges a link back to Oedipus, though also, it seems, forward to one of the two poles of hospitality, that is, to an unconditional hospitality that is always granted somewhat "blindly," beyond what can be seen, foreseen, or anticipated (*OH* 9/15, *H* 1 78/114).

4. Derrida cites *Apology* 17c–d and refers his students to Henri Joly's *Études platoniciennes. La question des étrangers* (Paris: Vrin, 1992). Joly remarks upon the fact that foreigners were able to appear as foreigners in Athenian courts, allowed, at least, to speak in their own language.

5. See Derrida's "Khōra," 111.

6. Both terms are used by Plato to describe *khōra* (see *Timaeus* 49a, 50d, 51a, 52d, 88d, as well as *Republic* 414e).

7. Stranger Things

1. I take up the question of hospitality in the work of Derrida from a more personal perspective in a chapter of *Derrida from Now On* (New York: Fordham University Press, 2008), 18–36, that was written not long after Derrida's death in October 2004. I there recall this very first phrase Derrida ever addressed to me, and I argue that it was precisely a sort of threshold question, a question that risked becoming an irritated demand for information but was instead, as I heard it, an invitation.

2. See Samir Haddad's excellent essay "Questions of the Foreigner in *Of Hospitality*," *Poetics Today* 42, no. 1 (March 2021): 69–83.

3. I cannot really explain why the title of the fourth session as published in *Of Hospitality* is not "Question de *l'*étranger," as it is in the seminar, but "Question d'étranger," which means "it is a question of the foreigner," a "matter of the foreigner." Derrida seems to have rewritten the phrase for *Of Hospitality*, though the seminar version is, to my ears, more economical, more suggestive, and more powerful.

4. I recall in passing that while Levinas is briefly evoked at several points during the first year of the seminar, Derrida will devote several sessions to him during the second year, which was given at the same time he was writing *Adieu to Emmanuel Levinas*.

5. Derrida in "The Principle of Hospitality" refers to his own "Violence and Metaphysics" of 1964 to show his longstanding anxiousness—his questioning—of the question (see "PH" 86).

8. Conditional and Unconditional Hospitality

1. Judith Still in her *Derrida and Hospitality: Theory and Practice* (Edinburgh: Edinburgh University Press, 2013) very helpfully suggests that between the extremes of conditional hospitality and unconditional hospitality one might imagine a series of gradations that run from (1) simple commerce, to (2) more complex commerce, (3) direct social exchange, (4) indirect social exchange, (5) invitation without reciprocity, (6) hospitality to animals, and (7) absolute hospitality, where "the door is open—even, there is no door, but rather perfect openness" (16–18).

2. As for the other common phrase or cliché—"you can't just let everyone in"—Derrida in "The Principle of Hospitality" gives a rather powerful rejoinder to the former French prime minister Michel Rocard's version of it, namely, that France cannot "take in all the wretched poverty of the world." Derrida says that either this is a truism—so true that no one ever thought it was possible or ever asked France to attempt it—or a merely a rhetorical phrase aimed at justifying cutbacks and protectionist and reactionary attitudes of various kinds (see "PH" 68–69).

3. This is also related to what Derrida calls *distinterrance*, that is, to the ineradicable possibility of erring, of wandering: "The possibility of misunderstanding, failure of comprehension, making a mistake is in its way a chance." It is this, says Derrida, that "gives time." ("AIP" 89)

4. In one of his more evocative and powerful references to "civil" or, as he calls it there, "civic" disobedience, Derrida *imagines* a Socrates who (despite everything he says about obeying Athenian law in the *Crito*) engages in acts of civil disobedience (see "US" 118).

5. In "The Principle of Hospitality" Derrida tries again to clarify or concretize this notion of making effective or concrete. After characterizing an absolute or unconditional hospitality as "a welcome without reservations or calculation," as "an unlimited display of hospitality," he adds: "But a cultural or linguistic community, a family or a nation, cannot fail at the very least to suspect if not to betray this principle of absolute hospitality: so as to protect a 'home,' presumably, by guaranteeing property and 'one's own' against the unrestricted arrival of the other, but also so as to try to make the reception real, determined, and concrete—to put it into practice" ("PH" 67). And yet, as Derrida reminds us in "Not Utopia, the Im-possible," this is not easy, because "it is not a question of simply applying a program." One must pass through the "trial of aporia or undecidability" ("NU" 128).

9. Unconditional and Conditional Hospitality

1. For an excellent restatement and reframing of this relationship between conditional and unconditional hospitality, see the exchange between Derrida and Penelope Deutscher in *Deconstruction Engaged*. Deutscher there poses a series of poignant and well-formulated questions to Derrida (*DE* 93–97), who answers in kind with an exceptionally lucid and pointed summary of the relationship between the two hospitalities (*DE* 97–104).

2. See *For What Tomorrow* for this opposition between a hospitality of "visitation" and a hospitality of "invitation" (*FWT* 59–60/101–2).

3. *Penser, c'est dire non*, transcribed and ed. Brieuc Gérard (Paris: Éditions du Seuil, 2022).

4. Later in the seminar, Derrida tries to rethink the relationship between conditional and unconditional hospitality in terms not of the one unconditional law and a plurality or multiplicity of conditional laws but in terms of *singularity* and *repetition*. He there argues, in conformity with the logic we see deployed in texts such as *The Work of Mourning* (*Chaque fois unique, la fin du monde*), that each act of hospitality has to be unique even if each must also be inscribed in a series. Each time unique or uniquely, we might say, we welcome an other across the threshold. And that other is, of course, always a singularity. It is always a singularity that/who is welcomed, even if that singularity must be repeated, compared, put in a series, etc. (see *H* 1 231–32/308–9).

5. There is a related passage toward the end of the seminar where Derrida speaks of unconditional hospitality as a *lever* for deconstructing the distinction between public law and private hospitality: "I must offer absolute hospitality to every arrivant, whatever the public or private law may be. This unconditional Law is then the lever or inspiration for a deconstruction of this distinction" (*H* 1 204/273). Though this lever of absolute hospitality might thus allow one to deconstruct the distinction between private and public law, it would not or should not lead to the complete erasure of it, for without such a distinction there would be no place for secrecy or singularity.

This term "lever" is, interestingly, the same one Derrida once used to describe "archē-writing," a "lever" that would allow him in *Of Grammatology* and elsewhere to deconstruct, for example, the distinction between speech and writing, inside and outside, life and death, and so on. Derrida speaks of this in a powerful and surprisingly moving way in an outtake from the movie *Derrida* (see the YouTube clip, https://www.youtube.com/watch?v=BSsDRf2wnOk). It is thus the "lever" of absolute hospitality, in the one case, and of archē-writing, on the other, that brings us to the limit of oppositions such as speech and writing, self and other, law and justice.

6. Derrida writes of this notion of invention: "Political invention, political decision and responsibility consist in finding the best or the least bad legislation; that is the event that remains to be invented each time. One must invent in a concrete,

determined situation, in the France of today, for example, the best legislation so that hospitality is respected in the best possible way. . . . There are no criteria given in advance, no preestablished norms" (S 71–72).

7. In a short text in *Paper Machine*, Derrida says something similar about this pure, absolute, hyperbolic, impossible hospitality and the "desire" to which it gives rise: "The 'impossible' I often speak of is not the utopian. Rather, it gives their very movement to desire, action, and decision: it is the very figure of the real. It has its hardness, closeness, and urgency" ("NU" 131/360–61).

8. Another one of these mediating schemata would be the *"jeu"*—the play or give—between the unconditional law of hospitality and all conditional laws. In *Sur Parole*, Derrida says that this *jeu* is the "place of responsibility" (S 71), that is, it seems, the place of a negotiation or an exchange, a place of hospitable interaction, between the two regimes. For a brilliant analysis of this "jeu" in Derrida's work, including, and especially, "jeu" as play and humor, see Elizabeth Rottenberg, *Derrida en jeu* (Montréal: Presses de l'Université de Montréal, 2023).

9. This is a first, rather enormous difference between the two years of the seminar. In *Hospitality* 1 and *Of Hospitality*, which is based on two sessions from *Hospitality* 1, the relationship between those two regimes seems to be the backbone of Derrida's entire analysis and thinking of hospitality. While that relationship is not completely absent from *Hospitality* 2, it does not have the pride of place that it had in the first year. There are several good reasons for this. First, much of the second year will be devoted to an analysis of Levinas, no doubt in large part because Derrida was working at the same time on *Adieu*, a work written in the wake of Levinas's death on December 25, 1995. Second, that work on Levinas—and there are already traces of this in *Hospitality* 1—led Derrida to begin thinking more about forgiveness, the topic of the next two years of his seminar, than hospitality, even if the two are clearly related. But there may be an even more internal reason for this shift in focus, namely, a need to rethink and deepen the question of *time* through Levinas and his thinking of *substitution*. For it would seem that, for Levinas, forgiveness is what temporalizes hospitality, or temporalizes the relation to the Other. Put otherwise, hospitality becomes forgiveness because of the intervention of time. In the end, what forgiveness gives is time. Time is given by the other as forgiveness.

10. Derrida underscores the same or a similar danger of unconditional hospitality and the concomitant need for conditional hospitality in his reading of the Levinasian third during the second year of the seminar.

10. The Art or Poetics of Hospitality

1. Derrida says in this same passage, "this is what will always link hospitality to poetics." For an act of pure hospitality, if there is such a thing, would have to be poetic, or better—because *poiesis* can always be understood as the creative, self-mastering act of a poet—*poematic*, the poem, the act, being somehow always made and received from the other (see *H* 1 157/215).

2. Since Blanchot jokes are relatively rare, this one, which makes reference to Blanchot's *Infinite Conversation*, clearly amused the seminar audience.

3. See *Statesman* 283c–284e. Already in the *Phaedrus*, Socrates reports that Prodicus once said that speeches should be neither long nor short but always "of reasonable length [*metriōn*]," that is, of moderate or fitting or appropriate length (*Phaedrus* 267b).

4. Toward the end of *Hospitality* 2, Derrida speaks of the way giving food and drink to a guest out of hospitality is not simply a question of giving sustenance but of "entertaining," and of doing so with a certain "grace" and "art." He then goes on to ask, "To what extent does hospitality presuppose improvisation?" The answer is, of course, that "one must improvise, but not too much" (*H* 2 231/318).

5. It is as if Derrida were taking up Klossowski's line from *Roberte ce soir* (10–11), which he cited in *Hospitality* 1, namely, that "one cannot at the same time take and not take, be there and not be there, enter when one is already within . . ." (*OH* 125/111; *H* 1 116–17/162). And yet, this "at the same time [*à la fois*]" is exactly what happens, says Derrida, as if the law of noncontradiction were being perpetually undone by the logic of hospitality.

6. We see something similar in Derrida's analysis of the Jewish joke of the two Jews on the day of the Great Atonement, which goes from talking about an abyssal logic of forgiveness to, all of a sudden—in what seems like a leap—an "art de vivre" ("What an art of living!") (*H* 2 173/240). See Elizabeth Rottenberg's analysis of this joke, and of humor more generally in Derrida, in *Derrida en jeu* (Montréal: Presses de l'Université de Montréal, 2023).

7. While this vocabulary of "grace" and "graciousness" is not completely absent from the first year of the seminar, it is more prominent in the second, and it seems to have been added by Derrida in several places to the two sessions drawn from the first year and revised for publication in *Of Hospitality*. Derrida says elsewhere that he affirms this word "grace," except in those cases where it has some kind of "obscure religious connotation" ("NU" 132).

11. But Why So Much Kant?

1. Immanuel Kant, *Toward Perpetual Peace*, in *Practical Philosophy*, trans. Mary Gregor (Cambridge: Cambridge University Press, 1996), 328; see *H* 1 2/20.

2. Despite their many differences, this is one place where Kant and Levinas overlap. As Derrida recalls in *Sur Parole*, ethics—including hospitality, or indeed *as* hospitality—cannot be reduced to "good feelings" or "good intentions," to *les bons sentiments*. Derrida expresses worries in the very same passage about a moralizing appropriation of Levinas, one that would, it seems, lead us far away from Levinas's fundamental insight that "there can be no friendship, hospitality, or justice without what Levinas calls the alterity of the other, without this irreducible, infinite, absolute, incalculable alterity" (*S* 65). It is a thinking, Derrida here testifies, that has "accompanied" him his "entire adult life" (*S* 64).

3. Derrida refers throughout to Kant's 1797 essay "On a Supposed Right to Tell Lies from Benevolent Motives" (sometimes translated "On a Supposed Right to Lie because of Philanthropic Concerns").

4. This scene from Genesis 19 is largely repeated in Judges 19:20–30, where the master of the house, after giving up his virgin daughter and his guest's concubine rather than his guest to the men who wish to rape him, cuts up into twelve parts the concubine who has been abused by the men and sends those parts to the borders of Israel (*H* 1 127/175–76). Peggy Kamuf has a very powerful analysis of this scene within the context of a reading of Rousseau's *Le lévite d'Ephraïm:* "Author of a Crime," in *Signature Pieces: On the Institution of Authorship* (Ithaca, NY: Cornell University Press, 1988), 79–99.

5. This is a fundamental scene for "Abrahamic hospitality," and it is used extensively by Louis Massignon in *L'hospitalité sacrée* (Paris: Nouvelle Cité, 1987) and elsewhere. What thus appears as a mere example to contrast with Kant in the first year of the seminar thus becomes a central theme in the second year.

6. The question of sexual difference emerges not only in this biblical story of Lot and his daughters but also in Derrida's reading of Klossowski's *Roberte ce soir* and La Bruyère's "Le Distrait," provoking Derrida to say that the space of hospitality is always libidinally charged (*H* 1 194–96/260–62). The question also arises in Derrida's brief comments about the scene of "hospitality" that takes place in a house of prostitution in Nighttown (the Circe chapter of *Ulysses*), a strange scene of hospitality that Derrida relates to the second "coming" of Elijah (*H* 1 239/317–18). So close is this relationship between hospitality and sexuality that Derrida ventures at one point the even more unwieldy neologism "hospitasexuality" (*H* 1 195/261). For an excellent, Lacanian-inspired, though also very much Derridean analysis of hospitality in relationship to sexuality, with readings of both Klossowski and the biblical texts mentioned here, see Tracy McNulty, *The Hostess: Hospitality, Femininity, and the Expropriation of Identity* (Minneapolis: University of Minnesota Press, 2006).

7. As Derrida says in *Of Hospitality:* "Europe" is the place where "the *law* of universal hospitality received its most radical and probably most formalized definition—for instance in Kant's text, *Perpetual Peace*" (*OH* 141/125; see *H* 1 121–22/167–68).

12. Xenos Paradox: Hospitality and Autoimmunity

1. Derrida uses the verb *s'incarner* a second time in this same interview: "Even if the unconditionality of hospitality must be infinite and thus heterogeneous to legislative, political, and other conditions, this heterogeneity does not indicate an opposition. In order for this unconditional hospitality to be incorporated [*s'incarne*], in order for it to become effective, it must be determined and, as a result, it must give rise to practical measures, to conditions, to laws, and that conditional legislation

must not forget the imperative of hospitality to which it refers. There is here heterogeneity without opposition, heterogeneity and indissociability" (S 71).

2. For this question of the date and dating, the question of the singularity and repeatability of the date—a major theme in Derrida's work since at least *Shibboleth* (in *Sovereignties in Question*)—see also H 1 224/299, 230–32/307–9). With regard to this "opening to the future," Derrida draws our attention in the opening session of the seminar to the fact that so many of the experiences we commonly attribute to hospitality—calling or inviting the other, being called or invited by the other—are experiences of the future, expressions related to the future, promises of a kind related to the future (see *H* 1 17–18/38–39).

3. This is also what leads Derrida to ask whether Elijah—a privileged figure, of course, of hospitality—might not be thought in terms of a sort of messianicity that resembles the absolute or unconditional hospitality he has been talking about or whether the figure of Elijah is not already too determined, too limited, for that absolute hospitality (*H* 1 232–35/309–12).

4. The first of these texts, "The Uncanny," was probably written during World War I and published soon thereafter, in 1919 (see *H* 1 220/294). As for Joyce's *Ulysses*, Derrida, still emphasizing the question of the date—"*Il faut dater les choses*"—recalls that the work is signed and dated "Trieste-Zurich-Paris 1914–1921" (*H* 1 221–22/295–96).

5. See Georges Leroux's superb, indeed irreplaceable analysis of the second year of the seminar in *Hospitalité et substitution (Derrida, Levinas, Massignon)* (Montréal: Les Presses de l'Université de Montréal, 2020). Leroux's extensive knowledge of the works of Derrida and Levinas, as well as, and this is so much rarer, Louis Massignon gives him a unique perspective on the second year of Derrida's seminar. Leroux begins the book by speaking of his own genuine surprise at Derrida's decision to read Massignon during the second year of the seminar, calling it "an absolutely unprecedented gesture not only in the work of Jacques Derrida but in the entire history of twentieth century philosophy. For who, among philosophers, has read or still reads Massignon? Who has even wanted to refer to him?" (47; my translation here and in what follows). As he later asks, "what does this opening to Islam indicate?" (72). Much of the book is an attempt to respond to this question. Leroux underscores Derrida's emphasis throughout his two-year seminar on "The Plural Sites of Hospitality" (the title of the book's opening chapter), on "The Biblical Site: The Scene of Abraham" (the title of the following chapter)—a scene that is common, of course, to all three monotheisms—but then, with his rather unique and unexpected turn to Massignon, on "The Islamic Site: Sacred Hospitality" (the title of the final chapter). Leroux is able to show in detail and with authority the places where Levinas's and Massignon's commitments and interests intersect (in particular with the shared themes of hospitality and substitution) and where they diverge (Massignon's emphasis on the mystical Body and the communion of the saints, for example, having no parallel in Levinas). He also shows how the theme

of substitution in Derrida's *Hospitality* seminar leads to the theme of the seminar that will follow hospitality, namely, forgiveness (*Pardon and Perjury*). As Leroux writes, "The intersection of Massignon's thought with Levinas's is founded on the analogy between forgiveness and hospitality, avowal and the gift" (111). Leroux's work is indispensable for anyone hoping to grapple with the second year of the seminar, particularly with Derrida's turn to Massignon, but also with Derrida's dense and difficult but crucial analysis of the themes of substitution and forgiveness in relation to time in Levinas. For if, as Leroux writes, substitution "constitutes the relay or the process by which the living being perpetuates itself by transmitting itself, indeed by substituting itself for itself [*en s'auto-substituant*]" (128), then it would seem that the ethical relation opened up by substitution (the substitution of "the one for the other") is essential to the very opening of time itself. It is as if Derrida recognized in the second year of the seminar both that the Islamic site of hospitality needed to be treated and that the relationship between hospitality and time needed to be more fully explored.

6. Translated by John Leavey as "As soon as it is grasped by writing, the concept is drunk [*cuit*: or cooked]" (233) and by Geoffrey Bennington and David Wills in *Clang* as "As soon as it is seized [*saisi*] by writing, the concept is done [*cuit*]" (260).

13. Dirty Foreigners: The Question of Purity

1. Derrida says elsewhere of this phrase, "at issue is a law that makes it possible to pursue, even imprison, those who shelter or help foreigners in what is considered to be an illegal situation" ("Q" 73). In an interview in *For What Tomorrow*, Derrida suggests that the phrase comes from Jacques Toubon himself (see *FWT* 59/101). Judith Still, *Derrida and Hospitality: Theory and Practice* (Edinburgh: Edinburgh University Press, 2013), 197, writes with the same repugnance as Derrida: "The expression 'crime of hospitality' is something that you don't want to have in your mouth—we can all think of things—that make you feel dirty just to have them pass your lips."

2. See the article in *Libération*, July 10, 2018, by Béatrice Vallaeys: https://www.liberation.fr/debats/2018/07/10/l-histoire-vraie-de-l-article-l-622_1665595/.

3. Derrida recounts hearing on the radio an interview with Ernst Jünger in which he says that during the First World War there was no hatred between French and German soldiers (*H* 1 138/190).

4. Derrida recalls certain Jews in Israel protesting the use of blood taken from Black (Ethiopian) Jews for their blood banks because of the fear that it carried the HIV virus. In the same passage, Derrida recalls that the AIDS crisis itself could be said to be the result of a certain "hospitality" to a virus (*H* 1 145/199).

5. Derrida is referring here to several yet unpublished seminars: "Philosophical Nationalism and Nationality" (1984–1988), "Rhetoric of Cannibalism" (1990–1991), "Politics of Friendship" (1989–1990), "Responding—for the Secret" (1991–1993), "Testimony" (1993–1994), and "The Secret and Testimony" (1994–1995).

14. Homing Devices: Teletechnology and the Question of Private Space

1. See Laurent Zecchini, "L'homme le babouin et le sida," *Le Monde*, December 19, 1995.

2. Derrida argues against a utopian discourse that would advocate simply getting rid of the police altogether ("defunding the police," as we might say today). Though the powers of the police must be limited, the police are nonetheless necessary, Derrida suggests, to counter terrorism, narcotrafficking, mafias, and so on (*H* 1 252–53/335).

15. Phantasms of Fatherlands and Mother Tongues

1. Derrida develops this analysis of language (in Arendt, though also in Rosenzweig and Levinas) in an extended footnote in *Monolingualism of the Other*, 78–93/91–114.

2. This discourse regarding the mother tongue needs to be put into relation with everything Derrida says in the seminar about the mother's *irreplaceability*, which Derrida characterizes as madness itself (*H* 1 159–61/218–19). The mother is irreplaceable, but, as Derrida adds during the session, "What is replaced is always the irreplaceable, that is the madness: that one has to replace the irreplaceable. . . . The unique is mad, what drives one mad" (*H* 1 160n15, 18/219n11, 4). Derrida goes on to say in a phrase that would take an entire dissertation to unpack, a dissertation that would have to include a long chapter on Derrida's reading of Freud's *Beyond the Pleasure Principle* in *Life Death* and elsewhere: "Absolute uniqueness drives one as mad as absolute replaceability" (*H* 1 161/220).There is madness, it seems, on both extremes, in both absolute irreplaceability and absolute replaceability. Derrida goes on to say that "there are two ways of being mad," "being mad because one is attached to the unique," because "there is only the unique," and being mad "because there is only substitution, because there is only replacement, because there is no unique at all. In both cases, there is madness" (*H* 1 161n19/220n11). All this is preceded by a long development on Arendt and the question of the mother tongue in relation to madness (*H* 1 157–59/215–18).

3. Derrida here remarks that we are not far from what Levinas calls "traumatism" or "trauma" with regard to the other (*H* 1 197/264).

4. Barbara Cassin, *Nostalgia: When Are We Ever at Home?*, trans. Pascale-Anne Brault (New York: Fordham University Press, 2016).

16. Phantasms of Mother Tongues and Mobile Phones

1. For an excellent reading of this text and of Derrida's rethinking of the mother tongue in relation to an "originary idiom," see Samir Haddad's "More Than a Language to Come," *Philosophy Today* 64, no. 2 (Spring 2020): 379–94.

2. One would also want to compare the language Derrida uses in these early

works with that found in "Above All, No Journalists!," a fascinating series of extemporaneous remarks made by Derrida in 1997, right around the same time he would have been revising for publication the two seminar sessions of 1995–1996 to be included in *Of Hospitality*.

3. Derrida's claim in early texts such as *Of Grammatology* that phonocentrism is a quasi-universal phenomenon is echoed in later texts, such as *A Taste for the Secret*: "From this point of view . . . logocentrism is something very Western, while there is a phonocentrism in practically all writing and especially in the relation, in the interpretation of the relation between speech and writing. In all writing in general. The authority of speech can be found at a certain point within every culture in general, as an economic phase of humanization, while logocentrism is linked not only to speech but, in the West—in the Greek West—to the authority of the *logos*" (*TS* 77).

4. The phantasm of language, of auto-affection, persists because it seems to us to be at the very *heart* of who we are. Derrida at one point even relates this interiority, that is, this supposed or putatively intact interiority, to what is often called in the West the "heart" (see *H* 1 114n26/159n1).

5. In the sixth session, Derrida adds to this comparison/contrast between Arendt and Levinas the figure of Rosenzweig, who asks, in effect, whether the Jewish people can have a *chez soi* or an at-home when they have no land and no language of their own, and to what extent blood rather than land or language can be the basis for community (*H* 1 167–73/228–35).

6. Georges Jacques Danton (1759–1794) was speaking to his friend, Louis Legendre, who was warning him in March 1794 of the dangers he was facing and urging him to flee abroad. See Alfred Rambaud, *Histoire de la Révolution française, 1789–1799* (1883), cited at http://www.histoire-en-citations.fr.

17. On Cosmopolitanism and Cities of Refuge

1. This title was clearly on Derrida's mind at the time. In a series of improvised remarks from December 1996, Derrida speaks at some length about the problems of immigration in France and about what are called the *sans-papiers*, that is, those "without valid papers," the "undocumented," as one might say in English. He says of this phrase, "one might already hear the call going out . . . *sans-papiers* of every country, unite" ("Q" 83). In *Sur Parole*, Derrida recalls that his playful title "Cosmopolitans of every country, encore un effort," which plays on Marx and Sade, means, first of all, that we are not yet cosmopolitan enough, that we must open the borders, etc., but also that cosmopolitanism itself is not enough. We must, says Derrida, "adjust our ethics of hospitality" in order to go beyond the hospitality offered by nation-states to *citizens* only. The massive problem of refugees without citizen status makes this abundantly clear (see *S* 69).

2. An article in the *Washington Post* from September 2020 reported on the Trump administration's plan to target undocumented immigrants in sanctuary cities, making

the very designation "sanctuary city" a danger rather than an assurance for those seeking asylum. Nick Miroff and Devlin Barrett, "ICE Preparing Targeted Arrests in 'Sanctuary Cities,' Amplifying President's Campaign Theme," *Washington Post*, September 29, 2020, https://www.washingtonpost.com/immigration/trump-ice-raids -sanctuary-cities/2020/09/29/99aa17f0-0274-11eb-8879-7663b816bfa5_story.html.

3. Georges Leroux underscores the importance of the Algerian civil war for the formation of this project in his *Hospitalité et substitution (Derrida, Levinas, Massignon)* (Montréal: Les Presses de l'Université de Montréal, 2020), 43.

4. We could add here the way in which refugees are being used across the globe as geopolitical weapons, refugees or immigrants in Belarus, for example, being brought to the Polish border, that is, to the European border, in order to create havoc and instability within Europe, or immigrants or asylum seekers in Florida or Texas being flown by the Republican governors of those states to northern, Democratic states such as Massachusetts or Illinois in order to score political points at home.

5. We see today's Europe trying to deal with this same problem by means of the so-called Dublin Regulation, adopted in 2003, whose aim is "to determine which State is responsible for examining an asylum application—normally the State where the asylum-seeker first entered the EU—and to make sure that each claim gets a fair examination in one Member State." UNHCR, "The Dublin Regulation," https:// www.unhcr.org/4a9d13d59.pdf. The fact that asylum seekers attempt to enter the European Union much more frequently through some states—Italy or Greece, for example—rather than others has produced sharp tensions among European Union members.

6. Were we to add a Greek tradition to the medieval and biblical ones, we might begin yet again with the *Iliad*, where we are told, as we recalled earlier, that both Phoenix and Patroclus were given asylum by Peleus, Achilles's father, because of an involuntary murder.

7. Emmanuel Levinas, "Cities of Refuge," in *Beyond the Verse: Talmudic Readings and Lectures*, trans. Gary D. Mole (London: Athlone, 1994), 34–52; "Les Villes-Refuges," in *L'au-delà du verset. Lectures et discours talmudiques* (Paris: Les Éditions du Minuit, 1982), 51–70.

18. Beyond Anthropo-Hospitality: Plants, Animals, Gods, and Clones

1. Derrida also speaks of Nietzsche's overman or superhuman to come in *Zarathustra* (see H 1 211/282–83).

2. Following a similar line of argumentation, Derrida later turns, albeit very briefly, to Heidegger's "Building Dwelling Thinking" in order to question once again the claim that only humans can die, which in this text seems to be related to the claim that only humans can dwell, and therefore only they can offer hospitality (H 1 242–43n43/322–23n3).

3. In a note in *Paper Machine*, Derrida imagines the founding of an internet

state "without territory" as a way of revealing the fictive, imaginary, or indeed—
though the word is not used here—*phantasmatic* origin of political communities:
"It reveals a *constitutive* imaginary or fiction: the supposedly legitimate occupation
of a fixed territory, if not the assumption of autochthonous origin, has up till
now been a condition of civic belonging, in reality the very being of politics, its
links to the nation-state, if not to the state" (*PM* 184n4). Elsewhere in the same
collection, Derrida argues that changing the laws of immigration is *not* asking for an
unconditional hospitality that welcomes everyone. It is simply a call to change the
law or the way the law is implemented "without yielding to fantasies of security or
to demagogy or vote seeking" (*PM* 116).

4. Speaking of the famous scene where Abraham, after being told that Sarah is
going to give him a son, Isaac, laughs, Derrida says, "To this question in the form
of an aporia, I know of no soothing response. Not even mad laughter. Nothing is
given in advance for a forgiveness, no rule, no criterion, no norm. It is the chaos at
the origin of the world. The abyss of this non-response would be the condition of
responsibility—decision and forgiveness, the decision to forgive without concept, if
there ever is any. And always in the name of the other" (*H 2* 176/244).

5. Derrida says in an interview in *For What Tomorrow*: "Like others, I argued that
there was much more space to welcome foreigners than people were saying, and that
immigration had not increased, contrary to the claims about the dreaded 'threshold
of tolerance.' It was imperative not to give in, because of electoral or other concerns,
to the fearful fantasies [*fantasmes*] of those who saw themselves 'invaded' by North
African immigration" (*FWT* 60–61/104; my emphasis). (Derrida seems to be referring
here to François Mitterrand's use of the phrase during an interview in 1991. See
https://www.mitterrand.org/le-seuil-de-tolerance-une-notion.html.)

6. In Derrida's original typescript there are five uses of *phantasme* (phantasm)
or some version thereof in the second year of the seminar, all from the session of
February 12, 1997: (1) "the phantasm of death," (2) the "phantasm at the origin
of meaning," (3) the "phantasm" related to "original sin," (4) a "phantasm that
consoles," and (5) "a phantasmatic return." There are then three uses of *fantasme*
(fantasm) or some version thereof, all from the session of May 7, 1997: (1) "the
fantasm of cloning," (2) an "ideological fantasm," and (3) "fantasmatic cloning."
What would go a long way toward establishing a genuine difference between these
two spellings would be a single session in which Derrida uses *both* terms, ideally
close to each other, so that one could test the difference in meaning that I have
suggested here. While no such session exists in the *Hospitality* seminar, there is a
session in *The Beast and the Sovereign* where Derrida does use both. Unfortunately
for my argument, it appears that the two terms are being used interchangeably
there, as Derrida speaks on the very same page of a "phantasm of living-dying" and a
"fantasm of the living dead" (*BS 2* 143/209). It thus seems that Derrida here, and no
doubt elsewhere, uses the two spellings interchangeably. (The editors of the second
volume of *The Beast and the Sovereign* note at one point: "Derrida spells this word
(in French) both as 'fantasme' and 'phantasme'" [*BS2* 77n3/122n4]). But this does

not mean that there are not two very different valences to this same word or these same words, as the foregoing analysis has aimed to show.

7. Derrida speaks in *Aporias* of the term *arrivant* in terms of "the neutrality of *that which* arrives, but also the singularity of *who* arrives, he or she who comes, coming to be where s/he was not expected, where one was awaiting him or her without waiting for him or her . . . without knowing what or whom to expect . . . —and such is hospitality itself, hospitality toward the event" (AP 33).

8. Derrida will speak in *The Animal That Therefore I Am*, first delivered at the conference in Cerisy that very same summer (1997), of a new experience of "compassion" (ATT 28). He comes to this thought in part through Jeremy Bentham, who asks whether animals can suffer, and he suggests that it is through the shared categories or experiences of mortality, finitude, and suffering that we can come to have a new experience of compassion based on these shared experiences. We may want to ask about the relationship here between this compassion and the *se sentir*, the *se mouvoir*, and the *s'émouvoir* that he goes on to evoke. And we may want to ask about what Derrida characterizes as our *denial* or *denegation* of that shared experience and that compassion. Derrida argues, for example, that "no one can deny [*nier*] the suffering, fear, or panic, the terror or fright that can seize certain animals and that we humans can witness. . . . No doubt either, then, of there being within us the possibility of giving vent to a surge of compassion, even if it is then misunderstood, repressed, or denied [*dénié*], held at bay" (ATT 28). The English reader might note that the notion of "compassion" is also central to Derrida's reading of Rousseau in *Of Grammatology*, though the favored term there is *la pitié* rather than *la compassion* (see, for example, OG 171–91/243–71).

9. This is more or less how the entire two-year seminar ends. Derrida simply adds, by way of conclusion of his own written and prepared seminar, since there were four remaining sessions devoted to student presentations: "Well, it is by the measure of this question that we will approach next time, first of all in a discussion, the problems of the double, the clone, of genealogy or family relation, of filiation and of sacrifice (animal and/or human), and of 'Thou shalt not kill,' which is for Levinas the commandment of commandments. Substitution begins there; the crime that I must expiate, in which I am involved in this originary substitution, is the crime against the face, but the human face; 'Thou shalt not kill' does not mean 'Thou shalt not put to death a living being,' it does not concern what we call an animal, it concerns the face. In principle, an animal does not have a face. Thus, the question of sacrifice and of 'Thou shalt not kill' on the basis of that ipseity I have just mentioned. / So I ask you to prepare for this discussion" (H 2 258/354).

Conclusion. From Threshold to Threshold—Derrida's *Démarche*

1. It may well be that Derrida is hearing echoes of Klossowski's *Roberte ce soir*, where the narrator, the nephew of a well-known professor of scholastic theology, says that he thought it "useful to note a certain number of [his uncle's] digressions

and to reproduce them in the context of the singular experience of my student years." Pierre Klossowski, *Roberte ce soir* (Paris: Minuit, 1953). English translation in *Roberte Ce Soir and The Revocation of the Edict of Nantes*, trans. Austryn Wainhouse (London: Dalkey Archive, 2002), 9. Given what follows, these "digressions" on the part of this famous professor will prove to be, or will become inextricably bound up with, his "transgressions."

Perhaps this is the place to note that while Derrida returns repeatedly during the first year of the seminar to this novel, where the host or master, the narrator's uncle, becomes a guest in his own home (see Klossowski, 13, 19), Derrida does not really comment on anything after the preface and the section titled "Difficulties," which includes a presentation of "The Law of Hospitality," those written laws that are put under glass and placed over the bed in the guest's bedroom. There are many other echoes between Derrida's seminar and Klossowski's novel, early references to the "threshold" (12), even to the "phantasm" (13), to name just two, but Derrida says almost nothing about the rest of this strange, pornographic novel that combines vivid descriptions of the uncle's "transgressions" (particularly those he encourages between his wife, the narrator's aunt, Roberte, and the preceptor who has been hired to tutor the narrator and who will take the place of the uncle as the master of the house in his relations with Roberte) with several lengthy "digressions" on Christian theology, from the incarnation to the trinity and the resurrection. See Judith Still's comments on Derrida's reading of Klossowski in her *Derrida and Hospitality: Theory and Practice* (Edinburgh: Edinburgh University Press, 2013), 122–25.

2. Much later in the seminar, Derrida moves, by metonymy, from the theme of the threshold to that of the door to that of the lock and key to, finally, the more contemporary phenomenon of the number or the code that opens the door and allows one to cross the threshold (*H* 1 187/252).

Index

Michael Naas is Professor of Philosophy at DePaul University. He is the author of *Class Acts: Derrida on the Public Stage* (2022), *Apocalyptic Ruin and Everyday Wonder in Don DeLillo's America* (2022), *Don DeLillo, American Original: Drugs, Weapons, Erotica, and Other Literary Contraband* (2020), *Plato and the Invention of Life* (2018), *The End of the World and Other Teachable Moments: Jacques Derrida's Final Seminar* (2015), *Miracle and Machine: Jacques Derrida and the Two Sources of Religion, Science, and the Media* (2012), *Derrida From Now On* (2008), *Taking on the Tradition: Jacques Derrida and the Legacies of Deconstruction* (2003), and *Turning: From Persuasion to Philosophy* (1994). He is co-translator of a number of books by Jacques Derrida, including *Life Death* (2020), and is a member of the Derrida Seminars Editorial Team.

www.ingramcontent.com/pod-product-compliance
Lightning Source LLC
Jackson TN
JSHW021958190225
79368JS00002B/15